INDIA'S
POWER
ELITE

INDIA'S POWER ELITE

CLASS, CASTE AND A CULTURAL REVOLUTION

SANJAYA BARU

PENGUIN

VIKING

An imprint of Penguin Random House

VIKING

USA | Canada | UK | Ireland | Australia
New Zealand | India | South Africa | China

Viking is part of the Penguin Random House group of companies
whose addresses can be found at global.penguinrandomhouse.com

Published by Penguin Random House India Pvt. Ltd
4th Floor, Capital Tower 1, MG Road,
Gurugram 122 002, Haryana, India

First published in Viking by Penguin Random House India 2021

ISBN 9780670092444

Typeset in Bembo Std by Manipal Technologies Limited, Manipal
Printed at Replika Press Pvt. Ltd, India

www.penguin.co.in

In memory of my father,
B.P.R. Vithal (1926–2020),
and my father-in-law,
A. Vaidyanathan (1931–2020)

Contents

Preface

It was during my graduate years at Hyderabad's Nizam College that I discovered C. Wright Mills's *The Power Elite* in my father's bookshelf. As a student of politics and economics, I was always fascinated by the study of power. While my discipline was economics, I took particular interest in political economy, which has its origins in the study of wealth and power. It was an interest stirred by the fact that for years I was a silent participant in conversations about policy and politics around me. My father was a civil servant and close to a succession of powerful chief ministers. Conversations about caste and class and the struggles for power were commonplace at home. The communist ideologue Mohit Sen, a friend of the family, argued vehemently about the centrality of class to an understanding of power, while our house guest, Professor Hugh Gray of the School of Oriental and African Studies, London, who was studying the role of caste in provincial politics, would insist on its recognition. I, therefore, grew up in a social milieu highly conscious of both class and caste as social dividers.

In 1974, when I moved from Hyderabad to Delhi's Jawaharlal Nehru University (JNU), I entered an intellectual space in which scholars seemed more familiar with class than caste. The study of caste was viewed as a preoccupation of sociologists. The communists accused 'right-wing' scholars of emphasizing the importance of caste, to shift the focus away from class. The left imposes Western theoretical constructs on India, its critics would retort, for caste is a more important institution of power and discrimination than class. These were familiar intellectual battles of the 1960s and 1970s. Caste politics was yet to graduate out of the provinces and overwhelm national politics. One event that brought a huge change to the way political parties and analysts thought about politics was the Emergency—a central political event of the 1970s. Prime Minister Indira Gandhi put almost every political group from the Rashtriya Swayamsevak Sangh (RSS) to the Maoists in jail. The all-in-one 'left and democratic unity' that was a consequence blurred the debate on caste and class.

The Emergency succeeded, however, in once again bringing out sharp intra-elite cleavages. National politics had witnessed this when Jawaharlal Nehru swerved to the left, and many among the elite moved to the right, joining the Swatantra Party. Indira Gandhi had similarly divided the ranks of the elite with her own leftward swing in the late 1960s. The Emergency united both the left and the right.

Then came the 1980s, and New Delhi woke up to the power of caste divisions when Prime Minister V.P. Singh tried to consolidate his political base by extending caste-based reservations in education and employment.

My interest in the dynamics of power was reignited when I returned to New Delhi in the 1990s as a journalist. I observed from close quarters the politics that shaped Prime Minister P.V. Narasimha Rao's five-year tenure and the rise of Atal Bihari Vajpayee. When Rao became prime minister (PM), journalist Saeed Naqvi declared him the 'last Brahmin prime minister of India'.[1] Within two years, Vajpayee, from the heartland of north-Indian Brahminism, took charge and, as of now, owns that title. He may well end up being the last Brahmin PM considering the direction the Bharatiya Janata Party (BJP) politics has taken under the leadership of Narendra Modi and Amit Shah, with its empowerment of the middle castes, referred to as Other Backward Classes (OBCs).

Unlike most economists, I did not see the economic liberalization of 1991 in purely ideological and economic theoretical terms. It was not just about neoliberal economics taking over Fabian socialism or free enterprise winning over state capitalism. The central element of the 1991 reforms was the end of the Licence-Control-Permit Raj, the original crony capitalism that had thrived in Indira Gandhi's centralized political regime. The policy shift was as much about changing power equations within the elite as it was about ideology.

A new post-Green Revolution business class with rural roots, located in states like Punjab, Haryana, western Uttar Pradesh, Tamil Nadu and Andhra Pradesh, had risen and was challenging the dominance of the essentially metropolitan Marwari business elite of Bombay (now Mumbai) and Calcutta (now Kolkata). I made my case in a paper on the role of 'regional business' and 'regional politics' in shaping national economic policy, viewing economic liberalization as a battle for space within the propertied classes and castes.[2] I saw the 1990s—dominated by Narasimha Rao and Vajpayee—as a turning point in Indian politics. From 1947 till 1989, the Nehru-Gandhi family had been at the apex of the pyramid of power in India. An entire class of the New Delhi-based elite that constituted the 'Delhi Darbar' of the Nehru-Gandhi dynasty was now being forced to adjust itself to the power shift.

When I was reading Mills's *The Power Elite* in the 1970s, in my home in Hyderabad's upmarket Banjara Hills, a relative who had lived most of his life in the Andhra districts and was ill at ease in the still-nawabi culture of Hyderabad mocked me by saying that I might have been reading a book critical of the American power elite, but was I not a member of Hyderabad's power elite? It is a remark that has stayed with me through the years as I have tried to understand the hierarchy of power and elitism in India.

When I moved to JNU in the 1970s, I came face to face with the country's 'national power elite'. Many of my contemporaries were from boarding schools set up by maharajas, and upmarket colleges in Delhi, Calcutta and Bombay, run by British missionaries.

They were more self-confident in their class than a Hyderabadi like me. That is in the nature of the hierarchy of power and elitism.

In the 1970s I was viewed as an 'outsider' by the power elite of Lutyens' Delhi. In the 1990s, as an editor at the Times Group and someone who knew Prime Minister Narasimha Rao well, I was welcomed into the charmed circle of the Lutyens' elite. I was invited to seated dinners, Hindustani classical *baithak*s and fancy cocktail parties in Lutyens' Delhi and homes around Khan Market. The Nehru-Gandhis had gone, but their *darbari*s survived the Rao-Vajpayee-Manmohan Singh era. When I became a member of the India International Centre (IIC), I had perhaps earned my credentials as a member of the national elite. I could leave my provincial past behind and become a card-carrying member of 'Lutyens' Delhi', a term that Narendra Modi gave currency to.

After having acquired membership of Lutyens' Delhi, I entered the sanctum sanctorum of the Delhi darbar as an adviser to the prime minister. One of the privileges of becoming an adviser to the PM, I discovered, was a temporary membership of the elite Delhi Gymkhana Club, a feudal vestige of the British Raj. For the period one was a member of the PM's charmed circle, the club had made a provision—one could become a 'VIP member' under the club's 'Eminent Persons' category. The day I quit my job, my membership ceased, and I was promptly reminded of it. When my book *The Accidental Prime Minister: The Making and Unmaking of Manmohan Singh* appeared, many readers around the country said it offered them an insight into the corridors of power, while most members of the Nehru-Gandhi darbar criticized me for doing precisely that—opening a window to the outside after having entered its door. The courtiers regarded it as betrayal. It is in the nature of elite clubs that once you are in, you keep other outsiders out.

Contemplating the response to the book from these two worlds—the outsiders to and the insiders in the corridors and avenues of power—I pulled Mills's book out of my bookshelf and reread it. Even while I was rereading Mills, Prime Minister Narendra Modi was exploring his love-hate relationship with Lutyens' Delhi. One day he would sport an expensive jacket with his name inscribed in gold thread while on another day he would rail against the Khan Market gang.

Of all people it was Rahul Gandhi, 'to the manner born', who accused the aspirational Modi of running a 'suit-boot-ki-sarkar'. Surprisingly, that charge seemed to unnerve Modi, illustrating the political appeal of anti-elitism.

Modi wanted to be loved by the denizens of Lutyens' Delhi, but he also loved hating them. He was willing to befriend and be interviewed by a journalist who hailed from that world, but he also disliked being questioned by those not overawed by his rise to power. Modi was not yet comfortable with becoming an insider, having been regarded as an outsider for so long. I compared the contrasting attitude of Lutyens' Delhi to Modi with that to Manmohan Singh. Singh, too, had risen from the ranks of the lower middle class. Many of his relatives, like Modi's, continued to live a middle-class life. But there was a difference. Singh had earned his elite credentials by securing an Oxbridge degree. Modi had not. Singh never failed to remind those who needed reminding that he had Oxbridge pedigree. Modi carried that chip on his shoulder.

Membership of Oxbridge, and subsequently of the US 'Ivy League' institutions, created the upper tier of the Indian power elite. The Nehru-Gandhi family and the members of the Nehruvian elite moved with ease within this globalized class. Modi may have hoped that by retaining the likes of Raghuram Rajan and courting the Indian diaspora in New York and London he could earn the admiration, if not regard, of not just Lutyens' Delhi but also the globalized elite of the Indian diaspora. But both were more demanding. They wanted more visible kowtowing and a declaration of allegiance to the values they held dear. Modi was not prepared. He had come to power mocking those values. He expected the elite to kowtow to him. Thus, was born the

Modi paradox—of seeking power while mocking the powerful. It was a subject I wanted to write about. This book is not exactly about that, but it does seek to shed some light on that paradox. It is an exploration of the foundations of power and elitism, inspired by Mills.

Mills, however, focused only on class and culture as the twin differentiators. In India, caste and language are equally important markers of power and elitism. As Ram Manohar Lohia, the anti-Nehruvian, desi socialist suggested, India is divided not just along class and caste lines, but also between the English-speaking and the vernacular Indian. Power and elitism in India are also defined by the role of the middle class through its dominance in the institutions of the state. The permanent bureaucracy, selected through merit-based examinations but increasingly mirroring the many diversities of society, leverages power in a manner not seen in the US. Political, social and economic change are redefining the parameters of traditional markers of the role of caste and class and shaping a new elitism in India.

The BJP's Hindutva politics seeks to paper over these divides in the hope of creating a pan-Indian Hindu consciousness and political constituency. To an extent the BJP has succeeded, but beneath the surface of a nascent and growing Hindu majoritarianism lurk long enduring divides along ethnicity, language, caste and class. Both academia and the media have been debating the recent rise of Hindu majoritarianism and there is no doubt that the impressive electoral victories of Narendra Modi are a consequence of increased communalization of politics.

The BJP justifies its Hindutva politics by drawing attention to the caste-based and linguistic politics of those who seek to divide rather than unite India's Hindu majority. The electoral marginalization of the left has convinced many that class-based political mobilization too has run its course. Consider, however, the possibility that Modi's political success has been made possible by his ability to conflate religion, caste and class. If there is a political platform that the north Indian-dominated BJP has not yet been able to conquer it is that of 'regional' or 'linguistic' sentiment. While Modi has made the BJP unassailable in Gujarat, the 'Hindu-Hindi' party remains vulnerable to regional sentiment in almost all non-Hindi states.

As the economist Joan Robinson once supposedly observed, every statement about India and its opposite is true. This assertion captures the diversity and complexity of a subcontinental nation and a civilizational state. I make no claims to have captured any of this complexity in this book. This book is not an academic enterprise. It is more a polemical tract, full of assertions aiming to focus on who matters and why in Modi's New India. I have also deliberately made it anecdotal in parts both to illustrate a point being made and to keep the reader engaged. Academics look down on anecdotal theorizing; journalists love anecdotes. I have used anecdotes as pegs to hang my arguments.

Most of this book was written during the Covid-19 lockdown—a period in which issues about caste and class attitudes came into play. The idea of 'social distancing' is inherent to the caste system, and its medical legitimization unleashed much comment on the 'wisdom' of traditional cultural practices, ranging from the simple namaste to the more complex *madee* and *muttoo*—Telugu words for physical distancing practised by Brahmin priests and menstruating women. Hindu–Muslim prejudices, always present below the surface and more visible during Modi's tenure in office, resurfaced with a large Islamic congregation in Delhi becoming a Covid hotspot. More than religion and caste, however, the politics of class became central to the discourse on the pandemic. Ranging from issues pertaining to employment security to health security, almost every major public policy issue has revolved around class.

The plight of migrant workers, on the one hand, and middle-class attitude to daily-wage earners, on the other hand, showed how the lockdown impacted different social classes differentially. While the middle class withdrew into the comfort of their homes, the working class walked the highways back to their rural homes. And while poor migrants walked to distant homes in search of security, Indians abroad were not sure if New York was safer than New Delhi. Influential business persons who had acquired non-resident status for tax purposes and set up home and office in the US and Europe, sending their children to schools and colleges overseas, were pulling strings in the Delhi darbar trying to get permission to return home—jumping quarantine requirements—from Covid-struck Western cities to the safety of farmhouses with high walls around Delhi and Mumbai. How the post-Covid world will be reshaped by class conflicts and caste prejudices remains to be seen. This polemic, though, is about pre-Covid India.

The first two chapters lay out the economic and political context in which this book is being written. It is defined by rising inequality and the increasing concentration of economic and political power. An examination of the nature of power and elitism is particularly relevant in this context. Chapters 3 and 4 offer a brief survey of relevant literature for the non-specialist reader. The rest of the book follows a structure similar to the one Wright Mills adopted but relevant to the Indian context. While Mills identified politics, business, military and culture as the four pillars of the power elite, the morphology of the Indian power elite presents a more complex structure. The permanent civil service is an important constituent of the power elite in India. So is the landed gentry and the remnants of the feudal elite, a class that surprisingly finds little mention in Mills' book. I also identify the overseas Indians, especially those who have migrated to the developed West over the past half century, as an important segment of the Indian elite, considering their 'roots and branches' relationships with the resident Indian power elite. It is important to note that the 'secession of the successful' is a more recent phenomenon with the well-off Indian, rather than labourers (blue and white collar), emigrating.

This book is aimed at the general, socially engaged reader but will also, hopefully, interest students and wielders of power.

A Cultural Revolution?

1

Bombard the Headquarters

Ideological and political struggles will continue to occur;
they will never cease. Disequilibrium is a general, objective rule.
Disequilibrium is normal and absolute whereas
equilibrium is temporary and relative.

—Mao Zedong

Narendra Modi came to power in New Delhi as the political leader who symbolized the upper-caste, capitalist, class-led development model of western India. Gujarat, earlier a constituent part of the Bombay Presidency, had been home to business, finance and commerce in British and even pre-British times. While Gujarat remained in the ranks of developed states in the post-Independence period, it was during Modi's tenure as chief minister (2001–14) that it became a symbol of private-enterprise-led industrial development.

Modi's tenure as chief minister began with the tragic death of Hindus at Godhra in Gujarat and the killing of Muslims that followed. Overcoming the setback to his political career caused by the communal situation in Gujarat, Modi focused on development administration and ran a business-friendly government. A key event that captured national attention was his invitation in 2008 to an embattled Ratan Tata, the most prestigious Indian business leader of his generation, to move his automobile manufacturing unit from the inhospitable environs of West Bengal to a business-friendly Gujarat. Five years later, in January 2013, every big industrialist present at the state's annual business summit, Vibrant Gujarat— from Ratan Tata to Mukesh Ambani, Anand Mahindra to Adi Godrej—praised Modi for his pro-business and pro-development leadership. Anil Ambani called him 'a leader among leaders, a king among kings.'[1] Clearly, India's business elite loved Modi.

His image as a development-oriented and business-friendly politician also won him support within the urban middle class that had migrated from the BJP to vote for Prime Minister Manmohan Singh in 2009, giving him a second term in office. By 2014, Singh's image had plummeted, and Modi sailed to power in New Delhi, accusing the Congress of promoting crony capitalism and corruption. Many hoped that as prime minister, he would balance the BJP's Hindutva agenda with the country's developmental needs, turning backward states of India, like Bihar and Uttar Pradesh, into developed ones like Gujarat, pursuing a strategy that I termed in an *Indian Express* column as 'developmental Hindutva'.

In many ways that was precisely the path that Vajpayee had taken as the head of a coalition government, interpreting the BJP's Hindutva in non-sectarian terms. However, Modi had delivered a single-party majority government to the BJP and no longer saw the need to walk Vajpayee's path of a more inclusive soft Hindutva. Vajpayee's inability to stitch together a coalition of adequate numbers in 1996, with many non-Congress political parties unwilling to extend support, may have encouraged him to adopt a more socially and politically inclusive approach that helped him form a stable government in 1998. In 2014, Modi was under no such compulsion.

However, despite the numbers, Modi adopted a more cautious approach in his first term, seeking to build a new image as a development-oriented leader with diplomatic skills. Consequently, throughout his first term in office, Modi did not identify himself with an overtly Hindutva agenda, distancing himself from some extreme forms of Hindu fanaticism like the lynching of Muslims by 'cow protection' vigilantes.

His initial focus in his first term was on securing a favourable global view of his leadership and consolidating the newly acquired support base of his party. Till he undertook the controversial, and eventually disastrous, experiment with demonetization, he seemed to be living up to his promise of remaining focused on development. Internationally, he reached out to the global Indian community, and courted Western powers and Japan, projecting himself as a globally admired leader. It is only in the second term, after his even more impressive electoral victory of 2019, that he and his party have mounted a more aggressive campaign to define India as a Hindu nation.

Most political analysts have come to believe that the turn in Modi's own politics, from being pro-development and pro-business to becoming more welfare-oriented and adopting anti-rich populist postures, can be traced back to the events of February 2015. When Modi sported a suit with his name inscribed on it in gold thread, gifted by the wealthy Gujarati businessman Rameshkumar Bhikabhai Virani, Rahul Gandhi was quick to mock the prime minister, calling his government a 'suit-boot ki sarkar'. This struck a raw nerve coming as it did soon after the BJP's electoral defeat in elections to the Delhi state assembly, won handsomely by the irrepressible anti-corruption campaigner, Arvind Kejriwal. That Kejriwal swept the polls by winning in the poorer districts of the nation's capital, with Modi's BJP picking votes in upper-class localities, gave the victory a David vs Goliath feel.

Till then, there had been no disparaging of the 'Khan Market gang' or the denizens of Lutyens' Delhi on Modi's part. In the 2014 campaign, Modi had been a business-friendly politician. But the BJP's defeat in the Delhi and Bihar assembly elections in 2015 forced him to become pro-poor. It was in this political context that Modi's anti-elitism was cast. It was, however, an anti-elitism that appealed to the BJP's urban and semi-urban middle class. The residents of Vadodara, Indore and Meerut, and indeed of Delhi's Patel Nagar and Rajouri Garden, loved his anti-Lutyens' Delhi rhetoric. It was a political strategy that Donald Trump adopted with his 'anti-Washington DC' and 'anti-Wall Street' rhetoric that an economically depressed Middle America came to so appreciate.

In a television interview in the run-up to the 2019 Lok Sabha elections Modi said his only regret at the end of his first term in office was that he could not win over the 'Lutyens' World'— *'Lutyens dunia jise mante hein, usko naa toh mein apne me la saka hoon, naa apna bana saka hoon'* (I could neither make the Lutyens' world part of me nor become a part of it.' Modi then added that he was in fact not interested in becoming a part of 'Lutyens' world' because he was from the 'non-elite' section of society.[2]

Unlike the anti-elitism of the left, Modi's anti-elitism has both a class and caste dimension. Modi unabashedly projected himself a chaiwallah, deploying a class concept in his favour and, if a bit hesitatingly, also deployed caste discrimination in his favour when he told an election rally in Uttar Pradesh, in April 2019, 'As you are playing the game of forward and backward caste politics, let me tell you I belong to the most backward caste.' With time, Modi's political platform has evolved as a mix of BJP's Hindutva nationalism, Ram Manohar Lohia's caste-based social welfarism and the left's class-based pro-poor radicalism. Equally, it has an anti-liberal, anti-left flavour that mimics Peronist populism.

These aspects of Modi's anti-elitism have been combined with the traditional anti-English-language cultural nationalism of the BJP to define a platform of populist nationalism captured by the slogan 'Hindu, Hindi, Hindustan' that stands in contrast to Modi's more liberal political platform of *'sabka saath, sabka vikas, sabka vishwas'*. The politics of the Modi government as it has evolved reflects a tension between these two identities. The high-minded inclusive platform seeks to mainstream the BJP and increase its support base while the more sectarian and chauvinistic slogan seeks to keep the BJP rooted in its origins.

Indian politics has always been defined by a mix of socialism and populism. Indira Gandhi epitomized this more than her father Jawaharlal Nehru with her famous political slogan *Garibi Hatao* (Remove Poverty), along with the abolition of privileges enjoyed by India's deposed feudal lords and the nationalization of banks controlled by members of the wealthy Baniya/Vaishya caste. While the Congress party pursued pro-business policies during the prime-ministerial tenures of Rajiv Gandhi and P.V. Narasimha Rao, in 2004, it returned to a left-wing platform, criticizing the BJP's 'India Shining' campaign, and unseating the Atal Bihari Vajpayee-led National Democratic Alliance (NDA) government with support from communist parties. The United Progressive Alliance (UPA) government headed by Prime Minister Manmohan Singh adopted a left-of-centre policy platform called the National Common Minimum Programme that promised right to employment, education and health care among other such welfare measures.

Taking a cue from the UPA, Modi also adopted almost all the welfare and pro-poor programmes launched by earlier governments, adding his own initiatives, like JAM (Jan Dhan cash hand-out linked to Aadhaar card and mobile phone). In defining the agenda for his re-election in 2019, Modi married his pro-poor welfarism and anti-rich populism to the BJP's traditional Hindutva nationalism. The 2019 political campaign was itself imbued with patriotism and nationalism pivoting around Pakistan's policy of sponsoring jihadi terrorism in India.

The 2019 victory encouraged Modi and the party president Amit Shah, now also Union home minister, to launch a more aggressive campaign of Hindutva, implementing long-standing promises of the BJP, like the introduction of a uniform civil code, a widely welcomed ban on triple talaq, a favourable verdict from the Supreme Court that facilitates the construction of the

Ram Temple at Ayodhya, the abrogation of Article 370 ending Jammu and Kashmir's special status within the Indian Union, and the legislation of a new law offering citizenship only to non-Muslim refugees from the Islamic Republics of Afghanistan, Bangladesh and Pakistan, combined to create a sense of unease among the minority Muslim community at home.

Taken together, this mix of Hindu nationalism and anti-elitism has become the basis of a new phase in Indian politics that many believe defines what Modi has termed as 'New India'.

This mix of policies and this turn in politics is rooted in the ideology of the BJP's parent body, the Rashtriya Swayamsevak Sangh (RSS), but is also aimed at consolidating the political base of the BJP. The BJP, like the communist parties, has always been an ideology-based political party. The Indian National Congress (INC) and various regional parties have also had their ideological platforms but most of them have come to be viewed as powermongers, easily willing to sacrifice ideology for power. The takeover of the Congress party by Indira Gandhi's sons and later by her daughter-in-law only reinforced this image.

Sonia Gandhi's laboured attempt at acquiring an ideological garb by surrounding herself with left-liberal and radical elements did help give the Congress-led UPA government an ideological platform and purpose before corruption scandals once again strengthened the image that the Congress sought power merely to perpetuate the privileges that generations of Congress persons had come to take for granted as members of a power elite.

The BJP, too, has modulated its ideology in pursuit of power, seeking to widen its support base. For example, it has eased off on pushing Hindi in non-Hindi states and has not banned beef consumption in north-eastern states where it has come to share power with regional political parties. It has also been corrupted by the spoils of office. Its chief ministers, Vasundhara Raje in Rajasthan, and Shivraj Singh Chauhan in Madhya Pradesh have been repeatedly accused of presiding over corruption in their governments. However, it has not given up the pursuit of its core ideological agenda of Hindutva.

Till date Modi has been able to successfully combine a commitment to ideological principles with political expediency aimed at securing and retaining political power. A succession of electoral defeats at the state level and the state of the economy suggest that the enthusiastic pursuit of an agenda of Hindu majoritarianism and cultural nationalism may have hurt the more immediate objective of promoting economic growth and ensuring political stability in a plural society. Clearly, even as the BJP pushes its Hindutva agenda, it continues to come up against the hurdles posed by class, caste, linguistic and regional sentiment. While the BJP's opponents who celebrate India's plurality seek to benefit politically from these divides, the BJP seeks to paper over them, creating a pan-Indian constituency of political Hindutva and India's own version of a cultural revolution.

If this aspect of the rise of the BJP under Modi's leadership has come as an unwelcome surprise to the traditional elite of Lutyens' Delhi it is because the earlier variant of Hindutva they experienced under Atal Bihari Vajpayee's leadership was more benign, not threatening to minority communities, and representing the more liberal and plural face of Hinduism. Vajpayee had also surrounded himself with like-minded members of Lutyens' Delhi. He was himself a long-standing member of the Lutyens' elite and indeed belonged to what Modi and his groupies would dub the 'Khan Market Gang', so to speak. For, my own first glimpse of Vajpayee in the early 1980s was in, of all places, Khan Market. He was carrying a Pomeranian in his arms and walking into a veterinarian's office. Even as many passers-by recognized and greeted him, he simply smiled and walked on, as if he was running an errand in a familiar neighbourhood.

I first met his principle aide in the Prime Minister's Office (PMO), Brajesh Mishra, on a Saturday afternoon in the early 1990s (long before he became the most powerful member of the Vajpayee government) at the bar of the IIC. It was a weekly ritual. Every Saturday, Mishra would turn up at the IIC bar and order his gin and tonic. Dileep Padgaonkar, then editor of the *Times of India* (TOI), and a few others would join Mishra at his corner table. I was then a senior editor at TOI. I would join Mishra and Dileep for a drink at half past noon, after winding up the editorial meeting for the weekend. Mishra's father, D.P. Mishra, was a senior Congress leader close to Indira Gandhi, and served a tenure as chief minister of Madhya Pradesh. Among Brajesh Mishra's important postings was his stint in Beijing when, in 1970, Mao Zedong walked up to him at a diplomatic event and greeted him, making it the first high-level contact between the two nations after the border war of 1962. After retirement he joined the BJP to head its foreign policy cell. In 1998, Mishra went on to become principal secretary to Vajpayee who was the prime minister then.

The ease with which senior BJP leaders, including Jaswant Singh, Arun Jaitley and Brajesh Mishra, interacted with a range of the IIC's usual suspects and then went on to become powerful members of the Vajpayee government further reassured Lutyens' Delhi. Lal Krishna Advani and wife were frequent diners at the IIC dining room, and Arun Jaitley loved his walks around the Lodhi Garden and the long chat sessions with friends over tea and snacks at the IIC lounge. Jaswant Singh was a regular in the IIC's seminar circuit. Even after Vajpayee became PM, one could find many PMO officials at the watering holes of the Gymkhana Club and the IIC. Vasundhara Raje Scindia was as comfortable raising Hindutva slogans in Rajasthan as she was partying in Delhi at the fancy homes of the Lutyens' elite.

Vajpayee's foster son-in-law, Ranjan Bhattacharya, was a businessman who frequented the Lutyens' cocktail circuit, making friends with cigar-smoking business barons and flashy journalists like Vir Sanghvi, demonstrating to Lutyens' Delhi that the BJP was not such a threat to their lifestyle. Vajpayee was also well-served by aides like Ashok Tandon, Sudheendra Kulkarni, Ashok Saikia and diplomat Ajay Bisaria. They maintained lines of communication with a wide range of influential people and helped consolidate Vajpayee's already high acceptability and popularity among the country's power elite. The hardcore within the BJP were not very comfortable with many in this more 'liberal' group around the PM and tried repeatedly to stage a coup, replacing Vajpayee with Advani. Just as the Rahul Gandhi loyalists tried to dislodge Manmohan Singh in his second term and get Rahul ensconced as PM, the Advani loyalists tried for a change of leadership midway into Vajpayee's term. But, the Vajpayee team, which soon included the inimitable bureaucrat N.K. Singh, warded off all challenges.

Many in Lutyens' Delhi had come to view the BJP's Hindutva through Vajpayee's liberal, benign and essentially secular personality. India's power elite had experienced a smooth leadership transition from Narasimha Rao to Vajpayee to Manmohan Singh. Not only had the framework of economic and foreign policies crafted by Narasimha Rao and Manmohan Singh in 1991–92 remained in place through successive changes of government, but even individuals who mattered in pre-Vajpayee regimes continued to remain influential in Vajpayee's. Bureaucrat N.K. Singh is a classic example. The son of an ICS officer, Sir T.P. Singh, NK rose to prominence in Delhi's power corridors during his stints in the commerce ministry where he became special assistant to Pranab Mukherjee in 1980. Mukherjee and Singh were both known to be close to industrialist Dhirubhai Ambani. Promoted to prominence in the 1990s by Prime Minister Narasimha Rao, Nandu Singh or 'NK', as many knew him, became Mishra's twin in the Vajpayee PMO. When Vajpayee was defeated and Manmohan Singh took over, there was a shake-up in the bureaucracy and many Vajpayee loyalists were moved out of important positions, but the Lutyens' elite very quickly adjusted itself to the new dispensation, with 'our friend Nandu' replaced by a 'our friend Montek'. Montek Singh Ahluwalia, a talented and influential policymaker who served successive governments in Delhi through the 1980s and the 1990s, returned to government in 2004 after a brief stint at the International Monetary Fund (IMF). NK and Montek were student contemporaries from the ultimate home of the Lutyens' elite—St Stephen's College.

Hence, the change of governments in Delhi between 1980 and 2014 did not result in any major changes in the social class that constituted Delhi's power elite. It was a revolving door, like in pre-Trump Washington DC—one set of friends went in and another set went out.

India's middle class who had come to love Vajpayee in the 1990s voted for Manmohan Singh in 2009 and helped him return to power with more numbers in Parliament. In 2014, that middle class switched to Modi. Most imagined this would entail a normal change of government. Lutyens' Delhi was prepared for that kind of change, secure in the hope that yet another of 'our friends' would be in the seats of power. Modi, on the other hand, marched to a different beat. While he did appoint a Lutyens' insider—Nripendra Misra, a retired IAS officer who became convener of the IIC Saturday Group after retirement—as his principal secretary, he surrounded himself mainly with people who were 'outsiders' to Lutyens' Delhi. For those who had imagined that the transition to a Modi government would be like an earlier transition to the Vajpayee government, many unpleasant surprises were in store. The power elite had been prepared for a change of government, not for a cultural revolution.

The notion of 'cultural nationalism' has been intrinsic to the ideology of the RSS, an organization that has always described itself as a 'cultural' organization that seeks to boost the self-confidence of a subjugated race. Drawing attention to the economic and cultural destruction of the Indian civilization caused by conquest and colonialism, the RSS Vision and Mission statement ends with high-minded sentiments:

> A lasting solution to the economic crisis can come only from cultural rejuvenation and re-assertion of Hindu values such as reverence for man and nature, a non-acquisitive and non-exploitative life-pattern, recognising mutuality rather than individual right as the basis of economy, voluntary austerity in consumption, and a premium on self-reliance. Sangh has been propagating this value-system based on self-knowledge and self-control, not merely because it is necessitated by the present state of the world, but even more basically because it is a source of individual joy, social harmony, cultural richness, spiritual advancement and universal peace.[3]

While decrying the poverty of the masses, the statement says, 'What should cause greater concern is the culturally induced poverty in the psyche of the people through endlessly repeating "you are poor", "you are backward", and "you are primitive". The need is to recreate the self-confidence of the people of Bharat.' In his more recent speeches, Mohan Bhagwat, the head of RSS, described Hindutva as a 'cultural idea, not confined to any religion or form of worship'. The idea that India is in need not just of cultural rejuvenation but of 'cultural purification'—washed of alien influences caused by foreign domination—has been an important theme of the RSS and its political arm, the BJP.

Interestingly, many on the political left also subscribed to the view that India's development as a post-agrarian society has been marked by a dualism that is captured by the binary India vs Bharat. India comprises the English-speaking, westernized, urban, middle and upper classes and 'upper' castes, while Bharat is the residue of vernacular-speaking, lower middle class, 'middle' and 'lower' castes, residing on the periphery of urban India. Indian politics has for long revolved around this binary with the INC trying to straddle both sides of this social and economic divide. The communist parties were also similarly intellectually conflicted, espousing an ideology rooted in Europe while fighting the westernization of the Indian elite. In 1981, West Bengal's Left Front government was among the first of the state governments to ban the teaching of English in the state's primary schools, mimicking a language policy associated till then with the more sectarian political parties like the Dravida Munnetra Kazhagam (DMK) in Tamil Nadu. Anti-westernism and anti-elitism have been very much the staple of both left-wing and right-wing politics and have fed cultural nationalism of both the left and right.

Such anti-elite cultural nationalism runs the risk of morphing very easily into anti-intellectualism. In the Indian context it has also been fodder for anti-upper-caste sentiments. Interestingly, more recently, Dalit leadership has inverted the argument, claiming that the switch from English language teaching in schools to the vernacular is an upper-caste plot against the weaker sections of society, depriving the latter of access to good jobs in the urban economy. The political scientist and Dalit rights activist Kancha Ilaiah has pushed for the teaching of English language, arguing: 'English education is the key to the modernist approach suitable to the globalised India. The upper castes have handled the contradiction between English and their native culture quite carefully. But when it comes to teaching English to the lower castes they have been proposing a theory that English will destroy the "culture of the soil".'[4]

Several state governments have also recently chosen to reintroduce the teaching of English in government schools. In early 2020, the state government of Andhra Pradesh decided to make English the medium of instruction for classes I to VI in all schools, replacing Telugu, and making Telugu or Urdu a compulsory second language. Chief Minister Y.S. Jaganmohan Reddy defended the move by saying, 'We will go ahead with English medium schools, come what may. We have to prepare the students to boldly face and stand up to the requirements of the technology-driven world and we should not be found wanting in it.'

The language politics of Ilaiah and Reddy play to caste and class identities while the 'Hindu, Hindi, Hindustan' slogan of the RSS plays to religious and nationalist sentiments. From a political perspective, both play into populist politics and the battle for power. Like religion, caste and class, language, too, has been a factor for political mobilization in India from the 1950s. What distinguishes the politics of the BJP during the present phase is the coming together of its anti-elitism with cultural chauvinism and religious sectarianism. In combining cultural nationalism with anti-elitism of the kind Modi identifies with 'Nehruvian India' and 'Lutyens' Delhi', the BJP may have willy-nilly unleashed an Indian variant of China's infamous 'Great Proletarian Cultural Revolution'.

———

Nowhere was the cocktail of anti-elitism and cultural nationalism more potent in its mix than in China during the Cultural Revolution. Faced with declining support for his leadership a decade and a half after he seized power, Mao Zedong, the founding leader of the People's Republic of China, unleashed an anti-elite 'cultural revolution', partly to consolidate his hold over the Communist Party of China, and partly to check what were dubbed as 'revisionist' tendencies within the ruling establishment, with a traditional 'mandarin' elite increasingly asserting control over the government. In this process. Mao was willing to disturb the social order that the communists had inherited without worrying about the consequences nor being yet ready to replace the old order with an adequately prepared new order.

While in theory, a communist revolution was about replacing an old order with a new one, and the organized communist parties of Europe stood in opposition to anarchists, Mao's Cultural

Revolution bordered on anarchism. Justifying the social and political destabilization caused by the Cultural Revolution, Mao once told his favourite China-watcher, Edgar Snow, 'Ideological and political struggles will continue to occur; they will never cease . . . Disequilibrium is a general, objective rule . . . Disequilibrium is normal and absolute whereas equilibrium is temporary and relative.'[5]

Mao encouraged an upsurge of the young with slogans like 'To rebel is justified' and 'Bombard the headquarters'. He defended attacks on party bureaucracy and established social mores seeking an end to 'Four Olds'—old ideas, old culture, old customs and old habits. The targets of such attacks were the mandarins and the intellectuals that had in fact helped legitimize the communist takeover of China. Kenneth Lieberthal, a distinguished chronicler of China's 'cultural revolution', believed that Mao lent support to the Cultural Revolution because he 'distrusted urban-based bureaucracies and China's intellectuals as a whole'.[6] Sharing this view, another distinguished China-watcher Roderick MacFarquhar hypothesized that Mao 'believed that until a huge new army of proletarian intellectuals was formed, it would be impossible to fully consolidate the revolutionary cause'.[7]

While the Cultural Revolution had many objectives and was motivated by many causes, its singular social impact on China was to subvert the social status of the professional class, the intellectuals and the cultural elite, and disturb the old social 'equilibrium' that the communists were challenging. It was Mao's equivalent of an 'anti-Lutyens'-Delhism', to deploy a Modism. While Mao spoke of 'disequilibrium' being the norm, Modi promoted the idea that 'disruption' would be the norm. However, when he was tagged with the moniker 'disruptor-in-chief', he mentioned in the India Today Conclave in March 2017 that the 'disruptor-in-chief' was not him, but that the role was being undertaken by the 1.2-billion-strong Indian population. Adding to it, he said, 'What is happening today is not a disruption, this is a transformation driven by the people of India.'

The two key differences between Mao's Cultural Revolution and that of Modi are, first, the former used a 'people's movement' to purge his own party of the 'old elite' who had become tired of his way of functioning, while Modi's 'disruptive' and 'transformative' politics is aimed at purging the influence of an 'old elite' outside his party; and, second, Mao's revolution was cloaked in Marxism-Leninism-Mao Zedong Thought, summed up in a 'little red book', while Modi's was painted in saffron and with the ideology of Hindu nationalism.

Mao's Cultural Revolution, with its slogan 'Bombard the headquarters' was a manifestation of intra-party power battles, while Modi's 'cultural revolution', whose slogan could well be 'Vacate the headquarters', is a manifestation of Modi's desire to create a 'Congress *mukt* Bharat'—an India in which the old elite, the 'Khan Market Gang', would no longer be the nation's ruling elite.

Both the impulses that drove China's Cultural Revolution—a distrust of the inherited bureaucratic and intellectual elite and the urge to create a new elite in its own ideological image—have defined Modi's anti-elitism. The Cultural Revolution also unleashed lawlessness and anarchy with Red Guards taking the law into their own hands. There have been echoes of such anarchism in the actions of self-proclaimed Hindu vigilantes who have violently espoused causes ranging from cow protection to charges of sedition against the Muslim minority and left-wing radicals, from villages in Uttar Pradesh to university campuses in New Delhi.

While the anti-elitist and anti-minority/anti-left movement has not yet attained the scale of the Red Guards' violence, they have also not targeted the rural rich, the focus of Red Guard campaigns. Mao's anti-elitism caused an upheaval in the very heart of China's power structure and disrupted the agrarian economy. Modi's anti-elitism has been less disruptive. Apart from the communist movement, no major political party in India has ever targeted its anti-elitism against feudal vestiges in rural India. The Congress party went through a brief phase of promising land reform and it did end the privileges of the top end of the feudal elite, the maharajas and the princes, but party-political anti-elitism has been a largely urban phenomenon. In Modi's BJP, too, this remains true and has been marked by a criticism of the bureaucracy and the established intelligentsia, including opinion-makers in the media. The terms 'Lutyens's Delhi' and 'Khan Market gang' defined the social groups that Modi campaigned against when returning to power in 2019.

China's Cultural Revolution had another dimension to it that one can discern in Modi's politics—the promotion of a personality cult. As Edgar Snow put it, 'One key to comprehending events of 1966 is the central role played by the cult of personality of Mao Tse-Tung, a factor he himself has freely acknowledged. In one sense the whole struggle was over control of the cult and by whom and above all "for whom" the cult was to be utilised.'[8]

On meeting Mao, Snow quizzed him on the issue. 'In the Soviet Union China has been criticized for fostering a cult of personality. Is there a basis for that?' Snow asked Mao.[9] Mao replied unabashedly. 'There perhaps was.' Mao conceded that Stalin had been the centre of a cult of personality, and that Khrushchev had none at all. Snow then quotes Mao as saying, 'Mr Khrushchev fell because he had no cult of personality at all.'

Observing the decline of the Congress party during Prime Minister Manmohan Singh's second term in office (2009–14), the inability of Rahul Gandhi to make a national mark and analysing his own rise to power in Gujarat to become its unchallenged leader, Modi may well have concluded that India was ripe for a strong leader and the promotion of a cult of personality around that leader. The combination of anti-elitism, anti-intellectualism and the cult of personality is what created the foundation for Mao's political consolidation after the reverses to the revolution in the late 1950s as a consequence of the Great Leap Forward. The death of 30 million Chinese had seriously threatened to undermine the revolution, and Mao needed a second wave of political consolidation.

Surely, political events in India in recent years and the 'disequilibrium' and 'disruption' in Indian politics caused by the BJP's pursuit of its Hindutva agenda are nowhere near that caused by the Cultural Revolution in China. However, if there is a parallel it lies in the nature of the beast—the combination of anti-elitism, cultural nationalism and personality cult of the leader. They have certainly combined to signal a power shift and have unsettled the existing social equilibrium, challenging the existing 'power elite', with consequences for economic growth and political stability. In doing so, however, Modi has worked hard to retain his base within the middle class. Modi's anti-elitism is Janus-like, mobilizing an aspirational middle class against a privileged elite—best represented by the Nehru-Gandhi dynasty and its courtiers—while, at the same time, ambivalent in its solidarity with the really poor.

This Janus-faced dualism in Modi's politics was most visible during the post-Covid lockdown when, on the one hand, the privileged elite, especially the business class, worried about their corporate bottom lines and asset values, while the poor migrant labour, with no assured employment, worried about their next meal, and the urban middle class clapped hands and lit lamps to express their support for Modi's handling of the pandemic and its fallout.

The top 1 per cent of India's population is estimated to own 51.53 per cent of all wealth nationally. The top 10 per cent owns 77.4 per cent. Is it then that India's elite and its 'power elite' are easily identified? Things are not that simple. The inhabitants of 'Lutyens' Delhi'—a mix of powerful politicians and officials, business billionaires and India's old rich, a legacy of the British Raj—would certainly be part of that 'top 1 per cent'. There are many provincial politicians who would share Modi's disdain for the privileged elite of Lutyens' Delhi but would certainly belong to the top 10 per cent

of the country's population and would display happily their newly
acquired political and economic muscle. Modi has climbed the
ladder of political power visibly targeting the upper echelons of the
'power elite', especially the 'old elite', to win favour with the poor
and the lower middle class, but he has allowed an upwardly mobile
nouveau riche among the middle castes to assert their presence in
the corridors of wealth and power.

The idea of 'elite' is complicated in India as it is influenced
by a mix of class, caste and language. The socialist ideologue and
political leader Ram Manohar Lohia identified three characteristics
to distinguish India's ruling class: 'High Caste; English education;
Wealth'.[10] This hierarchy is defined by economic and social
factors—class and caste; by socialization—urban and rural; and,
by language—English-speaking and Indian-language speaking.
Different forms of elitism are manifested in different forms of
power. Writing in the early 1950s, American sociologist C. Wright
Mills was able to define fairly easily the composition of the power
elite in the mid-twentieth-century US, but such a classification
cannot be easily done for India. In the US, Mills believed:

> The power elite is composed of men whose positions enable
> them to transcend the ordinary environments of ordinary men
> and women; they are in positions to make decisions having major
> consequences. Whether they do or do not make such decisions
> is less important than the fact that they do occupy such pivotal
> positions: their failure to act, their failure to make decisions,
> is itself an act that is often of greater consequence than the
> decisions they do make. For they are in command of the major
> hierarchies and organizations of modern society. They rule the
> big corporations. They run the machinery of the state and claim
> its prerogatives. They direct the military establishment. They
> occupy the strategic command posts of the social structure, in
> which are now centred the effective means of the power and the
> wealth and the celebrity which they enjoy.[11]

Mills viewed the 'power elite' as a more composite social set of the well educated and wealthy occupying the commanding heights of government, military, business, academia and culture. All these social groups would certainly constitute India's power elite, but then democratic politics gives play to religion, caste, region and language in a way that makes such a classification more complex. Even in the US, within the more homogenous social set of the power elite, there were cultural differences. The academic elite of the US East Coast were a very different social set compared to the business barons and the top echelons of the military-industrial complex. The form of power each group exercised varied, yet together they dominated the country's power structures. In India, however, caste complicates the picture as much as the social power of the middle class. We will talk more about this in the later chapters.

In all societies power has many dimensions. As Bertrand Russell put it, 'power is to social dynamics what energy is to the physical'.[12] It is the motive force of change. In India there is an additional dimension to the power system and that is caste. In a country of over 130 billion there are national elites and provincial elites. Modi caricatured the national elite as courtiers of the Nehru-Gandhi dynasty—the 'Khan Market gang'—and positioned himself against them. '*Modi ki chhavi, Delhi ke Khan Market ke gang ne nahin banayi hai, Lutyens Delhi ne nahin banayi hai. 45 saal ki Modi ki tapasya ne chhavi banayi hai. Achchi hai ya buri hai* (Modi's image has not been created by the Khan Market gang, or Lutyens' Delhi, but 45 years of his toil . . . good or bad.)' Modi claimed in an interview to the *Indian Express* newspaper.[13] 'Lutyens' media referred to Prime Minister Rajiv Gandhi as "Mr Clean", but how did his political career end?" asked Modi, alluding to the Bofors gun corruption scandal that contributed to his electoral defeat in 1989.

Every province of the republic has its provincial elites, and Modi was the darling of Gujarat's elite. With close to 16 million Indians living overseas, with many of them economically well off and enjoying globally enviable standards of living, there is now a global Indian elite. As they retain links with India as members of the families of India's power elite or as investors, they constitute the third tier. In short, India has a provincial, national and global power elite and their status is defined by political, economic, cultural and social power. Interestingly, religious institutions and leaders did not figure in Mills' definition of the power elite, even though Russell clearly identifies the clergy as a power centre. In BJP's India, religious leadership is gaining traction as a member of the power elite. Yogi Adityanath's ascendance to the office of chief minister of India's biggest province is only one, albeit highly visible, example.

In Russell's view, power in mid-twentieth-century Europe could take several forms—economic, political, priestly, military and opinion-making. The control of government gives a political party and its leadership access to all forms of power, even though in a democracy the diversity of opinion makes it difficult for governments to monopolize opinion-making power. This is where the ideological agenda and its articulation by the political party in power comes into play.

The Indian Constitution defines the manner in which the state can exercise power in its various forms in the pursuit of the nation's economic and social development. K Santhanam, a member of the Constituent Assembly, famously described India's Independence and its emergence as a sovereign, democratic republic as the beginning of three revolutions—first, a political revolution symbolized by the adoption of a democratic constitution; second, a social revolution liberating Indian society from the vestiges of medievalism based on birth, religion, custom and community with the establishment of the rule of law, respect for individual rights and merit and the inculcation of secular education; and, third, an economic revolution that would enable the transition from feudalism to a modern, science-based agricultural and industrial development. The history of the Indian Republic during its first three decades was one of realizing the promise of each of these revolutions. The inclusive politics of this period was best captured by political scientist Rajni Kothari's famous term, 'the Congress System'.

In 1976, Prime Minister Indira Gandhi launched a new phase of the republic, amending the Preamble to the Constitution by adding the words 'socialist and secular' to it. Thus, the Preamble now reads: 'WE, THE PEOPLE OF INDIA, having solemnly resolved to constitute India into a SOVEREIGN SOCIALIST SECULAR DEMOCRATIC REPUBLIC . . .' The idea that the state would pursue a 'socialist' agenda was first adopted by Jawaharlal Nehru in 1956 when he declared that his government would seek to establish a 'socialist pattern of society'. The constitutional commitment to secularism was introduced by Indira Gandhi in 1976 in response to the rise of religion-based political parties in the 1960s and after.

One could, therefore, argue that a Second Republic took shape through this change. It is this change that the Jana Sangh and its subsequent avatar, the BJP, have since challenged. With its stunning rise as the main pan-Indian political platform after the equally stunning decline and collapse of the INC, the ruling BJP seems to have decided to inaugurate a Third Republic, completing a fourth 'revolution'—to use Santhanam's metaphor, a cultural revolution.

This Indian version of a 'cultural revolution' is also anti-elitist in the sense in which the elites are now conceptualized—as an urban, westernized class that is Nehruvian in its outlook. It is the product of the arrival of the 'vernacular middle-class Indian', so to speak, in the corridors of power. There are social implications of this change. But there are equally important political implications. While the RSS seeks a cultural transformation of India, that is Bharat, the BJP seeks political power. In acquiring that power, it is empowering a new power elite. It is moot whether Modi is riding this wave or promoting, if not creating, it. Clearly, he has been its biggest political beneficiary.

The Congress party, under the leadership of the Nehru–Gandhi family, has come to represent the old elite whose influence is waning in the corridors of power—in politics, government, business, culture, academia and media. Even though Rahul Gandhi has tried to project himself as the voice of youth and the leader of a new generation, he has not been able to attract any young political, intellectual or business leader of any significance to his side, save an odd Raghuram Rajan and a Rajiv Bajaj, to bolster his image as a symbol of change. Modi has succeeded in painting Rahul as a son of privilege, while projecting himself as a rebel with a cause. It is this transformation that is under way in the composition of the Indian power elite that we seek to capture. Who constituted the old power elite and who who will constitute the new?? Who will knock on the doors of Lutyens' Delhi?

2

Modi's Metaphors

He [Rahul Gandhi] says everyone having Modi in his name is a thief.
They abuse me because I am from a backward community. This is how
they view people from the backward castes.

—Narendra Modi at an election rally in
Akluj, Maharashtra, 17 April 2019

There are now only two groups of people I recognize—the poor
and those contributing to the alleviation of poverty.

—Narendra Modi at a victory rally,
New Delhi, 23 May 2019

Addressing the 90th annual general meeting of the Federation of
Indian Chambers of Commerce and Industry (FICCI) in December
2017, Prime Minister Narendra Modi alternated between praising
and admonishing Indian big business—the leadership of FICCI.
Alluding to FICCI's big business origins, Modi said, 'I have been
told that FICCI's micro, small and medium enterprises [MSME]
vertical was started in 2013. In a ninety-year-old organization, the
MSME vertical is only four years old. The money owed to MSMEs

by big companies, can that be given quickly? Large amounts are stuck with these big companies.' There was applause from the back of the huge Vigyan Bhavan auditorium even as FICCI's leadership, seated in the front row, took a few seconds to join in. Not to miss an opportunity like this to make a point, assuming that the representatives of MSMEs were seated at the back of the auditorium, Modi remarked that whenever he said anything good about Indian business he heard applause from the front of the audience and whenever he said something critical he heard applause from the back of the audience.

Democratic politics have always required politicians seeking power to position themselves as the defenders of the underprivileged against the privileged. India's complex social composition with class and caste hierarchies has allowed different political parties to deploy different metaphors in playing this political card. If the communist parties spoke for the working class and the peasantry against landlords and capitalists, the political platforms of the Dalits and the backward classes have rallied support, battling caste hierarchy and caste discrimination. The Congress party, which has tried to be 'all things to all people', has built its politics around a combination of class and caste issues. Some regional political parties have come up with a strategy of tapping into resentments based on linguistic and cultural discrimination. The BJP and its precursor, the Jana Sangh, created their political base around cultural nationalism, blaming British imperialism and Muslim rule for destroying the rich legacy of a Hindu India and holding the Congress party responsible for the partition of India along communal lines.

It used to be said that the core constituency of the BJP was the trading Baniya community. Atal Bihari Vajpayee extended that base, bringing the urban and semi-urban middle class, including the professional middle class, into the BJP's fold. It was this urban middle-class constituency that Manmohan Singh was able to bring back into the Congress fold in 2009, scripting the UPA's return to power with improved numbers. Modi restored this class back to the BJP, while encouraging it to believe in the slogan. '*Garv say kaho, hum Hindu hain*' (Claim with pride that we are Hindu).

The BJP's strategy of communal polarization of the electorate and the subsequent unification of a caste-ridden Hindu community into a unified Hindu vote bank met with success in Modi's home state of Gujarat. While Modi appealed to these religious sentiments in consolidating his power in Gujarat, he chose to seek power in Delhi by promising to focus on national economic development—always a winner with the middle class—and empowerment of the poor, while ending the hegemonic domination of a privileged elite that had been beneficiaries of sixty years of Congress rule.

Anti-elitism has always been grist to a power-seeker's populist mill. So it was not surprising that Modi, like the other great Indian populist Indira Gandhi, chose to construct his political platform in 2014 on the foundations of anti-elitism. Unlike Indira Gandhi, Modi's anti-elitist and anti-dynastic credentials were robust. Born into a lower middle-class and middle-caste family, he acquired political power by dint of hard work. Having given up family life and by choosing to remain single, Modi has not created the conditions for a dynasty to emerge.

Indira Gandhi was, of course, a dynast who perpetuated even more unabashedly the idea of dynastic succession. She had to, therefore, distance herself from her elitist origins that went back at least two generations by adopting a left-of-centre political platform. Narendra Modi entered the physical premises of Parliament for the first time in May 2014 as prime minister. He did so after defeating a Congress that was now being led by Gandhi family members—Sonia and Rahul Gandhi. Quite understandably he chose to target the dynastic politics of the Congress.

———

The metaphor of a Delhi darbar presided over by Jawaharlal Nehru and his family, and including its Nehruvian courtiers, was not just an inheritance from India's feudal past nor a legacy of the British Empire. It was an idea intrinsic to the evolution of democratic leadership within the INC. When Motilal Nehru's term as Congress president was to end in 1928, the expectation in the party was that either Sardar Vallabhbhai Patel or Subhas Chandra Bose would succeed him. However, as Mahatma Gandhi's grandson Rajmohan Gandhi records in a biography, while Jawaharlal Nehru declared that he was a 'republican and so no believer in kings and princes', Jawaharlal's mother Swarup Rani sought Gandhiji's intervention to in fact ensure dynastic succession. She wanted to see 'a king passing on the scepter of the throne to his logical successor'. As Rajmohan observes, 'Gandhi, champion of the rights of the halt and the lame, the last and the least, had unwittingly launched a dynasty.'[1]

Modi described this 'Nehruvian elite' as members of 'Lutyens' Delhi'—the families that have dominated national discourse for over half a century, cutting across the worlds of politics, business, culture and media. The 'us and them' metaphor has deep roots in the Indian psyche given the centrality of caste as a defining feature of one's social status. India's freedom struggle helped bridge this divide and succeeded in preventing caste identities and antagonisms from weakening the national, anti-colonial movement. Gandhiji's greatest political contribution was in fact to ensure that caste, communal and linguistic identities got subsumed under a wider national Indian identity.

However, in the years after Independence, not only has there been a resurfacing of caste sentiments, with caste identities and loyalties used in political mobilization and assertion, but communal, linguistic, and to an extent, class consciousness have all taken root, each posing a challenge to one's 'national' identity. The 'us vs them' binary has been reflected at the national level in a 'Bharat vs India' dualism, with the 'idea of India', so to speak, evolving at times independently of and at times in opposition to the 'idea of Bharat'.

In many parts of India, political mobilization has for long revolved around the theme of a privileged 'English-speaking urban' India vs a 'vernacular and provincial' India. Through the processes of modernization and urbanization the English-speaking urban Indian acquired values and attitudes that the small-town and rural India did not always identify with. In this politics of 'us and them', provincial politicians also rose on the foundations of linguistic identity, a process further facilitated by the reorganization of states on a linguistic basis. While an 'anti-Hindi' and pro-Tamil sentiment took root in Tamil Nadu, in most other states, including the Hindi states, the politics of language revolved more around an 'anti-English' sentiment of the newly assertive political class—the members of state legislatures.

The Dravidian movement in Tamil Nadu and the Lohia-socialists in Hindi states promoted a politics defined both by linguistic and caste impulses. This phenomenon spread to many parts of the country in one form or another. The compulsory introduction of vernacular-medium education up to high school in states like West Bengal and Karnataka, the renaming of Calcutta, Madras, Bombay and Bangalore (now Bengaluru) among many other cities, the use of provincial language in state administration and so on, contributed to a strengthening of what has been called in the popular discourse as a 'regional sentiment'.

When this sentiment took on a 'centre vs periphery (state)' character, the INC, a party that dominated national politics for four decades, found itself on the back foot, battling caste- and language-based 'regional parties'. In fact, through the 1950s when the opposition to Congress party rule was articulated mainly in class terms, with the Communist party of India (CPI) emerging repeatedly as the single largest opposition political party in the Lok Sabha elections of 1952, 1957 and 1962, the Congress managed to hold its own, as an umbrella political party of a diverse society, through what political scientist Rajni Kothari dubbed the 'Congress System'.[2] However, as linguistic and caste loyalties gained importance as organizing principles for an anti-Congress opposition, the national party found itself having to deploy class-based politics to defend itself.

Indira Gandhi's turn to the left, her famous slogan of '*Garibi Hatao*', the nationalization of commercial banks controlled by big business and the abolition of the privileges granted to erstwhile feudal rulers gave the 'us vs them' politics a class dimension, even when the real challenge to the ruling Congress coalition came from caste-based parties. By the 1980s, the rise of caste-based political parties, especially in Uttar Pradesh and Bihar, and of 'regional' parties based on linguistic and ethnic sentiments gave the 'us vs them' politics a new twist. The battle lines were drawn between those who ruled from New Delhi and those who took control of provincial capitals. The dramatic rise of Telugu Desam Party (TDP) under the charismatic leadership of actor-turned-politician N.T. Rama Rao, popularly referred to as NTR, gave a fillip to the regional sentiment in national politics. NTR famously called the Centre a 'conceptual myth'. Even before NTR, the Left Front gave respectability to regional sentiment in national politics by mobilizing state governments in a fiscal battle against the Centre in the name of promoting greater fiscal federalism.

Having entered the government as a member of a state legislature and in the capacity of a chief minister, Narendra Modi very quickly and with ease adopted an 'anti-centre' platform to strengthen his own regional political base, first within his own BJP and subsequently vis-à-vis other regional leaders. At meetings of the National Development Council and other conferences of chief ministers, Modi would be the most vocal defender of the interests of state governments. In his own party forums, he would stand his ground as a popular leader from Gujarat against his party's mostly rootless 'national' leadership. Even when he spoke in Hindi, he unabashedly spoke with a heavy Gujarati accent. From Lal Krishna Advani, the party's most important leader till then, to leaders like Murali Manohar Joshi, Sushma Swaraj, Arun Jaitley, Yashwant Sinha, Rajnath Singh and the like, most of BJP's 'national' leaders were identified with Hindi-speaking north India. Modi consciously projected himself as a leader of Gujarat, even speaking Hindi in a Gujarati accent, till 2013, when he mounted his campaign to challenge the leadership of his own party and that of the ruling Congress party—all the denizens of Lutyens' Delhi. Having risen to power by bombarding his own party's headquarters, so to speak, Modi became the new symbol of the politics of 'us vs them'— provincial politician from 'Bharat' challenging the national leaders of 'India'.

In this politics of 'India vs Bharat', the term 'Lutyens' Delhi' became a metaphor for the country's power elite. It is an elite inherited from the colonial era but one that has prospered and enjoyed power even after Independence. Modi's metaphor has struck a chord in almost every state capital where local elites, even those more globalized than Delhi's, have for long felt that Delhi's elites have been a particularly privileged lot.

Interestingly, this provincial attitude towards Delhi has been there through much of history from the era of the Mughals and then the British. It acquired a new resonance in post-Independence India, owing to the continuing domination over Delhi of the Nehru-Gandhi family and the 'darbar' they spawned around their successive regimes. From Motilal to Jawaharlal, on to Indira and Rajiv, and then Rajiv's widow Sonia and her children, the Nehru-Gandhi family symbolized this continuity in pre-Independence and post-Independence power elite. Nehru, with his Allahabad Brahmin origins and upbringing, British education and his circle of friends from the British upper class—including the last British viceroy and his family—was the quintessential representative of the pre-Independence upper class.

How ingrained the feudal and patriarchal instinct was within the Nehru family was brought out by the manner in which Swarup Rani, Jawaharlal's mother, defined and celebrated her son succeeding her husband. Gandhiji's seemingly unwitting launching of a dynasty may well have been shaped by the view that India's first prime minister should not only be a Brahmin from Uttar Pradesh—the so-called 'Hindi heartland'—but also someone acceptable to the sizeable Muslim minority whose loyalty to India had to be reinforced, given their decision to remain in India and not migrate to Pakistan. But there was clearly another dimension to the Jawaharlal vs Vallabhbhai choice—England-educated Jawaharlal was the darling of the globalized, metropolitan elite, the erstwhile rulers of India, while Vallabhbhai was very Indian and vernacular. Gandhiji knew the world. His 'loincloth' attire should not make us forget that he, too, was educated in London, and he had a good sense of how power is acquired and wielded by a nation's elite. Vallabhbhai was the 'iron man' who united India; Jawaharlal was the urbane gentleman who would convince the masses that their leaders had the class confidence to be rulers.

In opting for Jawaharlal over Vallabhbhai, Gandhiji chose an anglicized, globalized Indian to preside over the destiny of Bharat. After all, even after the British withdrew from India it was this elite, dubbed 'Macaulay's children', who manned the institutions of the state. Nehru was to the manner and manor born. Within months of becoming PM, Jawaharlal took over the impressive and palatial official residence of the commander-in-chief (C-in-C) of the armed forces and made it the prime minister's home, rejecting advice to the contrary from some traditional Congressmen. The President of the Republic, of course, moved into the Viceroy's Palace!

In most post-revolution societies, the new rulers make it a point to destroy the economic, social, political and cultural base of the old power elite. From the French Revolution to the Russian and Chinese, we have seen the dethroning, often killing, of the old power elite. In India's 'gradual revolution', the old elite of a feudal India survived into the new world of a democratic India.[3] The institutions of the state, too, merely readjusted themselves to the new order rather than being reinvented. Thus, the instrument of colonial governance, the Indian Civil Service, became the Indian

Administrative Service (IAS), and the Indian armed forces retained the pre-existing leadership hierarchy, facilitating a smooth transition to Indian leadership rather than an overturning of the inherited order.

The most British of Indian inheritances, apart from the English language, was the architecture of the nation's capital. Edwin Lutyens was a British architect who had designed the palaces, office buildings and government residences of the British Raj in a region adjacent to the 'Old Delhi' of the Mughals, and that came to be called New Delhi. In Nehru's time, Lutyens' Delhi was home only to the Government of India. Bombay remained India's business and financial capital, and the subcontinent had no one cultural capital, with cities like Calcutta, Madras (now Chennai), Pune, Hyderabad, Baroda (now Vadodara) and Lucknow being centres of culture. However, by the end of Rajiv Gandhi's tenure, in the mid-1980s, New Delhi had not only come to dominate the nation's politics, but the industrial Licence-Permit-Quota Raj that fostered what has latterly been dubbed 'crony capitalism' was the foundation of an Indian variant of 'state capitalism'. This had made Bombay subservient to Delhi.

The central government also became the dispenser of largesse as far as the world of culture was concerned, much like in any feudal darbar, and not just of high culture. Popular culture, too, began to be manufactured in Delhi with private television making the national capital's extension into Uttar Pradesh its base. Both news television and entertainment TV opened shop in Delhi after the 1990s. The country's political capital also became its media and mass culture capital. Taken together, Delhi's three worlds— of politics and government, of business and of culture/media— created a new post-Independence elite physically located in Delhi even if it was from different parts of India. This social group is what is known as the 'Lutyens' elite'.

New Delhi began its post-Independence life as a city of refugees and immigrants. India's pre-Independence elite were evenly spread across the centres of colonial urban life—Calcutta, Bombay, Madras, Lucknow, Patna and Bangalore. The capitals of princely states like Hyderabad, Mysore and Baroda had their elites and elitist institutions. After Independence, Delhi gradually acquired primacy, but it was only in the 1980s that it began to forge ahead of Calcutta as a cultural capital, and in the 1990s, as a business and media capital. Delhi's wealthy today are no longer from the families of colonial Delhi but from the upwardly mobile immigrant families that began as contractors, traders, lobbyists, and constitute Delhi's parvenu bourgeoisie. They have come to be increasingly identified as members of a postcolonial power elite.

If New Delhi had remained merely a government city, as it was well into the 1970s, with Bombay remaining the hub of business and commerce, Calcutta and Chennai the cultural capitals and so on, Lutyens' Delhi would not have become the powerful symbol of the era of dynastic rule of the Nehru-Gandhis. New business groups like the Munjals of the Hero two-wheelers fame and the Mittals of Airtel established their head office in New Delhi and many Kolkata-based Marwari business families moved to Delhi. From the 1980s, New Delhi also became the centre of big media. The Bombay-based *Times of India* and *Economic Times* decided to shift their editorial offices to New Delhi in the 1980s. National news magazines like *India Today* and private news television channels like NDTV were established in Delhi. With New Delhi becoming the home of big money and big media it also attracted big culture, and by the turn of the century, became India's publishing hub.

Till the 1970s, the University of Delhi was one among many good universities. Others like the universities of Madras, Bombay, Calcutta, Allahabad, the Banaras Hindu University, Osmania University, Andhra University, and MS University Baroda were all regarded equally good in terms of their faculty. By the turn of the century most provincial universities began to sink into regionalism, casteism, communal politics and corruption. The vice chancellors of many universities today would not get admission into the best universities of Asia, not to speak of the West. Even in a highly literate state like Kerala, vice chancellorships were handed out on a communal basis, with one university headed by a Hindu, another a Christian and a third a Muslim. Police officers started heading universities across India. In this milieu the Jawaharlal Nehru University (JNU), established by Indira Gandhi, emerged as a symbol of excellence combined with commitment to social justice and welfare.

Ever since the Union ministry of human resources development began ranking Indian universities, JNU was always ranked second best, next only to the highly regarded Indian Institute of Science in Bangalore. However, JNU also became a symbol of left-wing and liberal politics with the students' union always under the control of one left group or another. Given this context, JNU, too, became a metaphor. It was what the BJP did not want an Indian university to be. The rise of mediocrity in JNU's governance enabled the BJP to easily pursue its Hindutva agenda of pitting student radicalism against Hindu nationalism. The expected resistance from the left, liberal academics and students is precisely what the BJP wanted, for it made JNU an easy target. Ironically, a university that opened its doors to the economically weaker sections of society and the socially underprivileged is now projected as an elitist institution because its origins lie in the left-liberal elitism of the 1970s.

The metaphor of 'Lutyens' Delhi' no longer refers to a geographical entity limited to the tree-lined avenues in the vicinity of the palace of the President of the Republic. It has become a portmanteau phrase that defines India's post-Independence ruling class. Geographically speaking, this class lives not just in Delhi's government area or nearby localities like Jor Bagh, Chanakyapuri, Vasant Vihar, Shanti Niketan, Greater Kailash, New Friends Colony and Maharani Bagh, but also in distant Gurugram and Noida. As Ranjana Sengupta observes in her evocative account of social change in post-Independence Delhi, the national capital is many cities in one in which, 'The celebration of Lutyens' Delhi may be couched in the vocabulary of heritage, architectural aesthetics and history, but the values it asserts—consciously or not—are those of regimentation, hierarchy and exclusion.'[4] These attributes, common to many imperial capitals, define Delhi's elitism.

With time, elites in major cities, especially Mumbai, have joined the ranks of this class through business links, social networking and political links. Many Lutyens' insiders have gone global, living as far away as London and Manhattan, visiting home when the weather is pleasant! No one represented this elite better than the country's first political family—the Nehru-Gandhis—and the many families cutting across professions that benefited from serving the family's successive generations.

Modi was not the first to identify and mock the so-called 'Lutyens' elite'. Diplomat, writer and now politician Pavan Varma identified a class that was monolingual in the English language and socially alienated from the India around them. He cites the telling example of pyjama parties in swank farmhouses located in the middle of rural Haryana. But this social set is only a subgroup of the much wider Lutyens' elite.[5] Though, as Sengupta observes, 'There is no recent portrait of the machinations of the political class, the brittle angst of the haute bourgeoisie or the new ariviste post Partition class that is soaring upwards on the wings of fashion, media or politics.'[6]

The irony of Modi's metaphor is that it is an argument first and most widely used by his leftist critics. It was the left that wrote passionately about the divide between a westernized India and the indigenous Bharat. It campaigned for a more federal and less Delhi-dominated India, gave primacy to education in the mother tongue and championed the linguistic reorganization of states. The difference is that the Left's 'India vs Bharat' argument was defined in class terms, while the Modi metaphor is defined in class and caste terms, but equally in cultural terms. The Lutyens' elite are an English speaking cultural elite that are a colonial inheritance in postcolonial India.

Rahul Gandhi's political adviser and aide, a non-resident Indian living mainly in the United States, Satyanarayan Gangaram Pitroda aka Sam Pitroda, described this class graphically while defending his controversial statement on the pogrom against the Sikh community of Delhi following Indira Gandhi's assassination. Claiming that his insensitive remark, '*hua to hua*' (if it happened it happened), was on account of his poor command over the Hindi language, Pitroda said, 'I think in English and translate my thoughts into Hindi.'[7] Pitroda spoke for an entire elite that often fails to mentally connect with fellow Indians because they do not 'think' in their mother tongue.

English, as spoken in India, has become just another Indian language. Millions of Indians do function in English during their working hours. But the India that 'thinks and, indeed, dreams, in English' is getting increasingly marginalized by a Bharat that thinks and dreams in the mother tongue. Even the soft drink multinational Pepsi bowed its head to this class when it chose to market its global product with the Hindi line, '*Yeh Dil Mangey More*' (This heart desires more).

Modi belongs to this new 'Aspirational India' that also desires more, and, he believes, it belongs to him. It is a social class that does not think or dream in English. It is a class that prefers to eat with the hand and does not quite understand the differing purposes of a fork and a spoon. This class does not constitute India's 'power elite' but it has begun to matter more—socially, politically and economically. Through its ranks, members of a new power elite are emerging. The political transition in India can also be viewed as a battle for influence between an old and a new power elite. Modi has pitched himself as the voice of the new, projecting Rahul Gandhi's as that of the old.

Nothing symbolizes the power shift in New Delhi better than the history and destiny of the mansion of the commander-in-chief of the British Empire's armed forces. Situated in the vicinity of the palace of the viceroy—that then became Rashtrapati Bhavan—the C-in-C's mansion continued to house Sir Robert McGregor Macdonald Lockhart, the British chief of the Indian Army at Independence. Prime Minister Nehru was, however, staying at 17 York Road (renamed Motilal Nehru Marg). In August 1948, Nehru moved into the C-in-C's mansion that was renamed Teen Murti Bhavan. It is possible that Nehru felt that like the head of state, the head of government ought to also live in a stately building. After all, independent India's republican and democratic state adopted many of the symbols of power and privilege inherited from the empire. Congressman Jairam Ramesh has, however, found archival evidence to suggest that both Lord Mountbatten, then governor general, and Sardar Patel, then home minister, advised Nehru to move to a more secure premises after the assassination of Mahatma Gandhi, and this building was considered adequately secure.[8]

Following Nehru's death, Lal Bahadur Shastri could not gather the courage to move in to Panditji's mansion, and when Indira Gandhi succeeded him she was advised by her 'left-liberal' friends not to move into this stately mansion. It was then decided that the mansion would be turned into a museum and a memorial to honour Nehru. Indira Gandhi personally interviewed candidates shortlisted by her close advisers like Romesh Thapar, and the Nehru Memorial Museum and Library (NMML) took shape. Over the subsequent four decades, the NMML campus, with its impressive library and archives, became the centre of considerable intellectual activity that valorized India's Nehruvian legacy. Not surprisingly, therefore, Prime Minister Modi decided to alter the character of the premises as part of his campaign to liberate India from the Nehruvian intellectual inheritance.

Modi's task was, however, made easy by the manner in which NMML came to be governed over the preceding couple of decades. NMML's days of glory were during the two-decade tenure of historian Ravinder Kumar, from 1979 to 1997. Kumar was not just a respected liberal academic but a visionary institution builder who kept the doors of NMML open to the free flow of ideas and helped several generations of young scholars. Kumar was succeeded by a less-known career bureaucrat without intellectual credentials but who kept the place going. The real blow to NMML's hallowed reputation, assiduously built by Ravinder Kumar, was struck by Nehru's own family and acolytes.

In 2005, a selection committee that included Sonia Gandhi, Manmohan Singh, Natwar Singh and journalist Suman Dubey, picked a historian of no great distinction but known to be close to the old CPI and its intellectual camp followers. Appointed on the recommendation of JNU historian Bipan Chandra, Mridula Mukherjee failed to win the respect of NMML's many well-wishers. Her appointment caused a vertical split within the 'left-liberal' intellectual establishment with only a section of the left, especially those still loyal to the Congress, supporting her appointment. The anti-Indira section of the left, especially academics close to the CPI(M), and the liberal intelligentsia both in India and overseas, vehemently attacked the Manmohan Singh government for making this appointment. Mukherjee's tenure was riddled with controversy with several eminent scholars repeatedly petitioning the trustees to intervene and set things right. When the time came for a renewal of term, in 2009, an international campaign was mounted to thwart it.

An army of liberal scholars including Rajmohan Gandhi, Sanjay Subrahmanyam, Sunil Khilnani, Sumit Sarkar, Neera Chandoke, Ramachandra Guha and many others from around the world wrote a letter seeking Manmohan Singh's intervention to 'save one of India's great national institutions' that had been 'trapped in a culture of apathy and mediocrity'.[9] Praising the long tradition of 'pluralism and ecumenism' associated with earlier directors, this letter alleged that, after 2005, NMML had become increasingly associated with one political party, with photographs of its leaders on display in the building and the youth wing of the Congress party allowed to hold its meetings there. Trustees including Suman Dubey, a friend of Rajiv and Sonia Gandhi and at the time corporate head of the US media firm Dow Jones, were accused of acquiescing in the conversion of NMML into a Congress party outfit.

Despite such protestations, Mukherjee's term was extended. In her second term, Mukherjee teamed up with her sister and husband, both historians, to produce a Congress party publication, *Congress and the Making of a Nation*, with Pranab Mukherjee, then finance minister, as the editor, and Anand Sharma, then commerce minister, as convener of the editorial board. The virtual takeover of NMML, a national institution with an international reputation, by the Congress party and in the face of protests by several distinguished scholars, presented Narendra Modi with a perfect opportunity to expose the underbelly of Lutyens' Delhi.

Early into his first term, Modi ensured that an IAS officer, with an interest in research, Shakti Sinha, who had worked as a personal secretary to the PM in Atal Bihari Vajpayee's PMO, was appointed director of NMML. While those who protested Mukherjee's appointment once again protested Sinha's, Modi and the BJP only drew attention to the manner in which the Sonia Congress had converted a national institution into a family and partisan entity. If Congress faithful had dominated the NMML's board of trustees and its various boards and councils, they would now be replaced by BJP's faithful. People like journalist Suman Dubey, politician Jairam Ramesh, economist Nitin Desai, bureaucrats Gopalakrishna Gandhi and M.S. Gill, all appointees of Congress governments, were replaced by journalists Surya Prakash, Swapan Dasgupta and Arnab Goswami, BJP member Vinay Sahasrabuddhe, and linguist Kapil Kapoor.

In the seminar rooms and corridors of NMML, photographs of Congress leaders have been replaced by BJP leaders. Modi's final denouement was to convert Teen Murti Bhavan from being a memorial only to India's first prime minister into a memorial for all prime ministers. The Nehru-Gandhi family's desire to appropriate a national institution and convert it into a party- and family-dominated entity offered Modi the opportunity to pull down one more monument of a bygone era. Many academics had protested the appointment of journalist Arnab Goswami to the NMML council, but then, none of them had ever protested the role of another journalist, Suman Dubey, who was both a member of the NMML council and was secretary of the Jawaharlal Nehru Memorial Fund, a private trust housed within the Teen Murti Bhavan campus.

The conversion of NMML from a memorial to Nehru into one for all PMs was a move that few could object to. Even fewer could object to replacing one set of fellow travellers with another. Every constituent of Lutyens' Delhi knows that is how power works. Located at the heart of Lutyens' Delhi, the NMML became one more metaphor for the cultural revolution that Modi had begun to bring about.

Even as Modi targets the elite as denizens of Lutyens' Delhi he has begun the process of in fact reshaping Lutyens' Delhi by rebuilding its core, the central vista, of which Rajpath is the spine and the entire area around it presents the architectural persona of the Indian state. The reconstruction of the central vista symbolizes its political reconstitution. In a report presenting all viewpoints on the proposed changes, the *India Today* news magazine dubbed it 'Modifying Lutyens'.[10] Delhi's old elite, best represented by vocal critics like architect Gautam Bhatia, bemoan the tearing down of old landmarks that Modi's India views as symbols of the Nehru-Indira era. Bhatia would prefer the central vista to in fact be converted into 'a truly heroic space of cultural and social participation' rather than be cluttered with more imposing structures representing the state.[11] The highly regarded British Indian sculptor and artist Anish Kapoor, whose exhibition of his oeuvre in New Delhi in 2010 was inaugurated by Sonia Gandhi, was sharper in his denunciation. 'The destruction of Lutyens's Delhi is deeply misguided and comes out of Modi's political fanaticism. This is not the redesign of buildings, it is instead Modi's way of placing himself at the centre and cementing his legacy as the maker of a new Hindu India.'[12]

The change began with the iconic Hall of Nations, in Delhi's Pragati Maidan, opened by Indira Gandhi in 1972 to celebrate the silver jubilee of India's Independence, and described by the curator of London's Museum of Modern Art (MOMA) as 'the first large-scale concrete (spatial) structure in the world'. It was torn down by the Modi government on the plea that better use would be made of that space. Lutyens' Delhi reacted in horror. A group of eminent Indian architects issued a statement opposing these plans, calling the Hall of Nations and the Nehru Pavilion 'a vital part of India's contemporary heritage'. What they did not reckon was the fact that a new social set had come to power in Lutyens' Delhi that had no such aesthetic sensibility. From the periphery of Lutyens' Delhi the architectural reconstruction has moved to its heart—the central vista. Not surprisingly, the aesthetes of the old elite have been horrified. The barbarians, they believe, have entered the gates.

Digression into Concepts

3

Power and Elitism

In positioning himself as anti-elite Modi's politics has drawn attention to the paradoxical relationship between elitism and power. Modi was the all-powerful head of government and the unquestioned leader of his party when he claimed he was not one of the nation's elite. His critics questioned Modi's anti-elitism by drawing attention to his unparalleled political power. However, in berating the capital's elites even as he conquered the summit of state power, Modi drew attention not only to a long-standing debate among social scientists on who constitute the elite and who are part of the powerful and what distinguishes one from the other, but also to an important feature of the Indian state that had been elaborated by Michal Kalecki.

Writing in the 1960s, after his brief visit to India, Kalecki described the Indian state as an 'intermediate regime'—neither capitalist nor socialist but in the control of a middle class.[1] In Kalecki's view, Indian society was divided into three groups—at the top were the landlord and business classes, with 'big business', some of it foreign owned, the dominant class. At the bottom were the workers, the landless and the poor peasants. In the middle were positioned the 'middle classes' comprising the rich peasantry, small businesses and the professional middle class. Democratic politics and the national movement had succeeded in vesting power with these 'intermediate' classes. While the poor were both powerless and non-elite and the elite were not necessarily all-powerful, the intermediate classes had access to power through the institutions of the state but did not belong to the elite.

The turn in India's caste-based politics over the past quarter century, with middle castes acquiring greater political power compared to the lower and upper castes, has further cemented the foundations of the intermediate regime. India's elite may be its landed aristocracy, its capitalists and financiers, its upper castes and celebrities, but India's powerful are its politicians, of varied castes and regions, its permanent civil service and the occupants of the institutions of the state. In mocking the Lutyens' elite, Narendra Modi, a member of the middle class and from a 'middle caste', was speaking as a spokesperson of a new 'governing non-elite', an intermediate class of those who had acquired political power but were as yet excluded from the nation's economic and cultural elite.

In the literature on power and the elites this distinction between these twin concepts is not very often clearly drawn. For a Marxist the distinction would be irrelevant. The 'ruling class' would be a society's 'elite' that also exercises power in its various manifestations—political, economic and cultural. The many professions and professionals who constitute a society's elite would only be serving the interests of the ruling class. In a feudal society that privilege would be of the landed aristocracy; in a capitalist society the ruling class would be the bourgeoisie and the state would be a bourgeois state.

In communist societies like the erstwhile Soviet Union and China, the pre-revolution elite were not just unseated from positions of power, but many were physically eliminated or forced to leave the country. Even writers and artists, who had no share in state power but were regarded as members of a complicit elite were denounced and persecuted. In short, the communists did not recognize any distinction between the social and cultural elite and those who wielded power through economic and political means.

The revolution endeavoured to eliminate the economic and political ruling class as well as the elitism of the social and cultural upper class in order to establish a classless society and the dictatorship of the proletariat.

While Karl Marx saw power as a function of class, sociologist Max Weber believed that there could be multiple sources of power, with economic power being only one of them. Social status and political affiliations could also be a source of power.[2] The authority of the state, Weber argued, was derived from three sources: tradition, charisma or bureaucracy. Of the three, he saw bureaucracy as inherent to any organization—capitalist or socialist. In his classic treatise on power, Bertrand Russell suggested that the ability of an elite to wield power is based on a social contract defined by a 'general acceptance of authority'.[3]

Russell identified six forms of power—priestly or traditional, kingly, naked, revolutionary, economic and ideological.[4] Religious institutions and leaders exercise what Russell calls 'priestly' power. This is based on tradition and so may also be called traditional power. Such priestly power can acquire the features of other forms of power depending on what point in history one is examining a society and what nation one is referring to. After all, religious institutions and leaders have acquired 'kingly' power as well and have also enjoyed economic and ideological power. In some parts of the world they have also exercised 'revolutionary' power, that is power derived from ideological mobilization. Radical movements of the left and the right, like the RSS, exercise that kind of power.

Traditional power is the basis of 'social dominance', a concept we shall consider in the next chapter. While kingly (political power of governments) and naked (military and police) power are exercised by the institutions of the state, both priestly and kingly power are backed by tradition and general social consent. Russell called the power that is exercised against or without such social consent 'naked power'. It is the power of the military and the police. Economic power may be exercised both by the state and religious institutions, but in modern societies it is increasingly exercised by private capital. Ideological power, or as Russell termed it, the 'power over opinion' is exercised essentially by those who wield both priestly and kingly power but also by those wielding economic power. However, in modern democracies, the power over opinion is dispersed across many social institutions, including the media and cinema.

Power, Russell suggests, is to social dynamics what energy is to the physical. It is the motive behind change. To understand how societies are organized and how nations evolve, it is necessary to understand the structure and dynamics of power in its various manifestations. 'The men who cause social change are,' in Russell's words, 'men who strongly desire to do so. Love of power, therefore, is a characteristic of the men who are causally important . . . The laws of social dynamics are only capable of being stated in terms of power in its various forms.'[5]

The power of the elites was examined in interesting ways by three distinguished Italian scholars writing in the early twentieth century. The earliest of them was Vilfredo Pareto who proposed that all societies are indeed divided into 'elites' and 'non-elites' and that the former possess qualities that enable them to exercise power. Pareto defined the elite as 'a class of people who have the highest indices in their branch of activity . . . and . . . possess in marked degree, qualities of intelligence, character, skill and capacity of whatever kind'. He then divided the 'elite' into two categories— the 'governing' and the 'non-governing' elite. The governing elite exercise 'power' through their control of government and ownership of wealth, while the non-governing elite possess power derived from economic, social and cultural capital.[6]

Pareto was followed by Gaetano Mosca, an Italian political scientist, politician and journalist, who was regarded, along with Pareto, to be a 'founding father of elitism theory'. Gaetano defined the 'elite' as a 'class that rules' and proposed that such an elite is common to all societies. To quote Mosca:

In all societies from societies that are meagrely developed and have barely attained the dawnings of civilization, down to the most advanced and powerful societies—two classes of people appear—a class that rules and a class that is ruled. The first, always the less numerous, performs all political functions, monopolizes power and enjoys the advantages that power brings, whereas the second, the more numerous class, is directed and controlled by the first.[7]

The most interesting theorization on elites, elitism and power was conducted by Antonio Gramsci. Imprisoned by the Italian dictator Benito Mussolini for being a communist, Gramsci did most of his writing in prison, and his essays, titled the *Prison Notebooks,* have been mostly published posthumously. Rejecting the traditional Marxist view of the ruling class power being determined largely by economic factors, Gramsci emphasized the role of ideology and the cultural dominance of an elite. The ability of a ruling class to dominate society through the power of ideas rather than brute force was defined by Gramsci as 'hegemony'. Marx and Engels had famously said that 'the ideas of the ruling class are in every epoch the ruling ideas'.[8] Gramsci, made a distinction between the dominance of the ruling class over institutions of the state— executive, judiciary, military and the police—and within civil society, shaped by religious and educational institutions, political parties and the media. 'The methodological criterion on which our own study must be based,' suggested Gramsci, 'is that the supremacy of a social group manifests itself in two ways, as "domination" and as "intellectual and moral leadership".'[9]

In the Indian context, one could suggest that while most political parties, including the Congress, have sought political 'power', the BJP, under Modi's leadership, is seeking 'hegemony' and 'domination'. Modi's slogan of 'Congress-mukt Bharat' and his relentless campaign against the only two 'national' political forces—the Congress and the left (in its various hues)—while willing to accommodate regional political parties, suggests a political strategy of seeking Gramscian hegemony and dominance. Indeed, the cultural and intellectual project of the RSS is about seeking 'supremacy of a social group' through 'intellectual and moral' hegemony. Given this political imperative, Modi's BJP has felt compelled to not merely challenge the Congress politically, but also ideologically; to not merely win an election but to establish its political dominance and cultural hegemony.

———

It is not my intention here to be detained by a survey of the considerable literature on the definition of who constitute the elite and the power of that elite.[10] For the purposes of our discussion, it is enough to say that in modern democracies the elite constitute a recognizable social group, given their access to and possession of economic and cultural capital defined in terms of their earned and inherited income, assets and education. A ruling class rules not merely by dominating the institutions of the state but, à la Gramsci, by acquiring hegemony in the realm of intellectual and moral leadership. An elite is a social group that has acquired such hegemony. C. Wright Mills described this class as a nation's 'power elite':

> The power elite form a more or less compact social and psychological entity; they have become self-conscious members of a social class . . . There is a qualitative split . . . separating them from those who are not elite. They are more or less aware of themselves as a social class and they behave toward one another differently from the way they do toward members of other classes. They accept one another, understand one another, marry one another, tend to work and to think if not together at least alike.[11]

In other words, they are not merely a class in itself but a class for itself. In Mills' view, the power elite, as defined, exercise power in its varied forms—economic, political and military.[12] Democratic politics, however, provide an opportunity for non-elites to also acquire power, even if for brief periods of time. The powerful may then graduate to become elites in due course, though not necessarily so. On the other hand, many members of a nation's elite—its cultural czars and business moguls—may not have access to political power but wield cultural and economic power and, therefore, may remain part of the elite but exercise little power outside the realm of their own activity. Mills, echoing Gramsci's view of intellectuals, saw 'celebrities' as opinion-makers, and therefore, members of the elite, exercising power over opinion.

In examining the social structure of post-War America, Mills concluded that four social groups dominated the country's power system—business, military, politicians and celebrities. Mills described the 'elite' as 'those who have the most of what there is to have, which is generally held to include money, power, and prestige' and control of institutions that facilitate this. The 'powerful' are defined as 'those who are able to realize their will, even if others resist it'.[13] Given these definitions, Mills defines the power elite as 'those political, economic, and military circles which as an intricate set of overlapping cliques that share decisions having at least national consequences. In so far as national events are decided, the power elite are those who decide them.'[14]

Considering the structure of American society and his understanding of American politics, Mills believed the 'elite' were also the nation's power centre. That he regarded the military as an important part of the US's power elite is both a testimony to the role of the armed forces in American history and nation-building, and to its role in the Second World War and post-War US politics. Mills gave prominence of place to a class he dubbed 'the celebrities' that included the captains of media, opinion-makers and, of course, Hollywood. While the idea of a homogenous 'power elite' is appealing, the dynamics of electoral politics in an unequal society is such that power sometimes does pass into the hands of the non-elite.

While the elite exercise power in one form or another, those who acquire political power through democratic means may not always be welcomed into the ranks of the elite. In such a situation one can understand what we can term 'the Modi Paradox', so to speak, of the powerful despising the elite.

The 'love of power' of 'the elite that rules' is circumscribed in a democracy by the rule of law and constitutional and institutional checks and balances. In doing so, a democratic society gives power to those who man the institutions of the state—the legislature, the executive, the judiciary and the police. The class that is so empowered is the middle class. If we define the 'middle class' in Kaleckian terms, as including rich peasants, small businesses and professionals, and those who man the bureaucracy, we would then find that a large number of such people in India belong to the 'middle castes' as well. This is a proposition that we will return to in the next chapter.

Power and Elitism

While political power is exercised by members of a 'governing elite', to use Pareto's phrase, economic, social and cultural capital defines the power of the 'non-governing' elite. Indeed, 'elitism' is a social and cultural phenomenon shaped both by inheritance and by access to education. Pierre Bourdieu has given us a fascinating account of how elitism is constituted through the accumulation of cultural capital.[15] The power of a social class that defines taste and modes of consumption of ideas and habits, attitudes and prejudices is manifested in its elitism. In India, command over the English language has been a primary source of social and cultural capital. The schools, colleges and media that define social taste shape elitism, an attitude that in itself becomes a source and manifestation of power.

The definition of aesthetic and vulgar, high-brow and low-brow, modern and traditional, liberal and conservative, folk and popular, sacred and profane, legitimate and illegitimate, and what is socially acceptable and what is not, is a consequence of acculturation—the process by which elites acquire and retain their elitism. The power to so define is exercised by a class that may not have economic or political power but enjoys social status and cultural hegemony.

When Narendra Modi distinguishes himself from the 'Lutyens' elite', he speaks for a class that has not acquired the social capital that inheritance and education give to those who define what is acceptable and what is unacceptable. Modi is the first prime minister to have self-consciously distanced himself from India's post-Independence 'Nehruvian elite'. He is of course not the first prime minister to have come from that background. From Lal Bahadur Shastri to Manmohan Singh, many prime ministers have also had a similar social background that stands in contrast to the upper-class, upper-caste, English-educated elitism of the Nehru clan. However, while most of them, including Atal Bihari Vajpayee, also came from a non-elite background, they sought to become a part of 'Lutyens' Delhi' by wooing the Nehruvian elite.

In fact, Vajpayee was often criticized by some diehard ideologues of his own party for seeking the approval of the 'Nehruvian elite'. 'Build your elite,' Swapan Dasgupta, then a journalist and now a member of Parliament, advised Vajpayee through one of his media columns, 'a party looks commanding in office if it is seen to have its own experts, stars and style. Vajpayee is too wary of breaking the mould and developing a saffron counter-establishment.'[16] In yet another column, Dasgupta accused Vajpayee of wanting to ingratiate himself to the members of the IIC—a much-envied symbol of New Delhi's elitism.

The distinction between Vajpayee's prime ministership and that of Modi can be made in Gramscian terms—the BJP under Vajpayee was seeking power within the limitations imposed by an ideologically diverse coalition, while the BJP under Modi has sought to assert political hegemony, given the favourable parliamentary arithmetic.

Assured of the power of political office, Vajpayee sought the acceptance of the power elite. He accommodated them as much as he wanted to be accommodated by them.

That was also the impulse of another 'outsider'—Narasimha Rao. Rao was an 'outsider' to Lutyens' Delhi and the national power elite, but clearly wanted to be regarded an 'insider'—the title of his fictionalized autobiography.[17] Manmohan Singh, too, came from a middle-class family, but his Oxbridge education enabled him to accumulate the social capital required to enter the ranks of the elite. Among the few personal initiatives that Manmohan Singh took using his status as prime minister was to authorize the grant of Manmohan Singh scholarships to Indian students studying at the University of Cambridge, UK, funded, among others, by British Petroleum and Rolls-Royce. Clearly, he wanted to be remembered more by his Oxbridge connection than by his Punjabi roots.

Modi not only came from a non-elite background but made a virtue of it by consciously creating a distance between himself and the country's ruling elite. Modi's contempt for Lutyens' Delhi captured the sentiment of a new social class that democracy and development had empowered but had not yet endowed with the cultural capital of elitism. A class that is not seeking admission into the ranks of the power elite, but dominance over them.

The Elite in India

In India an important social institution that has defined power is the caste system. Sociologist Andre Beteille brought out the interplay between caste and class in determining power at the village level in southern India and inspired other such studies on the many facets of power and elitism in India.[18] Examining the interplay between state power and social dominance across very different parts of India, M.S.A. Rao and Francine Frankel brought together a large number of regional studies in their two-volume study. Rao proposed that 'a useful distinction can be made between dominance in the domain of society and political power in the arena of the State. The distinction between dominance and political power overlaps with that between society and State to a considerable extent.'[19]

The 'elite' in India can be defined as those who wield power either through the modern institutions of the state or through traditional institutions of civil society, or through both. The caste system is one such traditional institution of power that confers elitism on the upper castes and defines social attitudes of middle and lower castes. Indians at the bottom of the social pyramid confront multiple forms of power—economic, political, social and cultural. The hierarchy of caste in itself defines elitism at the community level and the process of 'Sanskritisation', as sociologist M.N. Srinivas termed it, has been an affirmation of upper-caste elitism.[20] However, it would be simplistic to presume that caste and class run parallel, given the economic empowerment of various middle castes and the economic decline of some of the upper castes.

At the top of the caste pyramid we see a differentiation emerging based on the separation of political power from economic power through the intermediation of democratic institutions. The political empowerment of intermediate castes through the institutions of representative democracy has empowered social groups referred to as 'backward classes'. Frankel summed up the general conclusion of the studies brought together by Rao and her as follows: 'As India entered the 1990s a discernible separation was taking shape between economic power and political power. The decline of a homogenous elite, rooted in status hierarchies erected upon devalued notions of purity and pollution, is likely to place even greater importance on access to the huge resources of the managerial state as a basis of rank and privilege in society.'[21]

New forms of social domination and a new hierarchy of privilege and elitism have been shaped in urban India by elite schools and colleges and, increasingly, foreign education. In a social democracy, access to education has been an important instrument of upward social mobility. During colonial rule, a new urban middle class entered the portals of power and elitism through the acquisition of English-language education. After Independence, education has remained an important means of social and economic empowerment. Even so, a highly differentiated educational system has ensured that certain class privileges are retained by the elite through their access to privileged and exclusive educational institutions.

In theory, therefore, entry into the new power elite is not closed, as it is in the caste system where entry is defined by the accident of birth. But entry barriers remain high. If traditional elitism is shaped by traditional institutions of power, like caste, modern elitism is shaped by modern institutions like privileged schooling. Till the turn of the century, privileged schooling meant boarding schools or high-cost day schools in India. Over the past couple of decades privileged schooling has meant sending one's children off to Singapore, Dubai or even the UK. Privileged graduate education certainly implies overseas education.

While power in traditional institutions of hierarchy is based on social sanction, the foundation of power in contemporary India is increasingly based on wealth, the control of political power through the institutions of state and civil society, and the accumulation of social and cultural capital through access to modern education. And so, even when wealth is concentrated in a mere 3 per cent of the population, and cultural capital in an even smaller segment, power in its various forms may well be exercised by a larger segment of the population.

4

Social Dominance and Political Power

As a member of a backward caste—the fourth tier in the four-tiered varna system—Modi has successfully taken control of what was for a long time an upper-caste-dominated political movement and party.[1] The RSS has always been viewed as a Brahmin-dominated organization, though the Brahminical hold over the RSS has been weakening. The BJP's first prime minister, Atal Bihari Vajpayee, was a Brahmin; its most popular leader till Modi came along, Lal Krishna Advani, is Lohana, a Sindhi upper caste; most party presidents, apart from the scheduled caste Bangaru Lakshman, were upper caste. Modi stormed into this upper-caste bastion and changed the party's fortunes. So, if there is a touch of casteism to Modi's anti-elitism, one should not be surprised. Caste is the identity through which elitism and social dominance have long manifested themselves in India. In democratic India, it has also become the vehicle for political power.

Whatever its origins and purpose, the caste system was traditionally hierarchical. The 'upper castes' were defined by three conceptions of power—ideological or knowledge (Brahmin), military and political (Kshatriya) and income and wealth (Vaishya). The lower/backward group, Sudra, covers a wide range of working people, including cultivators. Modi's caste is *teli,* a community of oil-pressers. Below the backward groups come the outcastes—those required to perform

57

menial duties—and the tribal communities living in forests. They remain outside the caste hierarchy. The 'power elite' in this ancient system of social gradation are the Brahmins and the Kshatriyas, underscoring the political, military and cultural foundations of power. The Vaishya community acquired salience and entry into the 'power elite' only in a post-feudal India in which wealth became an increasingly important means of acquiring and exercising power. From a village community to the national government, the ancient caste hierarchy continues to define the structure of power.

The hierarchical nature of the caste system has been the social foundation of elitism and power through history. There are, of course, regional variations in the composition of castes across the subcontinent, and caste identities have even penetrated non-Hindu religions practised in India.[2] It would, however, be a mistake to imagine that the structure and composition of the 'power elite' in India strictly mimics the caste system. To be sure, upper castes populate and dominate all major institutions. Elitism is built into the very idea of a social hierarchy based on the accident of birth since one is born into one's caste and does not have the option of graduating to a 'higher' caste.

However, the caste base of political power, and indeed of politically related economic power, has widened to include a range of what may be termed as intermediate castes. The Polish economist Michał Kalecki's rich peasants, government officials, small businesses and an assortment of middle classes do not necessarily belong to upper castes. In fact, over time, they have increasingly come from intermediate castes known as OBCs. As sociologist D.L. Sheth noted, 'The traditional [caste] status system is now thickly overlaid by the new power system created by elections, political parties and, above all, by social policies—such as affirmative action—of the state on the one hand and, on the other, by changes in the occupational structure of society . . .'[3] Economic and political empowerment has allowed many sub-castes to claim a higher status within the caste hierarchy.

The political clout of the OBC became manifest when the long era of Congress party dominance came to an end in the 1980s, the era of 'Mandal politics'. Following the decision of Prime Minister V.P. Singh to implement the recommendations of the Mandal Commission on Socially and Educationally Backward Classes, OBC leaders acquired centre stage in national politics. Karnataka's H.D. Deve Gowda became the first OBC prime minister, heading a short-lived coalition government in 1996–97. Constituted in 1979, the Mandal Commission report was submitted in 1983 but was implemented only in 1990 when Prime Minister V.P. Singh decided to extend reservations in educational institutions and government organizations to the so-called OBCs. The Backwards Castes have come to be called Other Backward Classes so as to distinguish them from the constitutionally recognized weaker sections, namely, the Scheduled Castes and Tribes (SC/ST).

Modi has been able to extend the BJP's support base beyond its traditional upper-caste base to bring OBCs into its fold. By doing this, he has followed the same path to power the BJP tried out in Gujarat, Modi's home state, where the party grew on the strength of such OBC support.[4] With the singular exception of Manmohan Singh, a member of the Sikh community, most other Indian prime ministers have belonged to the Hindu 'upper castes'. While Modi acquired immense political power and ran a highly centralized administration, as a clever tactical move in his first term in office, he chose to hand over key ministries—finance, home, defence, foreign affairs and human resources development—to upper-caste politicians, mostly Brahmins. Key officials within the Modi PMO, including the two Mishras—Nripendra and P.K.—who have been principal secretary to the PM, have also been Brahmins. While Modi's politics, like that of his party, has been based on the development and strengthening of a pan-Indian 'Hindu' electorate, in opposition to the caste-orientation of most other political parties, at the hustings he has had no hesitation asserting his OBC credentials. This has contributed to burnishing his anti-elite, anti-Lutyens' Delhi credentials.

Castes and the Elites

During colonial rule, and even during Muslim rule, the non-Hindu rulers made good use of the caste system by politically and economically empowering the upper castes and incorporating them into the institutional hierarchy of governance. Thus, the Mughal rulers of north India and the Nizam of Hyderabad filled important positions in their administrations with Brahmins, Kshatriyas and Kayasthas—a sub-caste constituted differently in different parts of India but by and large comprising Kshatriyas and Vaishyas. Many Muslim rulers in southern India appointed Madhwa Brahmins to the high office of diwan in their courts. As Rajmohan Gandhi notes in his survey of south Indian history, both Haidar Ali of Mysore and his son Tipu Sultan appointed the Madhwa Brahmin Purniah as the diwan of Mysore.[5] Haidar's treasurer was a Brahmin. A Khatri noble, Raja Kishen Parshad, was appointed prime minister of Hyderabad by the sixth Nizam Mahbub Ali Khan.

Continuing this Muslim precedent of appointing 'twice born' Hindu upper castes—*dwija*—to positions of power in their administration, the British, too, created a civil service that was populated largely by the upper castes. Thus, an ancient hierarchy sanctified by religious belief and social dominance got reinforced by medieval and modern forms of government in an essentially feudal society. Not surprisingly, contemporary attitudes towards power and elitism in India are still influenced by the inherited logic of caste.

However, even as caste ideology asserts the social dominance of upper castes, democratic politics has transferred political power to the more numerous middle castes. Making a distinction between 'dominance' and 'power', Francine Frankel suggests that the term 'dominance' is used to refer to 'the exercise of authority in *society* by groups who achieved politico economic superiority, and claimed legitimacy for their commands in terms of superior ritual status, or through alliances with those who controlled status distribution. By contrast, the term "power" is used to refer to the exertion of secular authority by individuals appointed or elected to the offices of the *state*, who claimed legitimacy, under law, to make and implement decisions binding on the population within their territorial jurisdiction.'[6]

This is a relevant distinction in democratic India that facilitates a more contemporary appreciation of power and elitism in a society where the hierarchy of power does not necessarily overlap with the hierarchy of caste, with intermediate castes increasingly acquiring political power—hence, the distinction between 'society' and 'state'. In analysing the institutional power of the state and its functionaries, one should make a further distinction between 'appointed' and 'elected' officials of the state, given the role of the permanent civil service in India. A large number, indeed, a dominant number, of the 'appointed' members of state institutions could still belong to the upper castes, but the 'elected' officials are increasingly from intermediate castes—the OBCs. Even as traditional forms of social dominance may persist, democratic politics has given power to new social groups. In short, the elites may still be from upper castes, while the powerful may increasingly be from intermediate ones. This distinction between 'elites' and 'powerful' is more in the realm of politics. The economic and cultural elite, however, drawn mainly from the upper castes, are also the economically and culturally powerful.

While at the ideological level the traditional hierarchy of caste defines status and elitism in society, democratic politics has intervened to disrupt, empowering the numerically larger backward castes and the so-called 'outcastes', referred to in the Indian Constitution as Scheduled Castes. Ram Manohar Lohia, the ideological guru of Indian socialists, recognized the political and electoral importance of OBCs in challenging upper-caste dominance. In his essay, 'Towards the Destruction of Castes and Classes', written in 1959, Lohia observed, 'Hundreds of other (sic) castes are there who, when taken separately, are not decisive for election purposes, but taken together constitute two-thirds of India's population. For parliamentary elections, such backward castes should get our attention and leaders should be created from their ranks, whose voice and action may infuse and inspire satisfaction, self-respect and fearlessness among them.'[7]

'Three characteristics distinguish India's ruling classes,' suggested Lohia, 'high caste; English education; wealth.'[8] English education is the legacy of colonial rule that has reinforced upper-caste dominance. Indeed, familiarity with the English language has been and continues to be an important feature of cultural elitism. It is, therefore, not surprising that access to English-language education has become an important demand of Dalit leaders as part of their fight for social justice and empowerment.[9] Knowledge of English, however, is not a sufficient qualification for entry into the ruling class or elite. It is, though, a necessary condition. The only change that democratic politics has ensured is that, at the national level, knowledge of Hindi, too, has become an important qualification for ascending the ladder of power.

While both the knowledge of English language and wealth can be acquired over time, caste is a non-acquirable. However, two factors have diluted the relevance of caste status to the acquisition of elite status. First, the increasing importance of political power in defining one's elite status. Second, the process of what has been dubbed 'Sanskritisation' in altering the perceptions of caste and elite status, especially of the numerically important OBCs.

Consider first the role of political power. Political office acquired through democratic means has become an important vehicle of social and economic advancement of OBCs. Francis Fukuyama sees the extension of old kinship loyalties into institutions of the state as means of what he sees as 'elite capture' of democratic institutions. 'In the absence of strong institutional incentives,' argues Fukuyama, 'the groups with access to a political system will use their positions to favour friends and family, and thereby erode the impersonality of the State. The more powerful the groups, the more opportunities they will have to do this. This process of elite or insider capture is a disease that afflicts all modern institutions.'[10] Given the role that caste loyalties have come to play in democratic politics, Fukuyama's 'elite capture' could become 'caste capture' of state institutions. This has been visible across India in the interplay between caste and political power at all levels of governance.

Thus, politicians who lack any of Lohia's three attributes—upper-caste status, English education and wealth—can still acquire wealth and status by first acquiring political office. While upper castes constituted over 50 per cent of the membership of the Lok Sabha in the 1950s, by the early 2000s, their share was below 40 per cent. On the other hand, OBCs increased their share of Lok Sabha membership from around 10 per cent in the first Lok Sabha (1952) to over 25 per cent in the ninth Lok Sabha (1989). In the post-Mandal era, after 1989, OBC membership share has further increased.[11] Many so-called 'regional' parties in India have in fact originated as or become 'caste' parties, given the dominance of one caste within the party's power structure. Thus, in the case of Andhra Pradesh and Telangana, it is often observed that the TDP is a *Kamma* party, the Telangana Rashtra Samiti is a *Velama* party and the Yuvajana Sramika Rythu (YSR) Congress is a *Reddy* party. Mulayam Singh Yadav's Samajwadi Party has long been viewed as a *Yadav* party, and Tamil Nadu has had caste- and sub-caste-based parties for long.

Consider next the data on the economic enrichment of politicians in power, including those from non-upper-caste backgrounds. Across the country, several backward-caste politicians have over time become wealthy by using their political influence to enter various fields of business activity. Some scholars wrongly attribute this phenomenon to post-1991 economic liberalization and even view what is called 'crony capitalism' as a consequence of the post-1991 'neo-liberal' economic policies.[12] Crony capitalism, or the accumulation of capital through the use of political influence, is integral to democracies with private enterprise. Politicians in governments favouring individual business persons is one form of crony capitalism, but a politician using political power and governmental office to accumulate capital and invest in business is a more direct form of cronyism and is becoming increasingly commonplace.

The original source of private enrichment through access to public office was the government's Public Works Department (PWD). Even in British India, private contractors from lower castes and minority communities enriched themselves by taking up civil work, including road and railways construction, irrigation projects, etc. Thus, it was not the wielding of political power but access to public funds that enabled the non-upper castes to become wealthy and secure English education for their next generation in colonial India. Within three generations, the Sikh contractors who built Delhi graduated from being merely public works contractors to members of the elite of Lutyens' Delhi. Across India, there are several such examples of non-upper castes using access to political power to become wealthy and educated.

In free India, public works contractors have used their direct control of political power to enrich themselves. The Reddy contractor-politicians of Andhra Pradesh and the Sikh and Punjabi builders of Delhi and Gurugram are good examples. In the caste hierarchy, Reddys would be regarded as 'Sudras'—though they are often referred to as 'forward' castes given their control of land, as opposed to the various craft- and profession-based 'backward castes'.[13] Lohia, in fact, equates the Reddys to the Kshatriya and Ahir castes of north India, and in doing so, regards them as 'upper caste'.[14] Whatever their intermediate status in the caste hierarchy, economically, they are a rich peasant community, and politically, their rise within the Andhra Congress was in opposition to the dominant Brahmin leadership. After Independence, Reddys dominated Andhra politics (Neelam Sanjiva Reddy, Kasu Brahmananda Reddy, Marri Chenna Reddy, to name a few) and used their political clout to enrich themselves as contractors for public works. Their newly found wealth gave them access to political power and their children access to English education.

In the late 1950s and through the 1960s, the Congress party governments of Andhra Pradesh headed by Reddy chief ministers enriched Reddy contractors engaged in the construction of the Nagarjunasagar and Srisailam irrigation and hydel power projects. The next generation of these contractor families secured English-language education at good schools and colleges, entered politics, film production and distribution, real estate and other lines of business. The third generation, like Sanjay Reddy of the GVK Group, goes abroad for higher studies and enters new fields of business, like pharmaceuticals and airports that gives them a metropolitan base, entry into the media's 'Page 3', and into the country's power elite.

Upward mobility of backward castes has also been facilitated by what sociologist M.N. Srinivas termed 'Sanskritisation'—a process by which low- and middle-caste Hindus change their customs and rituals, adopting those of the dwija upper caste, mainly Brahmins, and claim a higher social status in the caste hierarchy.[15]

While many may still vilify the caste system, with good reason, it should be recognized that the caste system has not been as rigid as often imagined, and the process of Sanskritisation has been aggressive in many parts of India with non-Brahmins becoming active in temple administration and organizers of major religious-cum-sociopolitical events like Durga Puja and Ganesh Chaturthi in different parts of India. Access to political power and enrichment through cronyism have also allowed OBC leaders to enter the ranks of the nation's power elite.

In the late 1950s, when Lohia postulated his trinity of power, he may have delineated the attributes of the power elite correctly but democratic politics has empowered intermediate castes and classes so that today being an OBC may be a more helpful route to political power than belonging to a higher caste. In any case, social and political forces have changed the status of caste, from being a purely hierarchical institution to a more horizontal one in which caste has become an instrument of political mobilization rather than social or economic exploitation. In the words of D.L. Sheth, 'Competitive politics has made it difficult to view caste either as a pure category of "interest" or of "identity". Its involvement in politics fused the dimensions of interest and identity in such manner that a number of castes could now share common interests and identity through larger conglomerates of which they had become parts.'[16] The macrosocial category of OBC was one such conglomerate that has empowered a larger number of intermediate castes.

Thus, Lohia's three requirements for 'ruling class' status have to be modified. Neither wealth alone nor familiarity with the English language are sufficient preconditions for entering the ranks of the ruling elite. On one hand, political power acquired through democratic means can be the route to wealth and entry into business of even the intermediate castes. On the other hand, along with wealth and knowledge of English, upper-caste status and a metropolitan social base with social capital accumulated over at least a generation are the necessary qualifications for entry into the ranks of the 'power elite'—a social set that enjoys not just political and economic power but also cultural power.

Democratic politics, social change and the role of the state in development have all combined to make political power a far more important attribute of the power elite than traditional forms of social dominance like caste. The political empowerment of the intermediate castes, in an economy defined by extensive state intervention in the development process, has reduced the significance of inherited social status through caste. It has resulted in imparting greater relevance to status acquired through political processes, as well as the process of Sanskritisation—the acquisition of cultural capital.

This is one reason why membership of state legislatures and Parliament has become a position of inheritance in so many cases across the country. Traditionally, and across societies, family wealth, business and cultural capital have been passed on from one generation to another. In many democracies, political capital, too, is transferred from one generation to another, till it gets depleted to the point where it no longer yields returns. The Nehru-Gandhis have set an example for generations of politicians across the country. From Motilal to Jawaharlal to Indira, there was accretion to family political capital over time. Since Indira, there has only been depletion. The fourth and fifth generations have used up inherited capital without adding value. With the exception of the two ideological political formations—BJP and the communists— in most other political parties, too, political power is more often than not inherited.

The Wielders of Power

5

Business and the State

In Nehru's time we called it the Tata-Birla ki sarkar,
Today it is an Adani-Ambani ki sarkar

—A communist leader

In his historic tract, *Communist Manifesto*, Karl Marx described 'the executive of the modern state' as, 'a committee for managing the common affairs of the whole bourgeoisie'. Be it a democracy or a non-democracy, there is more than just social intimacy between the wielders of political and money power. Politicians need money, business persons need governmental support, in one way or another and at some time or another. This mutual dependency confers on the business class what Wright Mills defined as the 'institutional powers of wealth'.[1] With the corporate world becoming more 'intricately involved in the political order', wrote Mills, 'corporate leaders have become intimately associated with politicians, and especially with the key politicians who form the political directorate of the United States government.'[2]

The relationship between business and political leaderships in India is, however, mediated through a bureaucratic state that is responsive to an array of middle-class and caste interests. This is why, as we saw in an earlier chapter, Kalecki and Raj described the Indian state as an 'intermediate regime'. These groups—business, politicians in power and officers of the state—constitute the core of the Indian power elite.

In India, the roots of the nexus between business and politics run all the way into the heart of the national movement. Public awareness of this is deeply seated and wide, for, after all, every politically literate Indian knows that Mahatma Gandhi, the Father of the Nation, was assassinated in the home of one of India's richest businessmen, Ghanshyam Das Birla, where Gandhi was residing at the time. Generations have since visited the opulent Birla House in the heart of Lutyens' Delhi to pay their homage to India's greatest political leader. People also know that India's first prime minister lived in the grand home of the C-in-C of the British Empire in India. Popular conceptions of the power elite are shaped by such symbols.

It was at Gandhi's behest that, in 1927, leaders of Indian business came together and formed the FICCI, to function as a voice of 'Indian' business. British and European businesses had already established their own chambers of commerce in Bombay and Calcutta. Addressing the fourth annual general meeting of FICCI in 1931, Gandhi spoke about his concept of trusteeship, urging business persons to 'regard themselves as trustees and servants of the poor', deploying their wealth in the service of the nation. Gandhi was averse to the communist idea of a 'class war' and urged the wealthy to win the trust of the poor by promoting the welfare of all. In return for such a benevolent outlook, many business leaders and wealthy feudals willingly funded the INC. Interestingly, though, many even within the communist movement came to accept an idea implicit to Gandhi's strategy of seeking the support of Indian business when they recognized the 'nationalist' credentials of the bourgeoisie. Helping Indian business grow then became an act of nationalism.

Many contemporary commentators on India's political economy have suggested that the phenomenon of 'crony capitalism'—a mutually beneficial relationship between politicians, officials in government and business persons—is a consequence of neo-liberal economic policies of the post-1991 era.[3] The fact is that the roots of crony capitalism run deep and all the way into the initial experiment of running elected governments in British India.[4] When the demand for protection of Indian industry gained momentum in the 1920s, Indian political leadership supported it. When a group of sugar manufacturers, for example, operated a cartel called the Indian Sugar Syndicate in the late 1930s, they secured the support of the Congress leadership and in turn contributed funds to the party. B.M. Birla, who was instrumental in operating the cartel, had no compunction writing a letter to Rajendra Prasad (later the first president of the Indian republic) that he had made a financial contribution of Rs 10,000 as a gesture of appreciation for the services rendered by the latter to sugar millers.[5] This is just one example of the close relationship that developed during the freedom struggle between business and political leadership, and historians have written copiously on this.[6]

In his incisive account of business–government relations in 1935–37, when the INC ran provincial governments, Claude Markovits concludes that 'an overall view of the two years of Congress rule in the provinces reveals that the relationship between Indian business and the Congress became more institutionalized and stabilised. In the long term these years contributed to the emergence of an alliance between business and the Congress . . .'[7] The business community's links with political leadership were forged by the fact that it did play a constructive role in the building of a free India. Indeed, as early as in 1902, Dadabhai Naoroji, not merely a businessman but a man of learning and great public standing, awakened the consciousness of educated Indians with his landmark book *Poverty and Un-British Rule in India*, published over a decade before Mahatma Gandhi's historic return to India from South Africa in 1915.

Many years later, in 1944, some of India's top business leaders came together and drafted what has since become famous as 'The Bombay Plan', laying out a plan for India's long-term development.[8] As we have argued elsewhere, the significance of the Bombay Plan derives from the fact that it became the basis for national economic policy after India attained independence, sidelining all the other contending visions of industrial development like the Gandhian Plan and the Peoples' Plan. Jointly authored by the most renowned leaders of Indian business including J.R.D. Tata, G.D. Birla, Purshottamdas Thakurdas and Lala Shriram, it also had the imprimatur of John Mathai who went on to become a finance minister in Nehru's post-Independence council of ministers.

The Bombay Plan was more than just an economic plan. It was a manifesto of postcolonial development as conceived by India's 'national bourgeoisie'. It was a prescient document. Nowhere in the developing world, in no colonized nation, was there a parallel to the Bombay Plan.[9] Native business leaders were seeking their place in the sun, battling colonial rule from Asia to Africa, from Latin America to Eastern Europe. The interwar years of the twentieth century witnessed many anti-colonial and anti-imperialist movements. Nationalism was on the rise and was a pervasive sentiment. Patriotic leaders and nation builders were dreaming of a new era of self-reliant economic development. India was not the only country battling for freedom. Yet, it was in India that a group of business leaders, among the most successful business leaders of their time, came together to write a manifesto for development that had no parallels. In Marxist terms, one could argue that the Bombay Plan showed how the Indian business class had evolved from being a 'class in itself' to becoming a 'class for itself'.

The model of 'mixed economy' developed during the First and Second Five Year Plan periods was constructed on the policy foundations offered by the Bombay Plan, making the latter the 'manifesto of state capitalism'.[10] As economist Amal Sanyal has argued, India's Second Five Year Plan, often referred to as the Mahalanobis plan because statistician Prakash Chandra Mahalanobis, a member of the Planning Commission, had drafted it, was in fact based largely on a strategy outlined in the Bombay Plan. Neither Nehru nor Mahalanobis were willing to give the authors of the Bombay Plan their due credit, perhaps for political reasons. Both Nehru and Mahalanobis were left of centre and would not have liked to be seen walking the path first laid out by the captains of industry. In many ways the Bombay Plan was a superior document and more far-sighted than the Mahalanobis plan, particularly in the emphasis it placed on public investment in education and health and on implementing land reforms.[11]

The authors of the Bombay Plan were not ideologically dirigiste, but viewed their strategy as transitional, a way station in the evolution of indigenous business from the colonial era of stunted development to a postcolonial future of private enterprise-led growth. They were clear in their mind that with the passage of time the role of the state in the economy would decline, giving greater space for the fuller play of market forces. There was as much emphasis on their part on the immediate need for state support to economic development as there was on the need for protecting individual freedoms and the eventual development of a free market economy.

While seeking state support for private enterprise development and for public services provisioning, the Bombay Plan reiterated the commitment of its authors to 'the freedom of the individual'. 'If a planned economy involves, as it necessarily must, the restriction of individual freedom in varying degrees, such restriction under a democratic government will be of limited duration and confined to specific purposes.'[12] Outlining clearly what they regarded as 'basic principles' defining their version of what we have termed 'state capitalism', the authors of the Bombay Plan conclude: 'Firstly, there should be sufficient scope for the play of individual initiative and enterprise; Secondly, the interests of the community should be safe-guarded by the institution of adequate sanctions against the abuse of individual freedom; and, Thirdly, the State should play a positive role in the direction of economic policy and the development of economic resources.'[13]

The document took care to clarify that 'public-sector' industries created through public investment should, at a later stage in the development process, be disposed of by the state and sold to private investors. Outlining the features of 'state ownership' of enterprises, the document made a distinction between state-owned and state-managed, on the one hand, and state-owned but privately managed, on the other.[14] While some industries may remain within state control, for strategic reasons, others can always be privatized. To quote, 'If . . . private finance is prepared to take-over these industries, state ownership may be replaced by private ownership.'[15]

The Bombay Plan defined the nature of India's post-Independence 'mixed economy', or what Marxist scholars have called 'state capitalism', in these words:

> We have set out some of the leading considerations by which the question whether an industry should be left to private enterprise or should be owned and managed by the State is to be determined. The application of these considerations in particular cases is bound to present difficulties and there will necessarily be a wide field in which decision will involve a nice balancing of various factors. It will probably be found in these cases that the arrangement which will best meet the situation is a compromise between the two principles so that while some units of the industry are owned and managed by the State, others are left to private enterprise.[16]

In defining the contours of a policy of government-supported private enterprise development, the Bombay Plan sought to set the terms for the relationship that business leaders sought with government leaders. However, the power and influence of the middle class and middle castes both within the bureaucracy and mainstream political parties meant that the postcolonial, democratic Indian state acquired a certain degree of autonomy from the capitalist class and was not quite the 'committee of the whole bourgeoisie' as Marx had characterized it. It was, therefore, the relationships of 'social intimacy' between the leaders of business and politics, and the gradual evolution of a relationship of mutual dependence between them, that came to define 'state capitalism' or 'mixed economy' in practice. The roots of what is contemporaneously described as 'crony capitalism' are embedded in this ground.

The experience with provincial governments in the late 1930s and the Bombay Plan initiative of 1944 are not just evidence of social intimacy between senior leaders of business and politics but also of their mutual dependence. Business needed political support and the politicians needed funds. Markovits calls this a 'de facto alliance between Indian big business and the Congress which was demonstrated by the efforts made by each side to accommodate the other'.[17] Many business leaders actively participated in the National Planning Committee of the Congress that was set up to draft a plan for post-Independence economic development. Indeed, the Bombay Plan initiative only reflected this cooperative relationship.

In many ways the political economy of the national movement and the social intimacy between Indian merchant and business classes and the emerging national leadership laid the foundation of an enduring relationship between business and politics in free India. To be sure, however, this relationship has always had its ups and downs depending on the changing fortunes of politicians in power and business leaders in the saddle. At different points in time different business leaders found themselves in favour in the Delhi darbar. Whenever the political leadership of the day had to distance itself from the rich and wealthy in order to present itself as pro-poor and pro-people, fighting the vested interests of the well heeled and the privileged, shunning the image of being, as Rahul Gandhi graphically put it, a 'suit–boot ki sarkar', this relationship would get strained.

This periodic social and political distancing is not new. It happened in Nehru's time as it did during Indira Gandhi's, and every prime minister and chief minister has been tainted by questionable association with one or another business person. Indeed, Nehru himself was tainted by his association with one Jayanti Dharma Teja, a shipping magnate from Andhra Pradesh. The case of Teja and his association with Nehru and his daughter was a high-profile scam but an exceptional one in its time. Today, few would raise an eyebrow at the kind of relationship Teja enjoyed with the powers that be of the day. Tried and jailed for various financial misdemeanours in 1972, Teja's was just an early instance of similar entanglements that would recur from one government to another between politicians in power and business persons in a hurry to get rich quickly.[18]

The famous Santhanam Committee, appointed to enquire into corruption in public life in 1962, had sharp observations on the conflict-of-interest relationships between business, politicians and civil servants. Santhanam frowned upon members of the hallowed ICS joining private-sector companies immediately after retirement and acting as 'contact men' between business and government.

> It is generally believed, that such employment is secured in many cases as a *quid pro quo* for favours shown by government servants while in service . . . The fact that some of these retired government servants who have accepted employment with private firms live in Delhi and perhaps operate as 'contact men' has further heightened these suspicions.[19]

If such individuals are so able to influence government policy in favour of individual businesses, it is also because politicians in power are willing participants in this arrangement. The Santhanam

Committee report and the revelation of several corruption scandals even in Nehru's time was an early alert, drawing attention to the deep-rooted nature of the business–politics relationship that has only become more brazen in recent decades. The number of senior civil servants becoming independent directors in private companies, months after retirement has grown exponentially. Many end up as advisers to company chairpersons, some even as paid employees in the corporate sector. Today, Santhanam's views would be regarded as quaint.

During what was called the 'Licence–Permit–Control Raj', the big corporates employed suave executives as 'liaison officers' and expected them to maintain regular contact with government officials and politicians. They would become members of private clubs, like the Gymkhana Club and golf club, securing access to neutral territory in which to socialize with government officials. However, in more recent times, the role of such private-sector 'liaison officers' is increasingly being played by retired civil servants and diplomats. If senior IAS officers build their corporate relationships while serving in key economic ministries or state capitals, diplomats do so as ambassadors, helping Indian and foreign companies.

One senior officer who was also a successful diplomat and set an enviable benchmark for many others to aspire for and emulate was none other than a former Union cabinet secretary, Naresh Chandra. A distinguished and highly respected officer from the traditional community of seasoned civil servants, the Kayasthas, Chandra belonged to the Rajasthan cadre of the IAS. After holding several important positions in the Union government, he retired as cabinet secretary, the top job of the civil service, only to continue as an adviser to the prime minister.

Prime Minister Narasimha Rao assigned him the task of securing a resolution of the Ayodhya temple issue and overseeing preparations for nuclear tests. While neither of the tasks were completed during Rao's tenure, Chandra went on to briefly become governor of the state of Gujarat and then India's ambassador to the United States.

Even though he chaired a committee on corporate governance, he had no qualms spending his years in retirement as an independent director on the boards of many companies including Coca-Cola India, Bajaj Auto, Vedanta, Cairn, ACC, amongst others. Portly and tall, Chandra had a larger-than-life presence. No serving official of the government would refuse to take a call from Chandra. No minister would say no to granting an audience. With access assured into the corridors of power, Chandra's personality and genial manner contributed to the ease of interaction. A lifelong bachelor, he could not be accused of seeking personal gain for his family. He just liked living the good life. Many officers and diplomats have walked in Chandra's footsteps, making the transition from government to the private sector seem like normal career progression, cementing the relationship between state and capital.

Business and Politics

If despite the intimate nature of the relationship between business, government and politicians in power, Jawaharlal Nehru, born and raised in an aristocratic family, turned ideologically left, he was merely walking in step with the intellectual fashion of his times. Influenced by Britain's Fabian socialism and the Soviet Union's impressive industrialization experience under Marxist-Leninist leadership, Nehru was socialized to be disdainful of the wealthy. A Marxist would say Nehru liberated himself from his class origins. Apart from the influence of liberal education and the international political Weltanschauung of the times, the Indian national movement too had that effect on many political leaders. Nehru was also a practical politician. He would have understood the political need to maintain a left-of-centre stance, given not just India's mass poverty and gross social inequality but also the simple fact that the principal political opposition to the Congress party came from the undivided CPI.

In the elections of 1952 and 1957, the CPI was the single largest party in the opposition. The other major opposition party, the Socialist Party, was also left of Congress. As left-wing opposition to the Congress became stronger, Nehru tilted even more to the left. It was after witnessing the arrival of the communists on the country's parliamentary firmament in the general elections of 1952 and in preparing to deal with this challenge in the ensuing elections of 1957 that Nehru crafted the famous Industrial Policy Resolution (IPR) of 1956. The IPR 1956 was preceded by the Congress party's decision, taken at the Avadi Session of the All India Congress Committee in 1955, to commit itself and its government to the establishment of a 'socialistic pattern of society' in India.

The Congress's turn to the left and the gradual drift towards governmental control and regulation of the private corporate sector divided Indian big business. One section, best represented by the Birlas, chose to retain a close relationship with the Congress and secure the benefits of such support—namely, allotment of industrial and import licences. Another section, led mainly by J.R.D. Tata, chose to rebel against Nehru's Congress and support its pro-free-market critics like C. Rajagopalachari who went on to form the Swatantra Party. The house of Tatas openly funded the Swatantra Party in the hope of strengthening a right-of-centre political formation in India. The Swatantra Party's manifesto had made that now famous declaration: 'The business of the State is not business but Government.' As late as in April 1965, one year after Nehru's death, G.D. Birla addressed a meeting of the Indian Chamber of Commerce in Calcutta:

> I can tell you from my political experience there is not the slightest chance for any Swatantra party or any Jana Sangh or any other party to come to power to replace the Congress. You can break the Congress. You can weaken it, but it is not going to help. You will be replacing this government by a Communist government and they will be the first to cut your throat . . . Therefore, I say that with all its faults I support the Congress.[20]

While Birla was openly critical of the right-wing Swatantra Party, claiming, 'Swatantra politics are not good businessman's politics,' J.R.D. Tata joined fellow businessmen like Dharamsey Khatau to fund the Swatantra Party. With time, however, the post-Nehru Congress under Indira Gandhi turned even more to the left, no longer out of fear of the communists but in search of their support, and Swatantra's chief ideologue and organizer Minoo Masani was left bitterly complaining about 'the supine and cowardly attitude of the larger part of Big Business'.[21]

The difference between the 'Birla line', so to speak, and the 'Tata line' was in its essence about whether business should learn to live with the reality of the politico-bureaucratic domination of the postcolonial state or seek to secure space for the free play of market forces and private enterprise. The Birlas did benefit from toeing the official party line. According to the report of the Industrial Licensing Policy Inquiry Committee (1969), the house of Birlas was the biggest beneficiary of licensing policy, cornering a disproportionate share of industrial licences. New Delhi's political-bureaucratic power elite used the licensing system, set up ostensibly to 'curb the concentration of economic power', to distribute patronage. The Licence-Permit-Control Raj also allowed a middle-class bureaucracy to wield power in alliance with the middle and upper castes that had acquired political power and keep the business class on short leash. It is through these instrumentalities of state capitalism that crony capitalism took roots.

Indira Gandhi's political turn to the left, following the split in the Congress party in 1969, further consolidated the power of the bureaucracy over the business class. The nationalization of private-sector banks, insurance companies and the coal industry was a blow to big business that controlled most of the banks and insurance companies, while the abolition of privy purses, enjoyed by feudal vestiges of the British Raj, was a symbolic attack on agrarian feudalism given the inability of the Congress to undertake genuine land reforms, redistribute land to the tiller and ensure security of tenancy.

While the Congress's turn to the left alienated a large section of the business class, many among them heartily welcomed the imposition of the Emergency in 1975, given that it came on the back of a massive railway workers' strike, an oil crisis triggered by the 1973 oil shock, and hyperinflation caused by a variety of factors. Business leaders were quick to recognize a change in the government's approach—even a long-standing critic of the Nehru family like J.R.D. Tata praised the government for its 'refreshingly pragmatic and result-oriented approach' to economic policy. Returning to power in 1980, Indira Gandhi carried this change in her approach to economic policy forward by seeking balance-of-payments support from the International Monetary Fund (IMF). It was a clear indication of a policy shift and was viewed as such by friends and foes. The decision was severely criticized by the communist parties but carried forward the new phase in her relations with the business class that began with the imposition of Emergency. Indira Gandhi also ticked off the Soviets on their disastrous invasion of Afghanistan and began a shift in relations with the US by travelling to Washington DC to meet Ronald Reagan.

Having been on the receiving end of criticism from most of the traditional Indian business groups, Indira Gandhi built bridges with emergent businessmen like Swaraj Paul, the Hindujas and Dhirubhai Ambani. Through the 1970s, Indira Gandhi had sought to reduce the Congress party's dependence on funds from traditional Indian big business groups by allowing the Congress party to accept financial support from India's biggest defence supplier, the Soviet Union. As revealed by papers in the Mitrokhin Archives, the strategic relationship with the Soviet Union, sealed in 1969, made Russia the biggest arms exporter to India and, in return, the Russian communists were happy to offer financial support to the Congress party.[22]

On her return to power in 1980, not only did Indira Gandhi seek to distance herself from the Soviets, but she also reached out to European suppliers of defence equipment and in turn strengthened relations with countries like France and Sweden. A substantial part of the IMF loan of US$5 billion contracted in 1981 was alleged to have gone into defence imports from France. Interestingly, when India approached the IMF for a loan in 1981, the United States was not willing to support the Indian application unless drastic economic reforms, including privatization and trade liberalization, were carried out. It was support from the IMF managing director, Jacques de Larosière, a Frenchman, that helped Indira Gandhi seal the deal.[23] It was perhaps a mere coincidence that in the months preceding and following the IMF loan, India had signed up to import defence equipment from France, reducing its dependence on the Soviet Union. India bought forty Mirage-2000 combat aircraft between 1980 and 1984. Buying defence equipment from the French has been long considered a political sweetener by foreign governments seeking political and economic support from the French. From 1981, yearly French arms sales to India increased significantly. They averaged $26 million between 1982 and 1984, and then peaked to $467 million in 1986.[24]

The 1980s also saw three interesting trends in the relationship between business and politics. First, the funds secured through defence deals may have reduced the Congress party's financial dependence on traditional domestic big business for political funding; second, newly emergent business groups like the Ambanis became an important source of political funding for Congress leadership; and, third, newly emergent non-metropolitan entrepreneurs, mainly in states like Tamil Nadu, Andhra Pradesh, Karnataka, Punjab and Haryana, with political links to provincial politicians became an important source of funding for regional political parties.[25] Among them were the more savvy and smart entrepreneurs who had their finger on the pulse of Lutyens' Delhi and knew who the new power brokers were. The leadership of the Congress party had become, to use a phrase coined by

P.V. Narasimha Rao, a proprietorship, and a new darbar of power brokers had become the new power dealers.[26]

A Regional Business Class

It was the early 1980s. The late Ashok Mitra, at the time finance minister of the Left Front government in West Bengal, was on a visit to Hyderabad. Apart from building political bridges with the TDP supremo N.T. Rama Rao, at the time chief minister of undivided Andhra Pradesh, Mitra also delivered a public lecture on his favourite subject of Centre-state financial relations, seeking a fairer fiscal treatment for state governments by the Centre. I was then a lecturer in economics at the University of Hyderabad and had organized Mitra's lecture. On the day of the lecture I received a call from Hyderabad's media mogul, Ramoji Rao, owner of the Eenadu group of publications with business interests in food processing, chit funds, film production and media, inviting me to a dinner he was hosting in Mitra's honour.

Ramoji Rao started life as a communist sympathizer. With the Reddy and Raju communities of Andhra Pradesh dominating the state's Congress party, many Kammas gravitated towards the communist party, the main opposition party at the time, contributing to the pun that the 'CPI was the Kammanist Party of India'.[27] Starting as a small-time businessman, Ramoji Rao acquired fame and power as the architect of film star N.T. Rama Rao's historic victory in 1982 when his newly formed TDP swept the polls and defeated the Indira Congress. It was the first major political shift in Telugu politics. Rama Rao hoped to emerge as a national leader uniting all non-Congress parties once again, after the failed Janata Party experiment of the 1970s. He relaunched the Janata Party in a new avatar called the National Front—hence, Ramoji Rao's outreach to Mitra.

Arriving at Ramoji Rao's palatial house, I discovered that there were only four of us around a huge dining table—Mitra, Rao,

a TDP member of Parliament, P. Upendra, and myself. Ramoji
Rao was dressed in his trademark white shirt and white trousers.
Upendra, a railway official who rose to prominence during the
brief tenure of the Janata Party government in 1977–80 as personal
secretary to the railway minister, was by then an influential aide of
Rama Rao, and in 1988, became convener of the National Front.
Rama Rao, Ramoji Rao and Upendra were all from the same
caste—Kamma—the landowning kulaks of the coastal districts of
Andhra Pradesh.

All four seated around the table were dressed in plain white
cotton clothes. The ambience of the Ramoji home was anything
but simple. The opulence of the new rich was on display. The food
on the large table around which the four of us were seated could
have fed a hundred! As we drove out of Rao's home after dinner,
Mitra turned to me and asked, 'Why did he have so much food
on the table?' Before I could answer he added, 'It's the *nouveau
riche*! They like to show off. In Calcutta no Marwari businessman
will have the courage to place so much food on the table, that too
before a communist!'

I told Mitra of a conversation that N.T. Rama Rao reportedly
had with the Haryana politician Devi Lal. Asked by Lal how one
would classify NTR's 'kamma' caste in the traditional Indian caste
hierarchy, NTR reportedly told Lal, 'We are the Jats of Andhra
Pradesh.' The 1980s was the post-Green Revolution decade in
which newly rich communities with agrarian origins were entering
the world of business and commerce. The Kammas of Andhra
Pradesh, like the Jats of north India, had accumulated capital in
farming and agro-processing and began investing in the education
of the next generation as well as in real estate, construction and
other businesses. The Green Revolution and public investment
in irrigation and other rural infrastructure that began in the late
1960s generated new rural wealth by the late 1970s. India entered
the 1980s with a new class of agrarian capitalists seeking business
opportunities in the urban economy.[28]

One such entrepreneur was K.V.K. Raju, the son of a landowner. Having received his school education in his village, he passed out of a Ramakrishna Mission school in Tanuku and graduated from a college in Bhimavaram of West Godavari district. His parents decided to invest in his education. Raju secured a BSc degree from Banaras Hindu University and an engineering degree from Madras Institute of Technology and was awarded a master's degree in mechanical and industrial engineering by the Michigan State University in the United States. After stints at Caltex and Associated Electrical Industries, he joined Union Carbide in India. In 1973, Raju set up Nagarjuna Steels Limited.

In the early 1980s Raju decided to start Nagarjuna Fertilizers and Chemicals Limited. He required a licence. His rival was a member of the Birla family. Everyone he met in Hyderabad and New Delhi told him that it was unlikely he would get the licence, given the political clout of the Birlas. Raju decided to prove the naysayers wrong. He knew that there were new power brokers in the Delhi darbar who could make files move. One of them was an Italian businessman, Ottavio Quattrocchi, a friend of the prime minister's son and daughter-in-law. Quattrocchi represented the Italian firm Snamprogetti S.p.A., which manufactured machinery for the fertilizer industry. Years after Raju sealed his deal, Quattrocchi came into prominence when he was alleged to be a beneficiary of the Bofors gun deal between India and Sweden during Rajiv Gandhi's prime-ministerial tenure. A Raju-come-lately worsted a second-generation Birla to procure an industrial licence.

I narrate these stories about Ramoji Rao and K.V.K. Raju as examples of the parvenu bourgeoisie who had come to challenge the clout of an established metropolitan big business class during the 1980s. There were others like Rao and Raju in states like Tamil Nadu, Gujarat, Maharashtra, Punjab, Haryana and Karnataka rising on the back of new regional politicians. The world that Kochanek explored in his classic study of business and politics was the world of big business and the Congress party of the pre-Emergency era.

It was a world in which organizations like FICCI played an important role as a link between the government and business. It was a world in which the likes of a Birla and a Tata could recall personal relationships built over decades with individual politicians. Indeed, the 1980s was a decade of change.[29] New business groups like the Ambanis had emerged as major players in the political economy of business. Smaller, regional, players, too, found space using new avenues of patronage—be it the popularity of TDP that Ramoji Rao made use of or the influence of powerful intermediaries like Quattrocchi that Raju reached out to. The real change, however, came in the 1990s.

When one considers the list of top fifty business groups in India, there is hardly a new name one encounters as one moves from the 1960s to the 1970s. The list of India's top 100 companies remained remarkably static through the era of the Licence-Permit-Control Raj. Names like Birla, Tata, Singhania, Thapar, Mafatlal, Bajaj, Modi, and Shri Ram appeared year after year in the list of top twenty business groups from the 1950s through till the 1980s. In the 1980s, Dhirubhai Ambani emerged as a big name. After 1991, however, Indian business entered a new era as new entrepreneurs joined the power elite. The 1990s was the decade of change. Following the 'bonfire of controls' that Prime Minister Narasimha Rao executed in July 1991, the share of the top fifty business groups in net fixed capital stock declined from 73.7 per cent in 1992 to 41.6 per cent in 2001, while that of the top four groups, including the Birlas and Tata, declined from 39.5 per cent in 1992 to 23.1 per cent in 2001.[30] On the other hand, the business groups that increased their share of fixed capital included the Ambanis, TVS group, Mahindras, Jindals, Ruias, Munjals, Wipro's Premji and Nagarjuna's Raju. In Modi's India, Gautam Adani has made his way to the top ten, along with Uday Kotak and Dilip Shanghvi.[31]

As India entered the twenty-first century, firms in telecom, energy, petrochemicals, automobiles, software services and information technology, pharmaceuticals and retail, climbed to the top of the league of India's big business. The end of the Licence Permit-Control Raj had two consequences for the distribution of power within the business class. First, new and regionally dispersed business groups entering new areas of business challenged the supremacy and the political clout of the old, metropolitan business families that were mainly based in Bombay, Calcutta, Delhi and Madras, and remained largely confined to traditional industries. Second, the political class found new ways of ensuring access to political funding, deploying new instruments of patronage. State capitalism of the old variety gave way to new forms of crony capitalism, including the entry into business, often clandestinely, by politicians.

Power did slip away from the Delhi darbar during the 'era of coalitions' of the 1990s and the early 2000s, but wealth became more concentrated as India entered the age of billionaires. It was no longer rival business persons seeking favours from politicians, but competing politicians seeking funds from billionaire businessmen. The new rich were not just displaying excessive amounts of food on their lavish dining tables but were now building obscenely palatial homes and travelling around the world in private jets and yachts.

The New Cronyism

Much has been written about the rise of the new rich and the nexus between business and politics in the post-1991 period.[32] None of it represents a qualitative change from the earlier era of state capitalism. What is evident is a quantitative change. The Indian economy grew at a paltry rate of 3.5 per cent per annum through the era of the Licence-Permit-Control Raj of 1950 to 1980. After 1980, the rate of growth picked up, registering an annual average of 5.5 per cent, thanks to the improved performance of all three sectors of the economy—agriculture, industry and services. The new rich came from these three sectors, especially in the states that registered rates of growth above the national average, like Gujarat,

Punjab, Haryana, Maharashtra, Tamil Nadu, undivided Andhra
Pradesh and Karnataka.

The post-2000 years of high growth, referred to by many
analysts as 'the gilded era', created a new class of the super-rich
whose political clout increased as speedily as their wealth. Their
ability and willingness to finance politicians increased the stakes in
political office. The cost of getting elected went up and, in turn, the
clout of those capable of financing such rising costs also increased.
Several books have captured this new reality but none as starkly as
journalist Josy Joseph's *The Feast of Vultures: The Hidden Business of
Democracy*.[33] In this new era of crony capitalism, the relationship
between business and politics became two-way. It was no longer an
equation in which businesses helped politicians acquire and retain
power while politicians helped businesses make money. Politicians
discovered how they or their family could use political power to
build business empires and ensure wealth for several generations
going beyond a single term in office.

When K.K. Birla joined the INC in 1984, he was among
a small group of prominent business persons who had entered
Parliament. Both Parliament and state legislatures had a high
representation of the wealthy from their very inception with rich
landlords and the feudal gentry using their local clout to contest
and win elections. Several members of royal families like the
Scindias of Gwalior and the Rajas of Vijayanagaram entered public
life more as a continuation of their feudal status in democratic
India. Many legislators and MPs were rich landlords. However,
few business leaders found the time or the necessity to directly
enter the legislature given their access to the executive.

Post 1980s, business leaders began seeking seats in legislatures
and Parliament. It was, however, only after 2000 that billionaires
found it helpful to devote time and money to secure political
office. Following K.K. Birla's example, many others like Praful
Patel, Navin Jindal, Vijay Mallya and Lagadapati Rajagopal decided
to enter Parliament. Then there were those in Parliament whose

membership was the direct gift of a friendly businessman like the Reliance Industries functionary Parimal Nathwani, first elected to the Rajya Sabha from Jharkhand and recently from Andhra Pradesh. In both cases, a regional party obliged billionaire Mukesh Ambani to get his aide Nathwani elected.[34] Journalist Aman Malik has collated data that shows close to a hundred members of Parliament from across political parties have significant equity stakes and business interest in a range of businesses.[35]

The more insidious trend, however, has been that of politicians becoming capitalists using the clout of public office. Several elected representatives own private medical and engineering colleges, hotels, media and an assortment of dealerships, ranging from autos to petrol. This is at one level of wealth. Going up the ladder of capital accumulation, the more successful politicians have built bigger businesses. The Maran brothers of Tamil Nadu's DMK party best represent this trend. Andhra Pradesh's rival politicians Chandrababu Naidu and Y.S. Jaganmohan Reddy are both businessmen of considerable wealth whose corporate interests grew in tandem with their political clout. In such cases the nexus between business and politics is in full public view.

For a politician who is a lawmaker and a minister, having declared business interest is legal, even if it can constitute grounds for conflict of interest in some instances of policymaking. Thus, for example, when a Sharad Pawar and a Nitin Gadkari seek to influence ethanol policy or sugar pricing as senior members of the Union government, they are shaping public policy that can have direct or indirect benefits for them given their business interests in sugar and sugar cane. Political scientist Aseema Sinha gives a number of examples of such conflict of interest in the legislative role of politicians with business interests.[36] These are examples of declared business interest of politicians holding public office. The really insidious nexus between business and political power is, however, to be found in what are called benami holdings of ministers. The undeclared income of politicians in power is invested through third parties in corporate entities. In the cocktail circuits of metropolitan India, many know who the benami owner of a prominent firm is and who in business 'handles' the money of which politician.

The classic example is that of the now defunct Jet Airways. No one openly identified as the 'owner' of the airline is regarded to be the real owner. Speculation has revolved around several prominent politicians from across different political parties and underworld dons, including Dawood Ibrahim. In his graphic account of the rise of businessman Naresh Goyal and Jet Airways, Josy Joseph concludes that the political clout of this private airline was considerable on account of the fact that its real owners were politicians in power.[37]

Naresh Goyal began life as an office assistant in an airlines ticketing firm. Diminutive, moustachioed with a gruff voice, Goyal looked more like a Bollywood extra than the Mumbai business baron that he eventually became, before the institutions of law caught up with him. Taking advantage of the government's new liberalized civil aviation policy, Goyal set up the private airline Jet Airways in 1993. Many believed that the funds sourced from offshore accounts and foreign investors belonged to influential Indian politicians and that the foreign investment in Jet Airways was nothing more than round-tripping of undeclared income of powerful politicians. What was for long rumoured and suspected received official endorsement when the Enforcement Directorate of the Government of India detained Goyal under the Prevention of Money Laundering Act (PMLA) after first having charged him with violation of the Foreign Exchange Management Act (FEMA).

Modi's deliberate distancing of himself from billionaire businessmen, along with the official pursuit of high-profile billionaires like Vijay Mallya and Nirav Modi, and more recently, the banker Rana Kapoor, have upset many business leaders who had become used to social intimacy with influential politicians. Modi's love-hate relationship with big business reveals the dilemma of a populist politician who has to retain his legitimacy with his anti-elitist constituencies and, at the same time, has to ensure that the wealthy and powerful switch loyalties permanently to the BJP, away from rival political platforms. Without this shift in wealth in his favour, a politician's hold on power can easily slip.

Those familiar with the cocktail party circuit of Lutyens' Delhi rue the good old days when business persons, government officials and politicians in power could meet freely at the fancy homes of 'contact men' and 'liaison officers' that the Santhanam Committee wrote about in 1962. As one veteran of that era told me, 'Modi has taken the excitement out of Delhi's party life.' But then, few billionaires waste their time pursuing officials and ministers when they can so easily get work done by judges. 'When I entered this liaison business,' this veteran told me, 'I chased joint secretaries. Then I had to get to know senior officials. Then we had to deal directly with ministers. Now all I need to do is to make sure I know enough number of friendly judges.'

Chambers and Lobbyists

One institution that has survived the transition from the Licence-Permit-Control Raj to the era of big business cronyism and overt business-politics nexus is the chamber of commerce and industry. While business chambers like the Bengal Chamber of Commerce and the FICCI represented the old guard of traditional big business, the CII is a product of the liberalization era. Changing its identity and focus of activity in early 1992 from being a Confederation of Engineering Industry, the CII grew in size and stature, admitting members from sunrise sectors such as information technology (IT) and IT-enabled services, pharmaceuticals, and banking and finance. Under the leadership of its dynamic director general Tarun Das, CII identified a new avenue of corporate influence—policy research and advice. The government of the day was still in the grip of the ancien régime of permit-wielding bureaucrats, comfortable with the old ways of the Licence-Permit-Control Raj.

The advocates of reform and liberalization were few and mostly non-IAS, like Montek Singh Ahluwalia, Rakesh Mohan, Jayanto Roy and Shankar Acharya. The CII inserted itself into policy debates, hiring qualified economists like Omkar Goswami and Rajiv Kumar and converting itself into a policy think tank. It invited influential economic journalists, pro-reform economists, government officials, politicians and business leaders to seminars and conferences, pushing the agenda of reform and liberalization.

Not to be left behind, FICCI also entered this policy space hiring a pro-reform economist, Amit Mitra, who also happened to have been a student of the then finance minister, Manmohan Singh, at Delhi School of Economics (DSE). Both CII and FICCI sought to actively influence public policy not through old methods of lobbying and corruption but by adopting more intelligent and subtle tactics. They offered platforms that helped build the stature of favoured individuals in government, both at the national and provincial level, funded the foreign travel of journalists whenever important ministers went abroad to ensure favourable media coverage, and functioned as a bridge between business, government and media.

Both CII and FICCI, and other such organizations, actively helped retired officials find things to do and be gainfully employed. The two-way relationship between these organizations and the government manifested itself in diverse ways. For example, when a minister wished to travel abroad, especially to places like London, Dubai, Singapore and other centres of business and finance, he would get a business organization to arrange a meeting, a seminar, a lecture at that place and invite the concerned minister. The prime minister would then permit such 'official' travel, and the minister would attend to his 'personal' work, after completing the stated business. Business leaders who would find it difficult securing an appointment with a minister in New Delhi would turn up at such foreign capitals and manage friendly conversations with the minister over a drink and a meal.

Business persons pay hefty sums to become office-bearers of these organizations mainly because it offers them plenty of opportunities for informal and private conversations with ministers and senior civil servants, both at the national and provincial levels. Many business leaders, however, stay away from such leadership roles in business chambers opting to maintain access to government in less visible and discreet ways. One business leader who understood the game well and used the presidentship of a business chamber to build profitable links with policymakers was Rana Kapoor, the disgraced co-founder and CEO of Yes Bank. Becoming president of the Associated Chambers of Commerce and Industry (Assocham) in mid-2013, the last year of the Manmohan Singh government, Kapoor stayed on in that office till end of 2015, building bridges with the newly formed Narendra Modi government.

Modi initially took a dim view of CII because some of its members, led by its former president Anu Aga, had criticized his handling of the situation in Gujarat in 2002. After 2004, CII came to be regarded as being closer to the Manmohan Singh government than FICCI, and after 2009, Anu Aga was made a member of Sonia Gandhi's National Advisory Council. While Modi had a good equation with FICCI's leadership, which quickly managed to elect business leaders supportive of Modi (including a succession of two Gujaratis) as its president, Kapoor positioned Assocham as a strongly pro-Modi association.

As on so many other fronts, here, too, Narendra Modi has made a difference. Discovering the fact that most business chambers are increasingly dependent on government patronage—of both the central and state governments—to retain their membership and relevance, he has been able to bend these organizations and their leaders to his will. He has encouraged them to lobby on behalf of the government, supporting and promoting government policy, rather than only lobby with the government for change of policy. When the World Bank helped push India up on the Ease of Doing Business ranking, the government organized a celebratory event at which the bank official who helped make it happen, Kristalina Georgieva, presently managing director of the IMF, was feted. The business chambers were asked to provide the audience. Most business persons who turned up were personally not enthused about the improvement in India's ranking. In private, they would complain that little had changed on the ground. At the celebratory event, however, they felt obliged to cheer the government.

As secretary general of FICCI, I found it difficult to get the organization and its membership to stop affixing the prefix 'honourable' while addressing ministers and senior officials of the government. Do we refer to an academic as 'hon'ble professor' or to a scientist as 'hon'ble Scientist', I would ask my colleagues. So why do we refer to a minister as 'hon'ble minister'? A simple 'mister' or 'madam minister' would do. Few bought into my 'socialist talk'. While agreeing in private that the 'hon'ble so-and-so' was in fact a 'dishonourable so-and-so', they knew which side of the power equation they were on in India's semi-feudal state capitalist system.

An Enduring Nexus

In any democratic society control over wealth and public office are two sources of power. A nexus between the two enhances the power of those who benefit from it. However, when the wealthy become politically powerful and the politically powerful become wealthy, the combination of two forms of power transforms a democracy into a plutocracy. Indian democracy entered this phase in the first two decades of the twenty-first century. Popular anger against this plutocratic system has forced the Narendra Modi government to launch an assault on it, albeit a feeble one. It has been weak perhaps partly on account of the fact that the BJP has been the biggest beneficiary of corporate funding of political parties, cornering almost 95 per cent of legal and direct financial contributions made.[38]

Reviving economic growth, rejuvenating the 'animal spirits' of private enterprise, and settling the problem of non-performing assets of big companies have animated government policy, leaving the Modi government open to the opposition's charge of being pro-rich. From the days of the Santhanam Committee (1964), corruption and the nexus between business and government have been recurrent themes in public and academic discourse. Equally, there has been periodic concern about the clout of individual business persons and companies on government. Every now and then, someone or the other is hunted down by the keepers of law. However, the fact remains that wealth and power have always been intricately linked in Indian public life. Governments may come and go, businesses may grow and shrink, the economy may rise or retreat, but the nexus between wealth and power endures.

This is not to suggest that there is no social, political and economic change under way. The composition of the power elite—the members of the wealthy and powerful, of the 'committee of the whole bourgeoisie', as it were—has changed and will continue to change. The old wealthy are being edged out by the newly rich. The caste composition of the wealthy is changing as new social groups enter business and politics and straddle both worlds. The regional origins of the wealthy and the powerful, too, are changing. The ups and downs of both business and politics changes the fortunes of individuals but it has not altered the nexus between the wealthy and the powerful. If anything, the dynamics of capitalism and democracy have made the wealthy more powerful and the powerful wealthier. Pursuing the politics of anti-elitism and the economics of increasing the 'ease of doing business' presents its own challenges to a populist politician. Modi has been able to bridge this gap partly thanks to the social composition of Indian business. As one veteran business leader said to me, 'As a businessman I am not happy with many of his policies. However, as a Hindu I will vote for him.'

6

The Landed and the Feudals

He just could not see how he could take away lands from the landlords
and survive as chief minister.
And what could be more important than his survival as chief minister?

—P.V. Narasimha Rao, *The Insider*, 1998

Land was power. Land was the summum bonum of the rural context. Land was the omnipotent, omnipresent, omniscient entity in village consciousness, admits Anand, the hero of former Prime Minister P.V. Narasimha Rao's fictionalized semi-autobiography *The Insider*. 'Land was a supreme force that could not be opposed, a fact that could not be denied, a matrix that could not be destroyed. This had been proved over and over again for centuries.'[1] Through several chapters of his book, Rao uncovers peel by peel the hypocrisy around land reforms in post-Independence India.

Through the freedom struggle, native landed gentry continued to owe allegiance to the empire and its native feudal vassals. The British had created a hierarchy of power and privilege based on the possession or the control over land. In areas defined by the zamindari settlement, mainly the Bengal presidency and Bihar, the intermediary between the peasant and the state had little incentive to invest in the improvement of land or its tiller. In areas defined by what was called the ryotwari settlement, mainly the Madras and Bombay presidencies, the peasant proprietor had an incentive to invest in land and improve his lot. In many Indian states, like Hyderabad, the zamindari system prevailed.

Once India became independent, the landed elite used the institutions of democracy to retain their economic power and their social and political influence. There was a constituency for land reform in the national movement, but it was divided between moderates and radicals. Acharya Vinoba Bhave, the Gandhian from Maharashtra, was a moderate who campaigned for voluntary land alienation by the landlords. The Bhoodan Movement he led sought to convince the landed feudals that it was in their best interest that they parted with some part of their estate and transferred land to the tenants, the peasants who tilled the land. At the other end were the communists who advocated an armed struggle and forced seizure of land from the feudals. Telangana was home to one of the biggest such armed struggles of the communists. Standing between the two, Jawaharlal Nehru opted for a compromise. The feudal system of revenue collection instituted by the colonial state system was abolished, security of tenure was sought to be ensured, and access to credit and other forms of institutional support to the peasant were provided by the state.

Zamindari was abolished, but the zamindars did not go away. They got themselves elected to state legislatures and Parliament. A vestige of the British Empire, zamindars had been empowered as the foundation of the colonial revenue system. Democratic India withdrew their feudal privileges but gave them entry into the nation's power elite through its representative institutions. The story of land reforms in Rao's book is a tale of political duplicity. National leaders promised land reform, but state governments were not committed to delivering on that promise. Rao's hero, Anand, tried as chief minister of his state to sincerely implement the Congress party's promise of ending landlordism by imposing a ceiling on landownership and redistributing surplus land, so acquired, to the landless. The party bosses revolted. The prime minister was told that Anand, the enthusiastic reformer, had become a liability. He was removed from office and given organizational responsibilities, and the party retreated from its promise.

'When elections came,' writes Rao, 'the party sank or sailed by the leader's charisma that was the sole device used to woo the electorate. Elections results thus became largely unrelated to performance.'[2]

In New Delhi, Nehru's, and later Indira's, council of ministers had many urban liberals espousing land reforms, but in state capitals, the party's provincial leaders, mostly from the ranks of the landed gentry, resisted such moves. It was not just the liberal urban leadership of the Congress party that was committed to ending feudalism in the countryside and empowering farmers. Even the manifesto of Indian big business, the 'Bombay Plan', keenly advocated an end of landlordism, wanted security of tenure for peasants and a ceiling on land that could be owned. Acutely aware of the feudal nature of colonial revenue systems, the authors of the Bombay Plan believed that to increase agricultural production and productivity, 'ownership of land and its taxation, that is, land tenure and land revenue, are the two principal problems which require to be tackled'.[3] The document advocated ending landlordism, empowering peasants—direct cultivators—and imposing a normal income tax on agricultural income above a certain threshold level.

The Bombay Plan's advocacy of land reforms was only to be expected. The emerging class of industrial capitalists around the world have always sought to promote the transition from feudalism to capitalism in the countryside, given their need for land, agricultural raw materials and low-cost food. For long, land has been the primary source of wealth and power in pre-industrial societies. In densely populated, industrializing India it still remains a source of both wealth and power. The distribution of power in rural India did not, however, remain static. Politics intervened to shape social and economic dynamics. Recall Kalecki's definition of an 'intermediate regime'—landlords and big business occupied the top of the class pyramid, workers, landless and poor peasants constituted its bottom, and the middle was home to rich peasants, small businesses and the professional middle class.

While feudal landlords retained some of their economic and social power and authority, democratic politics increasingly empowered the rich peasants—dubbed 'bullock capitalists' by political scientists Susanne and Lloyd Rudolph in their classic treatise on India's political economy, *In Pursuit of Lakshmi*.[4] Many zamindars and *jagirdars* survived land ceiling and tenancy laws, mainly by evading them, and managed to retain sizeable lands as well as their inherited social and political influence. Members of the middle peasantry were able to increase their landholding as well as their political influence to emerge as the 'bullock capitalists'—self-employed, independent cultivators. 'The balance of power between these groups,' the Rudolphs concluded, 'lay with landlords in the sixties but in the seventies it shifted towards bullock capitalists and backward classes.'[5]

The Rudolphs saw bullock capitalists emerging as the 'hegemonic agrarian class', considering their share of both land and population across the country and also, more importantly, their social and political clout. Hailing not just from upper castes but also the numerically larger middle castes—or 'backward classes' in Indian political parlance—the bullock capitalists were set to grow in importance as members of the rural power elite.

Rise of the Kulaks

Two important developments of the 1970s shaped the dynamics of power in rural India. First, the Green Revolution, and, second, the emergence of rich peasants as powerful politicians in different parts of the country. The economic enrichment and empowerment of the middle and rich peasants was an important consequence of the

Green Revolution—adoption of high-yielding varieties of food crops. Their political empowerment was ensured by the fact that they came to proliferate and subsequently dominate the political leadership of the ruling Congress party at the state level in almost all major states. In the Nehruvian '50s the provincial leadership of the Congress party was still predominantly English-speaking and urban. By the end of the 1950s, this began to change, and by the mid-1960s, the Congress party came to be dominated by land-owning castes like the Reddys, Jats and Marathas.

In Uttar Pradesh, where in the 1950s, provincial politics was dominated by the urban and the urbane, Brahmins and Kayasthas, a rustic peasant leader from the Jat community emerged in the 1960s to challenge Congress dominance. Chaudhury Charan Singh quit the Congress to form the Bharatiya Lok Dal (BLD) and became the first non-Congress chief minister of Uttar Pradesh in 1967. He took several measures to economically empower farmers including the state takeover of sugar mills, belonging mostly to Calcutta-based Marwaris, so as to benefit sugar cane farmers who were now offered a higher price for cane. Charan Singh's BLD merged with the Janata Party in 1977, and he had a brief stint as prime minister in 1979–80.

Recognizing the rising political importance of the rich peasants post Green Revolution, Indira Gandhi nationalized private commercial banks in 1969 ostensibly to make more credit available to farmers. It had been alleged that the Indian banking system had neglected the peasantry, and being controlled by metropolitan bourgeoisie, had an urban, industrial bias. Between 1951 and 1961, the share of the agricultural sector in the total credit issued by private commercial banks remained static at 2.0 per cent while that of the industrial sector had doubled from around 34 per cent in 1951 to 67 per cent in 1967. Apart from nationalizing commercial banks and instructing them to open new branches in rural areas and lend more to the farm sector, the government of the day promoted the growth of several rural credit institutions, many of which came under the control of politically powerful agrarian classes.

The post-Green Revolution period brought into sharp relief the growing clout of the surplus-generating rich peasant class, especially in agriculturally prosperous states like Punjab, Haryana, Andhra Pradesh and Tamil Nadu. The growth of agro-processing industries like sugar empowered sugar cane farmers with large tracts of land in a state like Maharashtra. There are many ways in which one can see this newly acquired wealth of the more prosperous peasantry manifesting itself in terms of power relations. During her radical phase (1967 to 1976) Indira Gandhi's ministers for agriculture were a Dalit and a Muslim politician—Jagjivan Ram and Fakhruddin Ali Ahmed. Neither shared the interests of large landowners and rich peasants. By the mid-1970s, the surplus-generating rich peasants—India's kulak class—had become politically powerful.[6] While the political architect of the Green Revolution, the Union agriculture minister of the mid-1960s, C. Subramaniam, hailed from a land-owning farming community of Tamil Nadu, the Kongu Vellala Gounders, all successive Union agriculture ministers, from 1977 to 1991, hailed from the Jat community of Haryana and Punjab.[7]

Economist Ashok Mitra wrote eloquently about how the rising surplus-generating kulak class had acquired decisive influence on the central government's agriculture pricing policy in the post-Green Revolution period. 'The State is hardly a neutral entity. It reflects the concentration of power and authority. This authority can be directly deployed for affecting the terms of trade between classes,' wrote Mitra in his treatise on how the state manipulates terms of trade between agricultural and industrial produce to benefit surplus-generating rich farmers—the rural oligarchy, as he called them.[8] It was not the farming community as a whole that benefited from a shift in the terms of trade between manufacturing and agriculture in favour of the latter, argued Mitra, but the surplus-generating rich peasants, a class that he saw as an ally of the urban business class. 'The bourgeoisie depend on the rural oligarchy not just for the supply of food and raw materials, but more importantly for the supply of votes, they also recognize that certain payments are due to the affluent farmers in lieu of the crucial service they render; the apparatus of State power is used to organize these.'[9]

In her radical phase in the late 1960s, Indira Gandhi invited the highly regarded liberal economist K.N. Raj, long-time director of the Delhi School of Economics, to chair a committee tasked to examine the possibility of levying a tax on agricultural wealth and income. The Raj Committee recommended that the existing system of land revenue be replaced by an agricultural holdings tax. It would mimic the urban economy's income tax, while not exactly being a tax on income. It would be a tax on the presumed income of a holding in different agroclimatic regions. In 2016, farmers with more than four hectares of land constituted just about 4 per cent of the total farming families, but they were estimated to account for 20 per cent of total agriculture income. One estimate showed that as much as Rs 25,000 crore could be collected from these farmers if their income was taxed at the rate of 30 per cent.

The Raj Committee recommendations got buried under a heap of criticism both from the political left and the kulak lobby. There was severe political opposition to the proposal, and the idea of a direct tax on agricultural income has never been pursued since, attesting to the political influence of rich peasants. Since then farm income has not been subject to income tax. Whatever the pros and cons of taxing farmers' income, this exemption has provided an escape clause to taxpayers in the non-farm sector, allowing them an escape route from paying tax on non-farm income, declaring it falsely as farm income. This has also given an incentive to the urban rich to retain landholding and use it as a tax shelter. Many of the farmhouses of the urban rich along roads leading out of metropolitan India are also tax shelters that help avoid income tax. It should not, therefore, surprise anyone that many of the urban rich have agrarian assets, cementing an alliance between them and the rural rich.

With the increase in the cost of campaigning and winning an election, the barriers to entry into political office have also gone up.

While the Election Commission of India expects a candidate for a state assembly election to spend no more than Rs 28 lakhs, the fact is that in some states some candidates end up spending ten to twenty times as much. Rising entry costs have made politics the preserve of the rural super-rich. With the exception of the BJP, which has amassed huge sums of money for election campaigning, cornering nearly 95 per cent of all donations made through electoral bonds to political parties in the 2019 Lok Sabha elections, most other political parties expect candidates to raise and fork out funds for their campaigns. This further skews the electoral process in favour of the rural rich.[10]

Urban Landlords

Land is wealth. But land combined with caste and political influence yields power. The rural power elite are, without doubt, the big landowners from influential castes (Reddys and Kammas in Andhra Pradesh, Reddys and Velamas in Telangana, Marathas in Maharashtra, Patidars in Gujarat, Jats in Punjab and Haryana, Brahmins in Uttar Pradesh and so on), who have acquired membership of institutions of governance and finance—zilla parishads, panchayats, credit and commodity cooperatives, and state legislatures. It is a two-way relationship. Land gives access to political office. Control of political office facilitates acquisition of even more land. When that equation moves from the countryside to cities the 'wealth effect' of political power multiplies. Thus, rural landowning castes who have acquired political power are able to obtain urban land and become super-rich. Look at how politicians in power in Haryana, Punjab, Maharashtra, erstwhile Andhra Pradesh and Uttar Pradesh cornered valuable land in Gurgaon, Noida, Navi Mumbai and Cyberabad to graduate from being rich to becoming super rich. These are the new urban landlords.

Urbanization has become a new source of acquisition of wealth for the politically powerful landlord castes across India. In the new

state of Andhra Pradesh it has created new caste wars between the
Kamma politicians who acquired land in and around the proposed
new capital city of Amaravati and the Reddy politicians of the YSR
Congress who came to power after defeating N. Chandrababu
Naidu's TDP. They had, in their time, used control of public office
or access to public funds to finance buying land in Hyderabad.
In the triple city of Hyderabad-Secunderabad-Cyberabad a major
grouse of the Velama landlord caste that acquired political power
in the newly created Telangana state has been about the Kammas
and Reddys of Andhra cornering a huge chunk of prime real estate
in a booming metropolis.

Large tracts of land in New Delhi's satellite city of Gurugram
have been bought by the Jat politicians of Punjab and Haryana.
Punjab's Badal family and Haryana's Chauthala family helped each
other when in power in their respective states to amass land in
Gurugram before it became prime property. As the *Hindustan Times*
reported in 2004, 'Spanning over four decades, the Badal-Chautala
family ties have only grown stronger, cemented by a prime land
deal and unflinching support during jail stints and elections.'[11]

Every major urban conglomeration across the subcontinent is
now fertile ground for the enrichment of the provincial rich. Way
back in the early 1980s when a new wave of urbanization was
reshaping the colonial metropolis of Bombay, film director Kundan
Shah made the satirical movie *Jaane Bhi Do Yaaro,* portraying the link
between real estate developers, landowners, politicians and media
barons. Over the next four decades every urban centre has been
home to this nexus of the new power elite. Rapid urbanization and
the scarcity of urban land combined with complicated bureaucratic
procedures for the sale, purchase and utilization of urban land
have combined to create a nexus between politicians in power,
urban land mafias and the real estate business. Across the country,
politicians and government officials have been enriched by this
nexus, and in every major urban centre, local politicians have come
to be identified with real estate tycoons.

The media has over time featured the real estate interests and links of dozens of influential politicians across the country. In fact, the most telling evidence of private enrichment through public office is the land acquired by politicians in power. In every growing urban conglomeration around the country, real estate tycoons are seen to be associated with local politicians. From Gurgaon's K.P. Singh family to Mumbai's Wadhawan family, Hyderabad's Rameswar Rao Jupally and scores of such real estate developers around the country, the link between land and power is manifest. It is no coincidence that Sonia Gandhi's son-in-law, Robert Vadra, and Haryana's former chief minister Bhupinder Hooda's family have been identified as having business links with Gurgaon's major real estate czar K.P. Singh and his firm, DLF.[12]

Kushal Pal Singh was the son of a lawyer in Uttar Pradesh's Bulandshahr. After graduating from the Meerut College, he became an officer in the Indian Army. In 1961, he joined the firm American Universal Electric Company. Marriage into a landowning family helped him move into real estate, joining his father-in-law Chaudhary Raghvendra Singh's firm Delhi Land and Finance Limited that graduated into DLF Universal Ltd. An initial public offering in 2007 brought in the funds that enabled him to acquire large chunks of land in what was then a nascent urbanization programme in Gurgaon (now Gurugram), Haryana, on the outskirts of New Delhi. Gurgaon's emergence as an industrial and commercial district enabled the family to emerge as one of India's wealthiest families, with Singh named by *Forbes* magazine as the richest real estate baron and eighth richest person in the world in 2008. In the IIFL Hurun Rich List of 2020, Singh's son Rajiv Singh and family figure at the twenty-sixth position with their wealth estimated at Rs 32,800 crore.

Suave and urbane, K.P. Singh was the toast of New Delhi's power elite and an active member of business chambers who featured often in the media's power lists and on society pages in his impeccable suits and elegant attire. Honoured with

a Padma Bhushan in 2010, Singh was named in 2016 in the
Panama Papers exposé that listed Indian business persons with
offshore accounts in tax havens.[13] The political connections of
DLF's Singh and family came to the fore when Congress leader
Priyanka Vadra Gandhi's husband, Robert Vadra, was named as
a beneficiary in a DLF land deal.

Across urban India there are many such landowning rich in
the real estate business, most of them with intimate links with
local politicians. Many political families have amassed millions in
new urban developments around most major cities. Interestingly,
within one generation, these families evolve from being merely
land-grabbers involved in shady and benami deals to becoming
benefactors of art and culture, with the next generation often
educated overseas and living the good life of a globalized elite.
Often, the only consequence of a political regime change is that
members of the new ruling dispensation join the ranks of their
beneficiaries and benefactors. As P.V. Narasimha Rao notes in
his book, land is power and, in a rapidly urbanizing India, the
summum bonum of the wealth generated by urbanization.

Whatever the electoral fortunes of ruling politicians who
help them rise up the ladder of wealth, the bottom line is that
the landed wealthy manage to enter the ranks of the nation's
power elite. Within one generation they have grown out of
their rural roots to branch out into new urban spaces. From
being rural landowners they have become urban entrepreneurs—
like Andhra's G.V.K. family, moving from landownership in
Nellore district to civil construction in Guntur district, building
Nagarjuna Sagar Dam's right canal; then investing in Hyderabad's
real estate and moving on to biotechnology and management of
Mumbai's snazzy airport, entering the urbane world of a new
power elite. Somewhere along the way the family married into
politics and squared the circle. Hundreds of such business families
have graduated within two generations from grandfather's dhoti
to grandson's bespoke suits.

In all societies land is an important asset and source of wealth. In India, where the land–man ratio is adverse to man, where landownership remains a major desire of millions of the rural and urban middle class, the accumulation of land by a few, especially when such land has been alienated through executive fiat, is a highly charged political issue. This was on display when the Manmohan Singh government legislated a new law for land acquisition by the government to make such land available for industrial and other uses, and it created a major political storm. Much of the controversy revolved around the distribution of spoils. Who would gain more from the conversion of land from a commercially less profitable use to a commercially more profitable one. How can the poor peasant and the small landowner be protected from the adverse distributional consequences of the power imbalance between the one whose land is being acquired and the one who acquires—be it the state, in the form of a powerful politician, or private corporations with political connections. The alienation and subsequent accumulation of land is but a means of the accumulation of capital, and, eventually of wealth and power.

The Feudal Vestiges

The zamindars and the jagirdars constituted only the second rung of the colonial feudal hierarchy in parts of India that were under the titular reign of Indian rulers. With the integration of what were called 'Indian states' into the Indian state, these Indian potentates lost their status, even though they were allowed to retain their titles and many of their privileges. But they got these, thanks to the munificence of the new republic. In 1969, Indira Gandhi's government decided to withdraw these titles and stopped its financial contribution called a 'privy purse'. A bill introduced in the Lok Sabha in 1969 was eventually passed in 1971 as the Constitution (Twenty-Sixth) Amendment Act, stating its objective in these words:

The concept of rulership, with privy purses and special privileges unrelated to any current functions and social purposes, is incompatible with an egalitarian social order. Government have, therefore, decided to terminate the privy purses and privileges of the rulers of former Indian states. It is necessary for this purpose, apart from amending the relevant provisions of the Constitution, to insert a new article therein so as to terminate expressly the recognition already granted to such Rulers and to abolish privy purses and extinguish all rights, liabilities and obligations in respect of privy purses.

What the withdrawal of titles meant in simple terms was that the erstwhile Maharaja of the Indian state of Gwalior would no longer be addressed as His Highness Ali Jah, Umdat ul-Umara, Hisam us-Sultanat, Mukhtar ul-Mulk, Azim ul-Iqtidar, Rafi-us-Shan, Wala Shikoh, Muhtasham-i-Dauran, Maharajadhiraj Maharaja Shrimant Madhav Rao III Scindia Bahadur, Shrinath, Mansur-i-Zaman, Maharaja Scindia of Gwalior, but simply as Mr Madhav Rao Scindia. The heir to India's richest ruler, Mir Osman Ali Khan, the last Nizam of Hyderabad—who was deprived of his title 'Rustam-i-Dauran, Arustu-i-Zaman, Wal Mamaluk, Asaf Jah VII, Muzaffar ul-Mamaluk, Nizam ul-Mulk, Nizam ud-Daula, Nawab Mir Osman Ali Siddiqi, Khan Bahadur, Sipah Salar, Fath Jang, Faithful Ally of the British Government, 10th Nizam of Hyderabad and of Berar GCSI, GBE, Royal Victorian Chain'— looked at which side the bread was buttered and migrated to a sheep farm in the Australian outback. Many other erstwhile kings and queens used their inheritance to turn palaces into luxury hotels, invest in companies, continue traditional duties in family temples or build institutions of learning. The Maharaja of Baroda devoted himself to the building of The Maharaja Sayajirao University of Baroda. The Mysore Maharaja turned one palace into a hotel and another into the venue for the most colourful Dussehra festival that has since become a global tourist destination.

The many potentates of Rajasthan, big and small, have opened their palaces to India's new rich, offering them an opportunity to relive feudal grandeur at a price.

Not all feudals have been satisfied remaining in private and corporate spaces. Many sought to regain their lost public status by entering democratic politics.[14] In the very first general elections of 1952, as many as forty-five former heads of erstwhile princely families contested elections—with around 70 per cent contesting in elections to state assemblies. By the elections of 1967, the number went up to seventy-five. Interestingly, through Nehru's tenure, three-fourths of all MPs from princely families were members of the Congress party. However, with Indira Gandhi deciding to abolish princely titles and purses—a decision first taken in 1967 and then executed in 1969—many quit the Congress to join the Swatantra Party or the Jana Sangh.

The most prominent feudal to seek an early entry into democratic politics was the erstwhile Rajmata of Gwalior, Vijaya Raje Scindia. She began her political career in the INC, getting elected as a member of the Lok Sabha from Guna constituency in Madhya Pradesh in 1957. She later moved to the Swatantra Party, but in 1967, became a founding member of the Jana Sangh. She remained a member of Parliament till 1999. Her son Madhavrao Scindia also began his political life within the Congress, becoming an MP in 1971. He was a member of Rajiv Gandhi's and P.V. Narasimha Rao's council of ministers. It is both a reflection of the feudal mindset of most Indians and the false pretences of the deposed rulers that Madhavrao Scindia preferred to be referred to as 'maharaj' or 'shrimant' and his son is still referred to as 'shrimant' by his loyal subjects. A street named after the late Madhavrao in New Delhi is in fact called Shrimant Madhavrao Scindia Marg.

Both father Madhavrao and son Jyotiraditya exuded their feudal origins. Apart from the honorific status they liked, their physical demeanour, with rings and strings displayed on their persona, exemplified their royal inheritance. It was an example that other lesser feudals happily began to copy, confident in the knowledge that the voter in their respective fiefdoms was quite willing to vote them to institutions of parliamentary democracy and privilege out of age-old loyalties.

Thus, over the years, many other feudals, big and small in terms of their erstwhile status, have entered the political field, nursing inherited constituencies. From the twenty-one-gun-salute-commanding Maharaja of Gwalior to the nine-gun-salute-deserving Maharaja of Patna in Odisha (now Orissa) the Lok Sabha has been home to many feudal chiefs and chieftains over the years. Only one among them ended up being prime minister for a brief period—Vishwanath Pratap Singh, the erstwhile Raja of Manda. In the early years after Independence, some feudals voluntarily dropped the use of their titles, gave away their lands and even part of their wealth and tried to become republican in their public life. The Raja of Wanaparthy, in what is now the state of Telangana, was one such. Like many lesser feudals he opted to become a diplomat. Nehru was generous in making many senior officials of Indian rulers diplomats or governors. Rameshwar Rao was more republican than most. He divested himself of part of his land through Acharya Vinoba Bhave's Bhoodan Movement, stopped using his title, and joined active politics, becoming a Congress MP. He later launched a publishing house, and his wife ran a school.

Indira Gandhi's decision to abolish feudal titles and privileges prompted a large number of the erstwhile rajas and nawabs to mobilize themselves and join forces. On 15 August 1967, the twentieth anniversary of Indian Independence, an organization titled 'Rulers of Indian States in Concord for India' was formed in Bombay. The Maharaja of Baroda was named the organization's convener general, and the Begum of Bhopal was named pro-convener general. Referred to simply as 'The Concorde', the organization set up regional associations called 'Accords'. They failed in attaining their main objective of preventing the abolition of their titles and privileges by the Indira government. However, they succeeded in raising their public profile.

One of the paradoxes of urbanization has been that while the middle peasant sells his land and abandons an uneconomical farm life to move to the city—buying an apartment, educating his children and coping with the stress of urban life—the increasingly better-off urban elite invest their surpluses into acquiring orchards or farms or farmhouses or a home in the hills, on the beach or in the countryside. If in the pre-urban economy of a feudal past the ownership of landed estates was a symbol of wealth and power, in the new post-agrarian modern urban economy of today, it has once again become a symbol of wealth and status, not just in rural India, but for the metropolitan elite too.

Ownership and command over land and natural resources will remain an important determinant of wealth and power in India. The landowning class has retained power and influence through the years, with both the Congress and the BJP, and most regional parties dependent on them for rural votes and the cash that they have the capacity to raise and provide at election time. Interestingly, the rural rich, the landed gentry and the agrarian oligarchy have not been the target of Modi's anti-elitism. The BJP needs their support to retain power.

While most feudals continued to enjoy their wealth, some of it stashed outside India, many joined politics and continued to enjoy power. It took about a generation before they lost the stigma of their support for the British, their ill treatment of their subjects in many cases and other such negative attributes, to acquire a new image as members of a new post-Independence elite. Not all entered the new institutions of the state, but most became visible members of the upper class—a socially and culturally prominent set. Post-Independence cinema, influenced by left and liberal politics, depicted the old feudals as despotic villains. By the 1980s, they had evolved into socially awkward people. In twenty-first-century India they are celebrated as icons of fashion, elegance, hospitality and high living. Despite Indira Gandhi's decision to deprive them of their titles and purses, the Indian state did little to deny them their elite status. For instance, the government-owned airline Air India turned the servile, often despicable, maharajas of the past into a huggable, likeable gentleman of the modern world. Adopting a smartly attired maharaja as its mascot, Air India described him thus:

> 'The maharaja began merely as a rich Indian potentate, symbolizing graciousness and high living. And somewhere along the line his creators gave him a distinctive personality: his outsized moustache, the striped turban and his aquiline nose. He can be a lover boy in Paris, a sumo wrestler in Tokyo, a pavement artist, a Red Indian, a monk . . . he can effortlessly flirt with the beauties of the world. And most importantly, he can get away with it all. Simply because he is the maharaja!'[15]

The new generation of the old feudals play all these roles to the hilt. Indian cinema has been turned on its head. Gone are the despotic feudals of the movies in the 1950s. Contemporary cinema has made heroes and heroines of famous and forgotten feudals and celebrates the grandeur and glory of a distant, pre-republican past. In another social inversion of sorts, the Reddy and Kamma peasantry that fought the feudal nizam in erstwhile Hyderabad state now make money promoting the symbols of Hyderabad's feudal past to the nouveau riche from around the world. At fashion shows and in elegant soirees, the contemporary descendants of the old feudals are increasingly willing to step out in royal attire, sporting regal heirlooms to the awe of fashionistas and fashion victims.

From the maharajas of Mysore and Travancore to the Nizam of Hyderabad, common citizens of the republic are still referred to by their abolished titles. The famous captain of India's cricket team, Mansur Ali Khan, was better known in the media as the Nawab of Pataudi. His daughter-in-law, film actor Kareena Kapoor, recently tweeted about her happy marriage referring to her husband, actor Saif Ali Khan, as SAKP—the 'P' was of course a reference to Pataudi, the feudal possession of the family. How can SAK just be 'SAK' without the 'P'. A business newspaper reported a property dispute of a lesser feudal in a most matter-of-fact way, and, with no touch of irony, referred to the person involved as 'Mohammad Amir Mohammad Khan, better known as the Raja of Mahmudabad'.[16] The media clearly loves royalty.

The landlord class remained loyal to the Congress party as long as the opposition to the Congress was largely to its political left— the communist, socialist and backward-caste parties. With the rise of the BJP, and its softness towards Hindu feudal elements in different parts of the country, the landed gentry have moved away from the Congress, gravitating towards the BJP or other upper-caste parties. Like big business, big landlords, too, will go with the flow as the political ground shifts from the Congress to the BJP.

7

Shifts in Political Power

India is the world's largest psephocracy.
It is only secondarily the world's largest democracy.

—Ashis Nandy

Communist and democratic revolutions have all involved the displacement of old elites and the emergence of the new. In some countries the change was bloody. The French and Russian revolutionaries beheaded the monarch and members of the nobility. In China, the propertied were dispossessed. Across Asia, the overthrow of colonial rule and feudal regimes resulted in the decline of old elites and the rise of new. The sociologist Vilfredo Pareto had famously declared that 'history is the graveyard of aristocracies'.[1] As we saw in the previous chapter, in India, aristocracy did die, but the aristocrats survived the 'gradual revolution'.[2]

First, because the freedom struggle was largely non-violent, the transfer of power from imperial and feudal regimes to a constitutional democracy was gradual, negotiated and organized. There was some violence and use of force in parts, but it was nothing compared to the violence and loss of life that marked the establishment of democratic governments in many other postcolonial nations.

Second, the entrenched social order in India, defined by caste, proved far too resilient for any dramatic overthrow of the old elite as it made its transition into a new political system. While the new nation's republican constitution made the practice of untouchability illegal and unlawful, and offered constitutional guarantees of affirmative action to ensure the social and economic upliftment of weaker sections, the upper castes continued to dominate the many institutions of social, cultural and economic power.

Third, the absence of radical agrarian transformation meant that change in power equations in rural India were far too gradual—often reversible—and uneven across the very diverse subcontinent. The abolition of feudalism and redistribution of land was a defining feature of both the rise of capitalism in Europe and communist revolutions around the world. As we saw in the previous chapter, the Indian experience was limited in its scope. In the urban economy, too, traditional business and merchant communities that had begun to prosper in the interwar years continued to do so after Independence, despite Nehru's desire to usher in a 'socialistic pattern of society'.

Fourth, the new institutions of the democratic state continued to be manned by the old elite, namely the civil, police and military services inherited from the precolonial and feudal regimes. Thus, at the all-India level, the ICS, an institution created by the British imperial government, remained in place in republican India, and was transformed more in name, becoming the Indian Administrative Service. In the armed forces, British officers and generals continued to serve their tenures, and the name of the power game was continuity with change.

Given all these elements of the Indian revolution, the transfer of power from the old elites to the new emergent ones was gradual and orderly compared to many other postcolonial societies. Perhaps the single most important reason for this was the fact that what began as a 'national movement'—an all-in-one social and political mobilization that eschewed caste, class, linguistic and other divides that defined colonial India—morphed into a political party of government. In countries that experienced bloody revolutions, the new ruling elite belonged to one or another section of society that then sought to establish hegemony over those sections that had been displaced by the revolutionary change. In India, the INC became an umbrella party that remained open to all—including the feudal and business elite that had collaborated with the colonial regime.

Congress Dominance

What emerged as a consequence was a democratically elected regime that sought to be all things to all people. As the pre-eminent political theorist of his times, Rajni Kothari, observed in his essay on the 'Congress system', the party of the national movement retained its national identity as an umbrella party of all sections of society, 'representing a historical consensus and enjoying a continuing basis of support and trust'.[3] Apart from the legacy of the national movement, Kothari also credited Jawaharlal Nehru for sustaining this character of the Congress: 'The contribution of Nehru was not to have started a revolution but to have given rise to a consensus.'[4]

An interesting consequence of this was that the old Indian elite managed to retain their social and economic status, and, in many cases, their political power too. While their social and economic status was defined by caste and class elements that continued to define post-Independence society, the political power of the old elite was reinforced by their participation in democratic politics. For all his socialist ideas, Nehru himself came from an upper-caste, wealthy family with aristocratic pretensions. In opting for Nehru over Vallabhbhai Patel and Subhas Chandra Bose, Gandhiji may well have conceded the value of signalling to the traditional Indian elite that their caste and class interests would be safe in the hands of someone with Nehru's elitist credentials. Patel was not to the manner born, and Bose was far too radical in his thinking. Nehru's radicalism was manageable.

This is not to suggest that the traditional elites accepted Nehru's leadership blindly. Many resented it—whether they were upper-caste politicians like C. Rajagopalachari, Rajendra Prasad or Acharya Kripalani, or the business elite like the Birlas and Tata, or even the landed feudals. But none of them had any credible political option available outside the Congress during the 1950s. The non-Congress opposition was, therefore, confined to what were essentially 'regional' parties—the DMK in what was then called Madras, the CPI in Kerala and a couple of other states, and the Swatantra Party, with its mainly urban social base. In the 1960s, other parties came to the fore, including the Jana Sangh, but all of them were still 'regional' parties without a national footprint.

The Congress party was the only national party till the mid-1970s. As a consequence, even those who disagreed with Nehru and his policies remained within its expansive fold. The few who left the Congress migrated to marginal political outfits like the Swatantra Party. Given that the principal opposition political parties in the first two decades after Independence—1947–67—were the communist and socialist parties, the country's elite remained loyal to the Congress. It was only when the Congress itself moved left to position itself as a pro-poor party, with Indira Gandhi's famous slogan 'Garibi Hatao', that the elite social groups began investing in other formations like the Jana Sangh and regional parties. Following the same trend, in 1967, the Rajmata of Gwalior quit the Congress party and joined the Jana Sangh.

The era of Congress 'dominance', also a term we owe to Rajni Kothari, ended with the general elections of 1967. In the Lok Sabha elections of 1957, the INC won 47.78 per cent of the popular vote. The second largest party share of 10.41 per cent went to the Praja Socialist Party (PSP), and the third place was taken by the CPI with a vote share of 8.92 per cent. The Bharatiya Jana Sangh (BJS) clocked a share of 5.97 per cent. A decade later, in the elections of 1967, the Congress vote share was down to 40.78 per cent, the Jana Sangh became the second largest party with a share of 9.31 per cent, followed by the newly launched right-wing, pro-free market party, Swatantra, with a vote share of 8.67 per cent. Technically, the communists were still at second place with a combined vote share of 9.39 per cent, marginally ahead of the Jana Sangh, but the split in the communist movement with the formation of the CPI (Marxist) meant that the CPI was at fourth position with a vote share of 5.11 per cent, with the CPI(M) securing 4.28 per cent vote share.

The perceptible decline of Congress dominance occurred between the elections of 1957 and 1962. In the 1957 elections, four 'national' political parties—INC, CPI, PSP and BJS accounted for 73 per cent of the vote share, with independents accounting for as much as 19.1 per cent of the vote. In 1962, the combined vote of the four 'national' parties was down to 67.91 per cent, while a range of 'regional' or 'sectional' parties like the Akalis in Punjab, the DMK in Tamil Nadu, Republican Party of India and so on, made their presence felt. By 1967, the national parties (now including Swatantra) remained dominant with close to 70 per cent of the vote share, but a large number of regional parties made their presence felt in the Lok Sabha, including Kerala Congress, Bangla Congress, Forward Bloc, Muslim League and National Conference.

The picture changed even more dramatically in elections to the state assemblies in the mid-1960s, with the Congress losing power in Kerala and then in Tamil Nadu, and Swatantra and Jana Sangh making their presence felt across several states. Even within the Congress party the locus of power had shifted after Nehru's death from the party's 'national' leadership to provincial party bosses like Brahmananda Reddy in Andhra Pradesh, Mohanlal Sukhadia in Rajasthan, Y.B. Chavan in Maharashtra, C.B. Gupta in Uttar Pradesh, S. Nijalingappa in Karnataka, and so on. The political power elite of the early Nehru years were mostly those who had made their mark in public life through the freedom struggle.

As Nehru's influence over domestic politics began to gradually fade and with the promise of Independence giving way to concerns about social and economic development, the institutions of democracy allowed new provincial leaders to enter the ranks of the nation's political power elite.

Political Dynasts

The mid-'60s was a turning point for India in more ways than one. First, it was the period of transition from a Nehruvian to a post-Nehruvian political era. Second, the stature of the national political leadership came into question with China humiliating India in 1962. Questioning India's territorial claims along the Indo-China border, it sent its troops into India and then withdrew after making the point that they could walk in and out at will. Third, a war with Pakistan in 1965 imposed heavy costs on India in the middle of a food crisis caused by the failure of the monsoon and two successive drought years. Fourth, these crises—two wars and the two-year drought—imposed costs on the economy, forcing India to devalue its currency and seek foreign aid. All in all, the 1960s was a wasted decade.

The management of war and the national economy are both key responsibilities of the central government. Setbacks on both these fronts weakened the power of the Centre over the states. This, combined with the rise of provincial political leaders occupying a space vacated by a diminished national leadership of the Congress, was the first major challenge to the status of the metropolitan power elite that held sway for two decades after Independence. This social class hailing from the major cities of Nehru's India—mainly Delhi, Bombay, Calcutta, Madras, Patna, Lucknow, Bangalore and Jaipur—had been beneficiaries of Nehru's India even if they did not think much of Nehru's, and later, Indira's 'socialism'. The clout of the civil service inherited from the British, whom even Sardar Patel viewed as the Republic's 'steel frame', had only grown with time. This loyal civil service and the Nehruvian elite who had prospered along with them began to see the ground slip from under their feet through the turbulent '60s.

Apart from ensuring the support of the social groups that were empowered by their place in the state system, the political power elite of Nehru's India also ensured that they retained the support of the westernized, metropolitan elite. This small social set included the cultural and media czars of the time. Similar to them, their children, too, went to fancy schools in the Himalayan foothills and the Nilgiris, to colleges run by Christian missionaries and then, of course, Oxbridge universities. They had a 'love-hate' relationship with the Nehruvian state but were undoubtedly its beneficiaries. They went along with Indira Gandhi's politics in the hope of retaining their positions of influence and power.

Men like P.N. Haksar (prime minister's principal secretary) and Romesh Thapar (founder-editor of the journal *Seminar),* were the two legs of the power elite that facilitated the dynastic transition from Nehru to Indira. Haksar, a Kashmiri pandit who like so many of his social class went to England for higher studies and took to leftist politics, was inducted into the diplomatic service by Nehru and became the most powerful civil servant in Indira's government. Thapar, a Punjabi born in a merchant family in Lahore, became a Marxist in Bombay and launched a liberal journal, *Seminar.* He was a quintessential representative of New Delhi's Nehruvian elite—newly rich, England-educated, socialist in outlook, with prime property in Delhi. While Haksar was Indira Gandhi's trusted adviser, Thapar was thought to be a member of what came to be known as her 'kitchen cabinet'—an unofficial group of advisers to Indira that included Haksar, Thapar, Dinesh Singh, a minor feudal from U.P., and I.K. Gujral, who started his political life as a communist and ended up as the prime minister of a coalition government.

When Indira Gandhi chose to assert the power of the Centre by taking a series of policy steps that culminated in the imposition of Emergency in 1975, many among Delhi's power elite not only went along with it but encouraged it. As sociologist, Gyan Prakash, reminded us in his essay on the 'lawful suspension of law', it was the Haksars and the Thapars, and indeed so many others from Delhi's power elite—civil and military officials, business barons, media and culture czars and, to use Modi's favourite portmanteau, the residents of Lutyens' Delhi—who unleashed a Frankenstein that they 'could do nothing to control'.[5]

The multiple crises of the 1960s provided the context both for the decline in the 'dominance' of the Congress and the rise of a new provincial political leadership, both within the Congress and outside. The twin droughts and the consequent shortage of food, forcing India to import foodgrain and live what was dubbed a 'ship-to-mouth' existence, encouraged the pursuit of the Green Revolution. The Green Revolution, in turn, contributed to the enrichment of the rich peasants—the class that could produce more and sell more. The political leadership that this class of peasants produced began to assert its clout. Some—like the succession of Reddy chief ministers of Andhra Pradesh and Jat chief ministers of Punjab and Haryana—remained within the Congress. Others, like Charan Singh of Uttar Pradesh, floated their own political party.

Indira Gandhi's decision to suspend several types of freedom and impose a state of Emergency in 1975 has been explained in many ways, ranging from her desire to consolidate her family's dominance within the Congress party to her fear of a CIA-inspired political coup. Indira's supporters have long claimed that she regretted her decision within weeks of imposing the Emergency but continued to justify it on the grounds that external forces inimical to India and to her personally were planning to oust her and destabilize the country. Ravi Visvesvaraya Prasad, son of Indira's trusted aide and long-serving information adviser, H.Y. Sharada Prasad, has revealed, based on what he learnt from his father, that Michael Foot, a Labour Party left-winger and friend of the Nehru–Gandhi family, flew into New Delhi, rejecting advice to the contrary from the British Foreign Office and intelligence agencies, to warn Indira of a threat to her life and to the country. Prasad suggests that Soviet supremo Leonid Brezhnev also provided intelligence claiming the United States spy agency, the Central Intelligence Agency (CIA), had plans to organize Indira's overthrow similar to the political coup and assassination of Salvador Allende of Chile in 1973.

Sharada Prasad himself believed that the Emergency was the post-Independence State's knee-jerk response to a pre-Independence political tactic, namely 'satyagraha'. The government of the day just did not know how to deal with the forces unleashed by a later-day Gandhian, Jayaprakash Narayan. The Emergency, wrote Sharada Prasad in a 2006 column, was 'Indira Gandhi's coup against her own prime ministership'.[6] The Indian state was responding both to anarchy at home and imperialist conspiracy abroad.

Whatever the reasons for the declaration of a state of emergency, the fact is that it represented the first significant test of legitimacy of India's power elite. Could they continue to govern India in accordance with the letter and spirit of the constitution or had their governance come under such threat that, as in so many post-colonial societies, the power elite had to resort to non-democratic means to retain their power? Was the Emergency merely an individual leader's desperate act aimed at clinging to political office, or the consequence of a sense of collective siege on the part of an elite that had come to enjoy the fruits of democratic office without retaining the legitimacy conferred by democratic governance?[7]

The easy manner in which it was conceived and implemented by a loyal bureaucracy showed how willing the bureaucracy was to kneel when asked to bend. It reflected the ordinariness of an extraordinary situation.

What then motivated Indira Gandhi to finally end Emergency rule? Opinion is divided on this. Jurist Fali Nariman recalls being told that Indira was advised by US President Jimmy Carter to end the Emergency as it had hurt India's global standing. Others have suggested that she was aware of her declining global image and popularity, especially in Europe, and wished to retrieve it. Picking up from the late Kuldip Nayar's recollection that Sanjay Gandhi had told him that he had been kept in the dark on his mother's decision, many have argued that Indira was in fact unhappy with her son's doings and misdemeanours, and took the final decision to liberate her legacy from that of her son. Indeed, Sharada Prasad went to the extent of implicitly claiming that Indira had become a prisoner of her own son, when he wrote, 'Her secretariat, the home ministry, the cabinet, and indeed her government as a whole, were deprived of their effective power, and the prime minister herself was made a prisoner of the "palace guard".' The 'palace guard' being the coterie around the PM, led by her son Sanjay, that had come to acquire enormous power with neither legitimate office nor much responsibility.

It seems from these accounts that some conspiracy theories led to the imposition of the Emergency and other conspiracy theories led to its end. What do these theories tell us about the 'Delhi darbar' in the troubled 1970s? So much was happening around the world and across India that even an all-powerful leader like Indira, at the height of her power after the creation of Bangladesh, felt trapped in her seemingly secure position. Was the Emergency a response to the uncertainties of that era? Or was it just a palace coup by a cabal that had come to assume, after 1971, that 'Indira is India and India is Indira'? Either way, the Emergency was as much a consequence of the government's inability to govern, without resorting to extraordinary instrumentalities, as it was of the paranoia of India's power elite. It represented a breakdown of the Nehruvian elite consensus that had defined governance since Independence. A variety of changes—social, economic and political—had created new claimants of power who were challenging the Nehruvian consensus.

Sanjay Gandhi's entry into politics established the precedent that facilitated dynastic succession within the Congress, with

Rajiv Gandhi succeeding his mother, Indira. The 'Nehru Dynasty' was the first political dynasty in Indian politics. Others followed. If NTR was replaced by his son-in-law Chandrababu Naidu, Biju Patnaik, Devi Lal, Charan Singh, Prakash Singh Badal, Mulayam Singh Yadav, Lalu Prasad Yadav, Farooq Abdullah and many others have all been succeeded by their sons. Some became chief ministers, some remained party president. But the political phenomenon of dynastic politics has taken root, inspired by the nation's First Political Family.

The Era of Coalitions

The politics preceding and following Indira's Emergency reign represented fundamental changes in the social and political field. With the exception of the leaders of the pro-Soviet CPI, Indira Gandhi had imprisoned all other major opposition leaders. This was because the events leading up to the imposition of the Emergency, the imprisonment of most opposition during the Emergency and the victory of non-Congress parties in the elections held after the withdrawal of the Emergency, brought to the fore a range of traditional anti-Congress parties across the country. In the north, the Akalis, the BJP and the Lohia Socialists gained ground. In Bengal and Kerala, the communists improved their standing. In many other states, regional parties like the DMK in Tamil Nadu held sway. Each of them represented an alternative ideological strand in Indian politics. Morarji Desai, with his mix of Gandhian ideology and anti-left bias, became the prime minister heading a government that contained BJP's L.K. Advani and Atal Bihari Vajpayee, the kulak leader Charan Singh, the Dalit leader Jagjivan Ram, the socialists George Fernandes and Madhu Dandavate, a retired ICS officer H.M. Patel and a clutch of provincial politicians representing various sectional interests. The communists did not join the government but Morarji depended on them to sustain his parliamentary majority. Indira Gandhi's Emergency rule brought all of them together in an unlikely and unwieldy coalition that could, understandably, not last long.

The interesting feature of this experiment is that its political composition was at odds with the class preferences of the Nehruvian power elite. Very soon into the Janata Party's tenure, the elite of Lutyens' Delhi became disappointed and yearned for Indira's return. Jay Dubashi, a prominent journalist of his time, reflected this sentiment when he wrote in *India Today*, a magazine launched six months after the declaration of Emergency, 'If Janata Party does not seem to have made much of an impression on the city-folk including the city-bred intelligentsia it is because the party has apparently deliberately adopted a political style that contrasts sharply with the razzle-dazzle of Mrs Gandhi's populism.'[8] The publisher and editor of *India Today*, Arun Poorie, a contemporary of Rajiv Gandhi at Doon School, took a very pro-Emergency view in the magazine's inaugural issue of December 1975, pointing to all the good things that had happened since the declaration of Emergency in June that year:

What a handful would consider suppression, millions of Indians do seem to consider emancipation. Whereas six months ago visitors to India heard little else but complaints about the lack of consumer products and unbearable soaring prices, the average person is grateful he can now feed his family and get more value for his rupee.

There are few glaring signs of the emergency in India as most of the changes are subtle. A young television reporter visiting New Delhi from New York, asked in surprise, 'Where are the soldiers? Where are the guns? Where is the Emergency?'

Perhaps there is some wisdom in what a political leader in Delhi said recently, 'We can use the Emergency to boost tourism in India. The slogan for publicity campaigns should be: Come to India to see the Emergency. There has never been anything like this in any democracy before.[9]

Given its ideological incoherence, the patchwork alliance called the Janata Party, that came to power in January 1977, failed to hold ground, and its experiment of running the first-ever coalition government in New Delhi, in 1977–79, was aborted. But the politics they represented did not go away. The return of the Nehru-Gandhi dynasty in 1980–89, along with the restoration of the Nehruvian elite to positions of power and influence, happened in a different India. While Indira Gandhi and her son Rajiv Gandhi secured comfortable majorities in Parliament, non-Congress political parties had come to establish themselves in more and more provinces. The Left Front in West Bengal, Telugu Desam in Andhra Pradesh, the Akalis in Punjab and the Janata Party's constituents in Bihar, Madhya Pradesh and Uttar Pradesh began to grow roots, weakening Congress's hold over the country.

When Rajiv Gandhi was defeated in 1989 and the Congress government was replaced by a newly formed coalition, its leader Vishwanath Pratap Singh famously declared the dawn of an 'era of coalitions'. This experiment, too, was as short-lived as the one with Janata Party—with one difference. In 1977, the ground beneath the Congress had not fully shifted. Its defeat was not comprehensive. In 1989 two developments took place. First, in 1989, the Congress tally in the Lok Sabha collapsed dramatically from over 400 MPs, who had won the election for the party in 1984, to less than 200. Second, the BJP recorded its best-ever performance winning eighty-five seats. This was a dramatic improvement from the two seats it managed to win in 1984, in the highly emotive elections after Indira's assassination.

V.P. Singh grasped the significance of the 1989 result very quickly. He, like many others, saw in the result a contestation between the Hindutva politics of the BJP and the caste-based political mobilization by backward class (BC) and Scheduled Caste (SC) leaders. By offering to extend the constitutional reservations in educational institutions and government jobs offered to SCs and Scheduled Tribes (STs) to the BCs, Singh hoped to keep the

'Hindu' vote divided along caste lines to prevent the BJP's strategy of uniting it along communal lines. A sharp political contestation between caste-oriented leaders like Mulayam Singh Yadav and Lalu Prasad Yadav and the Hindutva-oriented BJP began in northern India. In the south, the BJP was pitted mainly against regional parties, which were also partly caste-based but essentially built around language and regional identity.

The 1989 elections have had a long-term impact on Indian politics and the sociology of the power elite. They signalled the arrival of Lohia's middle class on the national political stage. This phenomenon was already visible at the state level across many states with backward-class politicians asserting their political power even within the Congress. In response to the opposition, her kind of left-wing populism was facing from upper-caste politicians in the Congress, Indira Gandhi had begun encouraging backward-class leaders in many states. By 1989, several backward-class leaders had risen to prominence even within the Congress. But the arrival of Mulayam and Lalu at the national level, and the rise of Mayawati, a Dalit politician, signalled major changes in the social locus of power.

In 1979, Prime Minister Morarji Desai appointed the Second Backward Class Commission, under the chairmanship of a former chief minister of Bihar, Bindeshwari Prasad Mandal. The Indian Constitution had provided for affirmative action in favour of the weakest sections of Indian society—SCs and STs—but had not provided any scheme for the empowerment of other socially and economically less privileged 'intermediate castes' who came to be called 'backward classes'. In 1953, Prime Minister Nehru constituted the First Backward Class Commission that listed 2399 backward castes or communities, with 837 of them classified as 'most backward', creating a new social category of BC and Other Backward Classes (OBC). While political parties began winning their support by offering political office to members of these groups, there was no provision for reserved quotas in educational institutions and government service as there was for SCs and STs.

By the mid-1970s, these BCs had become politically influential, and it was in recognition of their political clout that the Morarji government set up the Mandal Commission. Mandal submitted his report in December 1980, by which time Indira Gandhi had returned to office. The report was placed in cold storage till August 1990, when Prime Minister V.P. Singh decided to implement its recommendation to extend affirmative action to BCs and OBCs. Weeks later, Singh's government fell, and some recommendations of the Mandal Report were finally implemented by the Narasimha Rao government in 1993.[10]

Between 1989 and 2014, a period in which no national political party commanded a majority of its own in Parliament, both the Congress and the BJP wooed the caste-based and regional parties to remain in power in Delhi. In 2014, the BJP took an important political step forward opting for a backward-class politician as its prime-ministerial candidate. While Karnataka's Deve Gowda was the first OBC PM, Modi was the first popularly elected OBC PM. Four of India's most popular and important PMs—Nehru, Indira, Narasimha Rao and Vajpayee—were all Brahmins. Modi's rise to power, that, too, within an upper-caste-dominated RSS-BJP organization was, therefore, an important turning point in the politics of the power elite.

Provincial Power

One consequence of the shift in political power in the post-Green Revolution, post-Emergency era was the rise of regional political parties, partly aided by the emergence of a regionally dispersed new business class. It was not, therefore, a coincidence that fresh demands regarding a rebalancing of Centre-state relations began to be made with greater force in the 1980s. The first salvo against the centralization of power during the Nehruvian era was in fact fired by the DMK in 1969 when Tamil Nadu chief minister, M. Karunanidhi, appointed the Centre-State Relations Inquiry

Committee under the chairmanship of a retired chief justice of the Madras High Court, Justice P.V. Rajamannar. Among its many recommendations aimed at reducing the arbitrary powers of the central government vis-à-vis state governments, a key suggestion was that Articles 356 and 357 of the Indian Constitution be entirely repealed. Rajamannar did not want a political party with an overwhelming majority in the Lok Sabha to arbitrarily remove elected state governments using these two provisions. This undemocratic act had in fact been committed for the first time by Prime Minister Nehru when his government dismissed the elected communist party government of E.M.S. Namboodiripad in Kerala in 1957. There were other instances of the misuse of Article 356 in the 1960s and 1970s, but by the 1980s the demand for an overhaul of Centre–state relations once again gathered wide political support.

After assuming power in West Bengal in 1978, the CPI(M) decided to mobilize non-Congress parties to demand a review of Centre–state economic and political relations and seek increased fiscal space for state governments. West Bengal's finance minister, Ashok Mitra, became the main spokesperson for a nationwide campaign for increasing the financial powers of state governments. Commenting on Mitra's campaign, *India Today* columnist Jay Dubashi observed, 'Frankly, it is doubtful whether all that CPI(M) wants is some more powers to raise revenues without reference to the Centre. The issue of the division of financial powers is merely a smokescreen—the gut issue is the division of political powers between the Centre and the states.'[11] Dubashi was not far off the mark. The reason why many regional parties, including the DMK and Telugu Desam, were willing to make common cause with the communists was because they, too, sought a change in the balance of power between the Centre and the state governments.

Joining the chorus of criticism against the over-centralization of financial resources and administrative authority in the central government, the founding leader of the Telugu Desam Party, N.T. Rama Rao, famously declared that 'the centre is a conceptual myth'.

He was not just drawing attention to the fact that almost everything that a citizen needs in her daily life, from water and power to sanitation and law and order, is provided by the state government. In doing so, NTR was also seeking a greater share of the financial resources at the disposal of the central government. The central government collects taxes but a large part of these taxes is distributed back to state governments through a variety of constitutional and administrative provisions. Apart from this fiscal function, the only other activities exclusively under the central government are defence, national security and foreign affairs.

Not surprisingly, NTR joined forces with other 'regional' parties in demanding more fiscal and administrative power for state governments. By the time he was swept to power in Andhra Pradesh, in 1982, the demand for more balanced Centre-state relations had already become a major political demand of non-Congress parties, reflecting changing equations within the country's political elites.[12]

Returning to power in 1980, both weakened and chastened, Indira Gandhi decided to concede to the demand for a comprehensive review of Centre-state relations. In 1983, her government appointed a commission under the chairmanship of Justice R.S. Sarkaria to re-examine Centre-state relations as specified by the constitution. The terms of reference stated:

The Commission will examine and review the working of the existing arrangements between the Union and States in regard to powers, functions and responsibilities in all spheres and recommend such changes or other measures as may be appropriate.

In examining and reviewing the working of the existing arrangements between the Union and States and making recommendations as to the changes and measures needed, the Commission will *keep in view the social and economic developments that have taken place over the years and have due regard to the scheme and frame-work of the Constitution* which the founding fathers

have so sedulously designed to protect the independence
and ensure the unity and integrity of the country which is
of paramount importance for promoting the welfare of the
people.[13]

It is worth noting that the government appointed as member of
the commission a distinguished economist, S.R. Sen, which points
to a recognition of the influence of changing economic reality on
Centre-state relations and a willingness to situate a review of the
constitution in the context of these changes. While only a few of the
recommendations of the Sarkaria Commission were implemented
both in letter and spirit, the fact we wish to draw attention to is
that of a political recognition in the commission's appointment of a
change in the balance of political power in the 1980s.

Over the years, different political parties with varying degrees
of power at the Centre have handled the issue of Centre-state
relations depending on the relative power of national and regional
parties. Everyone in power in New Delhi, from Indira Gandhi to
Narendra Modi, has not hesitated to ignore constitutional niceties
and morality if it suited their party to impose president's rule in
one state or another or interfere in the functioning of duly elected
state governments. Whether they did it or not was not decided by
their commitment to constitutional principles, but by the extant
balance of power between those in office in New Delhi and those
in state capitals.

Towards Plutocracy

While Lohia's three identities of the ruling elite were wealth, upper
caste and English-speaking, Narendra Modi positioned himself as
a leader who did not belong to any one of these three groups—
not wealthy, not upper caste and certainly more comfortable in
the vernacular. By contrast, Rahul Gandhi has been shown to be
wealthy, upper caste (his mixed parentage notwithstanding) and

certainly of the English-speaking elite. Indian politics has long since devalued the status of English as a language of power, even though its importance as a language of opportunity has grown. However, the social composition of the power elite remains such that, even today, Lohia's three qualifications continue to define the power elite.

Wealth remains, above all, the most important determinant of power. Several recent studies have focused on the role of 'money power' in politics and the nexus between crime, business and politics. The rising cost of election campaigns, the inability of the state to enforce rules pertaining to election funding and, more recently, the brazen manner in which political parties in power are able to corner the bulk of the funds provided by corporates and other donors, has made politics a game of the rich in which the wealthy become wealthier and are able to become politically more powerful.[14]

It is not, therefore, surprising that a disproportionate number of the elected representatives of the people are wealthy. There had been some dilution of this aspect after Independence, with more members of the middle class—especially rich peasants—entering politics. However, as election expenses have grown and with rising importance of political office as a source of both power and wealth, there has been a rise in the number of wealthy among the elected representatives of the people. Consider the social composition of the 17th Lok Sabha elected in 2019. It has more wealthy members than any other Lok Sabha in the past half century. Data collated by the Association for Democratic Rights shows that as many as 475 MPs (constituting 88 per cent of the 539 MPs for whom data was available) have assets upwards of Rs 10 million (1 crore), slightly up from 443 (82 per cent) in the 16th Lok Sabha. Out of 542 winners analysed during Lok Sabha 2014 elections, 443 (82 per cent) winners were *crorepatis*. In the 15th Lok Sabha (2009–14), the comparable number was appreciably less at 315 (58 per cent).[15]

The Association for Democratic Reforms (ADR) study shows that not only had MPs become richer during the five years they were members of the Lok Sabha but that in successive elections since 2009 the proportion of 'crorepati' candidates among the victors has also risen. In other words, the wealthy had a better chance of securing admission to political office, while the latter was an important source of acquiring wealth. In a country with a nominal per capita income of Rs 1,20,000 per annum, and at least a fifth of the population living in abject poverty, it is surprising that an overwhelming number of elected representatives, both in the Lok Sabha and in state assemblies, are millionaires if not billionaires.

The ADR data showed that with the exception of MPs from the communist parties, all other MPs of all other parties were millionaires, with the BJP having the largest number of them. As many as a third of MPs in the 17th Lok Sabha had assets worth more than Rs 50 million, while average assets per winning MP was Rs 21 million. The wealthiest MPs, however, came from smaller political parties like YSR Congress, Nationalist Congress party, DMK, Telangana Rashtra Samiti (TRS) and Akali Dal. These are, of course, declared assets, and that too, in the name of the specified individual and not of all family members taken together. Many wealthy Indians hold considerable wealth in the name of their spouse. The ADR data also shows, interestingly, that MPs from regional parties like the Akali Dal, TRS and the Nationalist Congress party saw the highest increase in wealth of sitting MPs between the elections of 2014 and 2019.

The rise of what have been called 'Mandal politics' has contributed to an increase in the share of OBCs in the elected members of the Lok Sabha and state legislatures since 1989, both on account of mainline parties like the Congress and the BJP picking winners from these social groups and on account of the increased presence of caste-based parties, like the Yadava parties of north India, in legislatures. However, it is also true that the upper castes have retained their dominance and remain the single largest group of MPs and MLAs in most states.[16]

The shifts in Indian politics over the past seven decades have, without doubt, shaped the composition of the political power elite. Their caste, class and regional composition has certainly changed. The rise of intermediate castes, the OBCs, has been one of the major structural changes in both the class and caste composition of the ruling political class. Yet, the landowning upper castes have retained their place of prominence and dominance in many regions. From the Jats and Rajputs of north India to the Marathas and Patels of western India and the Reddys, Kammas, Velamas, Chettiars and Nairs of the south, upper castes have retained their presence in politics.

The role of money power in politics has only increased with time, and this is reflected in the wealth of elected politicians. For all his anti-elitism, Narendra Modi presides, along with his colleague Amit Shah, over the wealthiest and and most cash-rich party in India today. With the decline of the Congress, the balance of power and wealth has shifted in favour of the BJP, which is one reason why the loss of power in wealthy and cash-rich Maharashtra would hurt the BJP. Politicians from the more developed states, like Maharashtra, Gujarat, Tamil Nadu and Punjab-Haryana, as well as politicians with roots in regions where their access to natural resources has enriched them—like the Reddy brothers of Karnataka—are valuable assets for political parties and their leadership. Politicians who have made their millions in mining, or politicians from the coal mining regions where they are hand-in-glove with the coal mafia, have greater access to financial resources than politicians from states with fewer rent-seeking, wealth-accumulating possibilities.

Where you come from and how you make your money determines where you are on the political power ladder. The wealth and power of the Maratha politicians of Maharashtra, the Reddy-Kamma-Velama politicians of Andhra Pradesh-Telangana, the Chettiars of Tamil Nadu, Vokkaligas of Karnataka and the Jats of Haryana-Punjab is thus explained. In every regime, at the Centre and in the states, there are individual politicians with more influence and clout than their counterparts. Their power is defined both by the electoral support they command as individuals, not dependent on their party machines, and the financial resources they are able to mobilize for their party. If the consolidation of a political base occurs in a political family's first generation, its conversion into wealth begins with the first generation but accelerates during the tenure of the second generation. The Karunanidhis, Pawars, YSRs, Badals, the Yadavs of Bihar and UP, the Gadkaris and the Chauhans of the BJP—the pattern is the same with every political family, from the Nehru-Gandhis to an Amit Shah. Political power accumulated in one generation is converted into family wealth over successive generations.

As the foundations of wealth accumulation shift—across sectors, regions and social groups—the composition of the political power elite also undergoes a change. With each passing decade, a new set of wealthy politicians becomes powerful and a new generation of the politically powerful becomes wealthy. For all their anti-elitism, Modi and the BJP have become increasingly dependent on the wealthy, the landed and the cash-rich to keep the wheels of political power well oiled. Corporate funding of political parties has sharply increased over the past decade and, in the run-up to the 2019 elections, the BJP cornered nearly 90 per cent of all corporate donations to political parties.[17] The gradual loss of power, on the other hand, has deprived the Congress party and its leadership of their funds. Their third position in the power equations of Maharashtra is not very reassuring for the Congress. Loss of power in Karnataka and Madhya Pradesh makes the party dependent on the Punjab and Rajasthan for funds. Many factors contribute to shifts in political power. Access to cash is certainly one of them.

It is over this political milieu that Modi's BJP has sought to establish its hegemonic dominance, so to speak. The use of both caste and class metaphors to project a political personality has been done with the larger political objective of ensuring not just the party's, or indeed even the individual's, but an ideology's dominance. The shifts in political power over the six decades after Independence have occurred against the background of declining Congress dominance—end of the 'Congress System'—and the rise of normal party politics wherein there are winners and losers and changes of government. That has been the norm in most democracies— the revolving door of governmental power. However, the rise of Modi's BJP appears thus far to be a combination of the rise of a new dominant political party, echoing the 'Congress System', and the assertion of political and cultural hegemony of a new power elite. Hindutva politics has also arrived with deep pockets, with the rural and urban rich bankrolling the BJP, making it the richest political party. The phenomenon is as yet nascent, and Indian democracy can still surprise those who view elections as revolutions.

8

Bureaucracy and the Military

The civil service is a professional service and
forms the backbone of our governance structure.
It must remain politically neutral and professionally competent.

—Manmohan Singh, 2007

An old adage says that the three key functionaries of the Indian government are PM-CM-DM—the last of the trio being district magistrate, also known as district commissioner or collector. For most citizens, the representative of the state is always the lowest functionary.

The recognition of the importance of the DM—also called the deputy commissioner in British India's imperial administration—encouraged the colonial government to begin recruiting highly talented individuals to this position. Thus, in 1858, the Indian Civil Service (ICS) was born. In 1861, the Indian Civil Services Act was passed, allowing the recruitment of natives into the colonial government. One of the consequences of the First World War was that fewer Englishmen were available and willing to join the civil administration of the British Imperial government in India. Subsequently, the British government decided to open up the colonial institution of the ICS to Indians who could qualify by passing a test. The test was initially conducted only in the UK and so required the Indians taking these tests to travel to England. Over time, the qualifying test started being conducted in India.

Prior to the First World War, 95 per cent of ICS officers were British; a decade after the war, they constituted less than half the recruits. However, a bulk of the recruits had either completed their education in the UK or had to train there to enter the service. Lloyd George, prime minister of the United Kingdom from 1916 to 1922, during whose tenure the ICS became more open to native Indian recruits, called it 'the steel frame on which the whole structure of our government and of our administration in India rests'.[1] It was a view that India's first home minister, Sardar Vallabhbhai Patel, is credited with having endorsed.

Rise of Meritocracy

Prior to Independence, Indian recruits to the ICS were expected to be trained, if not educated, in Britain's best institutions. Among the many colleges of Oxford and Cambridge in the UK that conducted this training, St Catherine's was one. In April 1938, St Catherine's College Society Magazine reported the passing away of my maternal grandfather in these words:

SIRUGURI JAYA RAO
Died April 20, 1938

Siruguri Jaya Rao, B.Sc, I.C.S., was born in 1905 at Vizianagram, Madras. He was educated at Hyderabad, was placed first amongst the matriculates, and was awarded a Scholarship for five years by the Nizam's Government. He obtained First Classes in the Intermediate and B.Sc. Examinations of Madras University; conducted postgraduate research under Sir C. V. Raman at Calcutta, passed the I.C.S. Competitive Examination held at

Delhi in 1928, and then proceeded to St. Catharine's, where he spent two years working for the Indian Civil Service. Jaya Rao then returned to India for Service in the Central Province, and in 1938 rose to the rank of Deputy Commissioner. He met his untimely death as the result of a motor accident. Mr. H. Bomford, then Governor of the Central Province, wrote: 'I feel that the Province has lost a man who can ill be spared.'[2]

I refer to this very personal example for two reasons. First, to draw attention to the pride the college took in the academic achievements of its Indian alumnus, and second, to emphasize the meritocratic nature of the ICS. We owe the idea of a merit-based civil service manned by natives but trained at the best institutions of the empire to Lord Thomas Babington Macaulay. Macaulay is largely remembered as the colonial administrator who introduced teaching of the English language to Indians so as to create a class of natives who would be 'Indian in blood and colour, but English in taste, in opinions, in morals and in intellect'. However, his other significant contribution was to encourage the colonial government to create a merit-based administration in India.

As one of Macaulay's biographers, Zareer Masani, observes, 'Whatever his views on Indians and their climate and culture, Macaulay remained ardently committed to the task of providing them with the best administration that Britain could offer; and his efforts resulted in an Indian Civil Service far superior in education, talent and integrity to Britain's own domestic service, for which it later became the model.'[3] It is, therefore, widely believed that the idea of a permanent civil service recruited through merit-based selection is a very British legacy. However, it is interesting to note that we actually owe the idea of meritocracy—a bureaucracy selected on the basis of merit—to China's Tang dynasty (618–907 AD).

The Tang rulers created a system of local schools whose students were permitted to appear for an examination that tested their knowledge of Confucian classics. Those who excelled by passing an examination would be recruited into the government and could rise to fairly high non-hereditary positions. The version of Chinese language they had to learn was Mandarin, hence this elite within the power hierarchy came to be referred to in Western literature as 'the mandarins'—precursors to the modern institution of the permanent civil service.

The idea of a ruler being served by experienced officials is, however, something that dates back to an even earlier period— that too, in Indian history—to a theorist of the state. It was in his classic treatise on governance and administration, the *Arthashastra*, that Kautilya, the friend-philosopher-guide of the great Emperor Chandragupta Maurya, explained to the ruler the usefulness of 'associates' who would man the emperor's administration. 'Rulership can be successfully carried out only with the help of associates. One wheel alone does not turn.'[4] The practice of the monarch appointing competent 'associates' to assist him in the governance of his kingdom was continued by the Mughal rulers who chose men of competence and capability from within their courts for positions of administrative power. Seeking such talent, the Mughals identified the Kayastha community as capable administrators. While the Nizam of Hyderabad also opted to employ Kayasthas of north India as his senior officials, some of the other southern rulers opted for Madhwa Brahmins. The British took a liking to both Brahmins and Kayasthas who became the single largest caste groups within the ICS. Interestingly, this social composition of the higher civil service endured after Independence. A study conducted in the mid-1980s showed that caste data was available for 3235 of the 4284 IAS officers in service at the time. Of these 3235 officers, 37.67 per cent were Brahmins and 9.56 per cent were Kayasthas. Another 13.33 per cent were classified as Kshatriyas. Taken together, over 60 per cent of the IAS in service belonged to those upper castes traditionally regarded for centuries as capable of being 'administrators', or what Kautilya would call 'competent associates' of the ruler.

While sociologists and students of public administration have credited Max Weber as being the original theorist of modern bureaucracy, it is entirely possible that Weber had himself been first exposed to the institution of mandarins in China and Kautilya's views on administration. The English translation of *Arthashastra*, first published in 1905, was available to Weber before he wrote his treatise on the institution of the bureaucracy. There is, however, an interesting difference between Weber's conceptualization of the role of a modern bureaucracy and a more likely Kautilyan view of bureaucrats as 'associates' of the ruler, a 'second wheel' of the chariot of state power. By contrast, Weber saw the 'main source of the superiority of bureaucratic administration' in the emphasis it places on 'technical knowledge'. To quote Weber:

> Bureaucratic administration fundamentally means the exercise of domination based on knowledge. This is the trait that makes it specifically rational. It consists, on the one hand, of technical knowledge, which is, per se, sufficient to ensure a position of extraordinary power for bureaucracy. On the other hand, it should be considered that bureaucratic organisations, or those in power who use it, tend to become even more powerful by the knowledge that comes from the practice that they attain in the function.[5]

Kautilya viewed officials of the state as intermediaries between the tribal chieftains who wielded autonomous power, the rising class of landowning cultivators and traders, and the mass of poor labour and subjects of the ruler. This autonomous status of a professional bureaucracy within a class/caste divided society gives it a character that Weber did not care to examine. Rather, it was the Marxist scholars who focused on this dimension of the civil service in a post-colonial context. Recall our discussion of Kalecki's characterization of 'intermediate regimes'. Kalecki saw bureaucrats hailing from the educated, essentially urban, middle class as members of an 'intermediate' class wielding authority over others due to their status within the state apparatus. The Kautilyan civil servant was not merely a professional administrator but a member of the power elite mediating between contending classes. As Deva concludes, 'The picture of the bureaucracy that emerges from the *Arthashastra* is one of a powerful, ubiquitous and parasitical ruling class.'[6] Some may believe that this would be a fitting epitaph for the civil service. Yet, democratic India chose to retain the 'steel frame' it inherited from the imperial state.

The Steel Frame

Like the ICS, the IAS, too, was powerful and ubiquitous. However, by deriving its powers and role from the constitution it was no longer 'parasitical' in the Kautilyan sense. That is, the IAS did not derive its power by being merely an 'associate' of the 'ruler' but was in fact defined by the constitution as an arm of the executive, to be recruited by a constitutional body, the Union Public Service Commission. By giving the IAS and IPS (Indian Police Service), along with the Indian Forest Service, this constitutional status, the architects of the republic underscored an important aspect of India's 'gradual revolution'—it sought continuity with change. While Patel did echo a widely held view that the ICS was neither Indian nor civil nor a service, both he and Ambedkar held a positive view of the role of an all-India service.[7] They did not see the permanent civil service merely as a vestige of colonialism but judged it from a Kautilyan prism. Ambedkar justified the continuation of an all-India civil service during an intervention in the constituent assembly, stating that the country needed a 'federal service' of capable officers who could man 'strategic' positions within the government. To quote Ambedkar:

It is recognized that in every country there are certain posts in its administrative set-up which might be called strategic from the point of view of maintaining the standard of administration. It may not be easy to spot such posts in a large and complicated machinery of administration. But there can be no doubt that the standard of administration depends upon the calibre of the civil servants who are appointed to these strategic posts. Fortunately for us we have inherited from the past system of administration which is common to the whole of the country and we know what are these strategic posts. The constitution provides that without depriving the States of their right to form their own Civil Services there shall be an All India service recruited on an All-India basis with common qualifications, with uniform scale of pay and the members of which alone could be appointed to these strategic posts throughout the Union.[8]

That the IAS would, like the ICS, attract young men and increasingly women from the upper castes with privileged access to education, was a given. During the colonial period, the ICS naturally engaged such individuals given the paucity of good employment opportunities for the upper castes and classes outside government service. Indeed, government service was much sought after. The fact that these officers were Oxbridge-trained and often went to good schools in India before going to England meant that the upper reaches of the civil service acquired the traits of a power elite early in their careers. Much of this elan and attitude was transferred to the IAS, but with a difference.

Independent India wanted its civil service to focus on development and not merely administration. The DM was no longer just a revenue collector and a law enforcer but also a development administrator. The Community Development Programme launched in 1953 by S.K. Dey, the minister for rural development, cooperation and Panchayati raj in Nehru's first council of ministers, enthused young recruits to the IAS to become instruments of development at the village level. Over time, the civil services developed a dual personality—its members enjoyed their privileged social status and the power and perks of the job, but many among them also became socially sensitized to the ground realities of an unequal and backward society in which democratic institutions were getting rooted.

Members of the service fell into three different categories— the liberal progressives committed to development and welfare; the bureaucratic file-pushers, cogs in the wheel of state; and, the high-flyers who went to elite schools and colleges and, either by marrying into wealth or into families of highly placed officials, made their way into key ministries, and secured foreign postings or international assignments. They were the elite within the elite. It is relevant to make this distinction because the permanent civil service of a democratic nation had the dual personality of both being the guarantor of national progress and interest and the instrument of state power.

India was fortunate to have had an educated middle class of adequate size and ambition, with access to good schools and colleges, so that it was able to recruit talented young people into the civil service. The fact that the private sector was still small, offering few exciting job opportunities, given the fact that managerial control in most business groups was restricted to members of the promoter family, also enabled the civil services to attract the best and brightest from the higher education system. Within this limited middle class, there was a subset of the more elitist who had gone to private schools known as 'public schools'—Doon Valley, Scindia, Sanawar, Blue Mountain, Lovedale—and to elite colleges like St. Stephen's in Delhi. A hierarchy of elitism was built into the meritocratic civil service system. Given the fact that one generation of such officers selected through an examination and interview process the next generation of officers, a scholar of public administration worried about the 'oligarchic character of the civil service'.[9]

The usual kinship networks including family, caste, religious and linguistic affinities continue to operate even within a meritocratic hierarchical system, creating an elite within an elite. In the early

1970s, a young IAS officer prepared a list of all the officers in key posts at the joint secretary level in the central secretariat in New Delhi and showed how they were all sons and sons-in-law (with few women at the time) of ICS officers and hailed mainly from Brahmin, Kayastha and Kshatriya castes.[10] Officers with roots in some states like Uttar Pradesh, Bihar, Tamil Nadu, Maharashtra, Kerala and Jammu and Kashmir had a higher representation in key posts. Over time, there have been changes but the role of kinship and family networks in privileging elites within elites continues. During Indira Gandhi's early years in office it was commented that Kashmiri pandits had come to occupy important positions within the Union government. However, when she returned to power in 1980, with Sanjay Gandhi and his Punjabi wife at her side, the media noticed the rise of Punjabi civil servants in various positions of influence.

When my father, who knew Prime Minister Narasimha Rao personally from their time in Hyderabad, told the PM that many in the IAS were commenting that Rao had surrounded himself with officers belonging to the Kayastha community, Rao was quick to defend himself saying that the Kayasthas had served the Mughals and the Nizam well and, as the first south Indian PM in Delhi, he felt it was best he relied on them to run his government. The reference was to the Union cabinet secretary, Naresh Chandra, the principal secretary to the PM, A.N. Verma, and industries secretary, Suresh Mathur. The view that Kayasthas end up in prominent positions in the Union government keeps coming up in Lutyens' Delhi's cocktail circuits. Finance Minister Yashwant Sinha, a Kayastha himself, was accused of placing Kayastha officers in key positions. During Manmohan Singh's tenure, officers with a Kerala or a Punjab connection were said to populate the corridors of power, just as a Gujarat connection is said to matter in Modi's government.

A cadre of government officials selected through an open, merit-based examination, hailing mainly from middle-class families, graduated into becoming members of a power elite by virtue of the fact that they served a state that had come to dominate a wide range of economic and social activity. The government, at the Centre and in the states, took on increasing responsibilities ranging from public investment in agriculture, industry, infrastructure, higher education, and science and technology development, apart from its basic duties like maintaining law and order, and collecting revenues. At the bottom of the administrative pyramid were officers committed to providing competent development administration, while at the top of the pyramid was an elite class that served its own interests, feathering nests, exercising power and carrying out the bidding of their political bosses.

On the foundations of this elitism was built what C. Rajagopalachari, the founding leader of the Swatantra Party, called the Permit-Licence Raj. The new 'Raj' created a 'nanny state' manned by middle-class bureaucrats, serving some power-hungry, some well-meaning politicians—that some have called bureaucratic socialism. Businessmen had to kowtow to the new nawabs of the Licence-Permit-Control Raj to secure permission to invest, manufacture, trade and conduct anything related to private enterprise. The power of the civil servant derives both from procedure—every officer at every level of decision-making can express an opinion and thereby influence the final outcome—and from protocol—the requirement of following procedure. Thus, the dynamics of democracy allowed the civil service to become entrenched as yet another constituent of the power elite.

A Committed Bureaucracy

In her unremitting quest for the acquisition and consolidation of power, Indira Gandhi did not leave any policy or institution untouched. In the realm of policy she turned left to put the Congress's old guard on the defensive, nationalized private banks, abolished privy purses, pushed for land reforms and tightened the screws on business by expanding the scope of the Licence-Permit-Control Raj. As far as external policies were concerned, she entered into a security alliance with the Soviet Union, broke up Pakistan and created Bangladesh, and took a step closer to declaring India a nuclear weapons state. In the political field, she converted the Congress party into a family enterprise, becoming the first national politician to normalize dynastic succession in democratic politics. Indira browbeat the judiciary, made fundamental changes to the Constitution and reduced Parliament to a cipher during the Emergency. Given this track record, securing the servility of the executive would have required very little effort on her part and she was quite brazen about it.

Addressing the All India Congress Committee meeting in November 1969, Indira Gandhi fired her salvo at the permanent civil service. 'The present bureaucracy under the orthodox and conservative leadership of the Indian Civil Service with its upper class prejudices can hardly be expected to meet the requirements of social and economic change along socialist lines,' complained the prime minister.[11] Therefore, she concluded, 'The country would be in a rut if it followed the British system in which civil servants were not supposed to be concerned about which political party was in power.'[12] By forthrightly demanding political loyalty from a professional civil service, Indira Gandhi gave currency to the theory of a 'committed bureaucracy'. Such a 'committed bureaucracy', concluded public administration guru S.R. Maheshwari, 'regulating its tune in accordance with which political party was in power, is apt to be a sinister and disruptive force.'[13]

The spreading tentacles of the Licence-Permit-Control Raj, the willingness of many civil servants to become courtiers of the ruling dispensation in the name of a 'committed bureaucracy' and growing proximity between officials and politicians in power certainly increased the power of the civil service, but did little to enhance its elite status in society. The elitism of the civil service was also dented by two other developments. First, the fact that

after the 1980s the 'best and brightest' coming out of the school
and college system were no longer attracted to the civil service,
with new avenues opening up globally and in the private sector.
The decision of governments to permit private medical practice
by doctors in public hospitals and the gradual emergence of a
private, for-profit, healthcare sector made medicine an attractive
profession. The expansion of the private corporate sector and the
hiring of students with engineering and management or finance
qualifications, as well as the opportunity for students from the best
engineering colleges to go to the United States for further studies
and employment, made the civil services even less attractive to
talented young students.

To make matters worse, populist pressure on governments
to dilute qualification standards for entry into the civil services,
including relaxation of the age limit for writing the civil services
examination, allowing candidates to repeatedly take the exam
(4 for general category, 12 for reserved), and the growing
perception that one entered government service in search of power
and money rather than to serve the society, further weakened the
quality of entrants to the civil service and dented their brand value,
particularly within the middle class.[14] The upshot of it all has been
that while the bureaucracy may have become more powerful, it
had lost its 'elite' status.

Nevertheless, given the extensive reach of various arms of
government in the daily lives of most people, the higher echelons
of the civil service remain firmly entrenched within the structures
of power. However, in seeking to retain power, the civil service has
had to yield space to the political leadership. Both at the national
and provincial level, the permanent civil service is permanent only
in name, ever ready to be transferred from one post to another
for not kowtowing to a political boss or surrendering to political
pressure to prevent transfer or worse. The transition from the
post-Independence generation of politicians in power to a new
generation of provincial politicians seeking power and wealth

through public office has also altered the nature of the relationship between the 'permanent' civil service and the political leadership in government.

As mentioned before, the concept of 'permanent' has itself undergone a qualitative change with 'difficult' officers frequently transferred and 'pliable' officers relied upon to do the political master's bidding. The decline in the quality of the entrants into the civil service has also enabled politicians to browbeat and play favourites.[15] As N.N. Vohra, a distinguished civil servant who was also governor of Jammu and Kashmir observed in his book on governance and security, 'To remain in power at any cost, the political executive consciously selects pliable officers.'[16] Equally damning was the remark of another distinguished civil servant, N.C. Saxena, Kayastha by caste, a liberal-minded officer who went on to become a member of Sonia Gandhi's National Advisory Council: 'In UP, the average tenure of an IAS officer in the past 10 years is said to be as low as six months. In the IPS, it is even lower, leading to the wisecrack that "if we are posted for weeks, all we can do is to collect our weekly bribe".'[17]

While the rot is deep and the 'civil service' has morphed into a 'bureaucracy', there are still many talented, honest and capable individuals manning the institutions of the state. A couple of decades ago, I asked Chandrababu Naidu, then the highly regarded chief minister of the erstwhile united state of Andhra Pradesh, how capable and efficient he found the civil servants in his government. 'One-third are "top class",' Naidu told me, 'one-third are "useless". Rest are average.' He depended on the top third to run the key ministries of his government. Prime Minister Manmohan Singh would often pose a rhetorical question, 'Where are the good officers?', in his constant search for talent in the government. He thought Naidu's categorization was fair. So, it is really the top third of a so-called 'elite' service that makes the grade and runs the country.

From time to time, some IAS officers come into prominence and their caste, regional and educational background tells a story about the changing composition of this segment of the power elite. In Nehru's time, the ICS dominated the upper reaches of the civil service. By the 1970s, powerful politicians from different parts of India brought their favourite officers from their state cadres to New Delhi, even as Indira Gandhi relied on Kashmiri Pandits and south Indian Brahmins to man her PMO. Tamil Nadu's C. Subramaniam, a minister for agriculture who distinguished himself as the architect of the Green Revolution, brought many Tamil Brahmins from his state cadre to New Delhi. During the period when Sanjay Gandhi ruled the roost, Punjabi officers were known to bag key posts. Some officers acquired a higher profile than others. Officers like L.K. Jha, Krishnaswamy Rao Saheb, Abid Hussain, T.N. Seshan, Gopi Arora and P.C. Alexander became public figures. In recent years, an IAS officer who has come to be identified with the nation's power elite is N.K. Singh, someone we spoke about in the very first chapter.

NK or Nandu Singh came from a privileged social and economic background. His father, Sir T.P. Singh, was a knighted ICS officer and Singh married into local royalty. His clout derived not merely from the fact that he was to the manner born and went to St. Stephen's, the alma mater of the more influential IAS officers, but also from his proximity to influential politicians in power. After being a trusted aide to the controversial commerce minister from Bihar, L.N. Mishra, NK became a trusted aide of another high-profile politician, Pranab Mukherjee. He was regarded as the IAS officer closest to the Ambani family. Not surprisingly NK titled his autobiography, *Portraits of Power: Half a Century of Being at Ringside*. He earned the unalloyed admiration of his batch of the IAS when he used his 'ringside' position as secretary in Prime Minister Vajpayee's PMO to get the age of retirement for the IAS extended from fifty-eight to sixty years within days of his own impending retirement. Like many civil servants who come to enjoy wielding power and are not ready to retire at sixty, NK entered the world of politics to become a member of Parliament. Among the handful of officers who survived the bureaucratic regime change under Modi, NK secured a prized post—chairman of the finance commission.

NK's signature events in his annual social calendar included garden parties on a Lutyens' Delhi bungalow lawn, with live piano music playing sixties' numbers, and sit-down dinners he hosted at the annual Davos meeting of the World Economic Forum. When his son got married, also into the family of royalty from Gujarat, the ceremony was solemnized at Jodhpur's Umaid Palace in the presence of the who's who of Bihari, Rajasthani and Gujarati feudal families, prominent political leaders from across party lines and business billionaires who flew into Jodhpur in their private jets. A very likeable and friendly person, NK endeared himself to friend and critic with his wit and charm. Few IAS officers have been able to emulate his act but not for want of trying.

A Politicized Police

My focus so far has only been on the IAS because the administrative service has always remained at the top of the civil service pyramid, with the cabinet secretary placed a peg above even the foreign secretary, the senior-most member of the foreign service. Officers of all other central services remain below the IAS within the civil service hierarchy. While formal hierarchies are defined by official protocol and procedure, from the viewpoint of power one could argue that both the police and revenue service—IPS and IRS— enjoy greater power vis-à-vis the citizen, given the nature of their job. Within the hierarchy of administrative power, officers of the IRS and other central and state services have been placed under the charge of IAS superiors. However, the politicization of top-level police appointments and political interference at all levels of the force have made the police particularly subservient to politicians. A ministry of home affairs report dating back to 1993 pointed to the nexus between the police, politicians, crime syndicates and the mafia.[18]

At the state and district levels, the police have acquired considerable clout given the fact that most politicians in power become indebted to the police fairly early in their political careers. At the national level, the IPS did not have the profile and influence that the IAS has enjoyed. However, two developments have given the police force greater visibility at the national level. First, the problem of internal security and terrorism. The citizen has become habituated to the pervasive presence of the police in one's daily life. In a metropolis like Mumbai, for example, the police force was routinely portrayed as corrupt and ineffective. The policeman always arrived in the last scene of a Hindi film after the film's hero had rescued the heroine. While stories of police sloth and corruption abound, the rising threat of criminality, with fake encounters and the summary delivery of justice, has made lawbreakers out of law enforcers.

A second development that has raised the status of the police as a member of the nation's power elite has been the decision of successive prime ministers to appoint an IPS officer as the national security adviser (NSA). While the first such officer, M.K. Narayanan, had a less than glorious term and an ignominious exit after the Mumbai terror attack, the second IPS officer, Ajit Doval, has not only acquired the reputation of being the most powerful NSA to date, but has also been given the charge of presiding over a defence planning committee, with the senior-most civil and military officials reporting to him. Being from an intelligence background, both Narayanan and Doval acquired clout by having access to information that served their political superiors from time to time. Narayanan made a point of letting everyone know that he had a file on them, even if this was said as a joke. Most police officers, however, have more regard for officers who have earned their spurs on the field, doing regular police work, like K.P.S. Gill, S. Anandram, Julius Robeiro, Vijay Kumar and Ashvini Kumar.

The growing clout of the police in the Indian state system is both a reflection of the politicization of the police and the emergence of the Indian state as a security and law-and-order state, more than a developmental state in which the IAS was top dog.

Military Brass

Writing in the 1950s, Wright Mills included the military brass in America's power elite, along with the political and business elite, referring to them as 'warlords'. He saw the US victory in the Second World War as being responsible for the elevated social status of military leaders and their influence on politics and government. After all, the American public had voted a war-time general to the nation's presidency in 1953 when General Dwight Eisenhower became the 34th president. Mills also worried about the excessive influence of military men on diplomacy and international relations, giving a military edge to post-War US foreign policy. He was nervous about retired generals joining company boards and creating a link between the military brass and corporate interests, a concern that gained in importance with the growth of a large defence manufacturing industry in the private sector.

The 'military-industrial' complex, as Mills put it, was the arena within which political, business and military interests combined, making defence production and defence diplomacy integral to US economic and political power. Mills believed the military 'warlords' with corporate links had become an important source of funding for research and development and in science and technology institutions. 'Yes, there is a military clique,' concluded Mills, 'but it is more accurately termed the power elite, for it is composed of economic, political, as well as military, men whose interests have increasingly coincided. In order to understand the role of the military within this power elite, we must understand the role of the corporation executive and the politician within it.'[19]

If US democracy was so concerned about the growing prestige and power of its military brass, the nascent democracies of most postcolonial nations were being overtaken by their militaries. India's post-Independence leadership was also wary about the intentions of its military brass, and the coup in Pakistan did little to set at rest nascent anxieties at home. Many scholars have written at length about the evolution of the relationship between civilian and military leadership in India. Most of them have noted the fact that India's civilian power elite—politicians and the bureaucracy—have kept military brass on a tight leash, allowing a degree of autonomy in professional and military matters.[20]

In the US the high social profile of military leadership was a consequence of the US victory in the Second World War and, perhaps, the public memory of its role during the Civil War. After Vietnam the brass lost shine. In countries where the armed forces played an important role in national liberation, like China, or during battles for national survival, like in Russia, they have enjoyed wide public support and, as a derivative, political power. Elsewhere, as in Pakistan, it is military coup and the economic power of the generals rather than popular support for them that has given the armed forces political power.

The marginal role played by Netaji's Indian National Army in the freedom struggle and the fact that the armed forces remained loyal to the British till the end, barring the single incident of the naval mutiny in February 1946, ensured that the military brass did not acquire a high social profile at the time of Independence. The profile of the armed forces was, in fact, dented by its performance in the border conflict with China in 1962. Their performance in the war with Pakistan in 1965 was also not particularly impressive, but Prime Minister Lal Bahadur Shastri's slogan of '*Jai Jawan, Jai Kisan*', the campaign to get citizens to contribute gold for the war effort and the exhibition of captured Pakistani Patton tanks around the country in celebratory melas, helped raise their public profile a bit. It was, however, the 1971 war with Pakistan, the creation of

Bangladesh and the consequent break-up of Pakistan, that gave the armed forces and the military leadership high social standing.

Subsequently, and despite the bravery of the forces in the Kargil war, Indian armed forces have produced few leaders who have been able to become national heroes on the scale required to make a successful bid for political power. The few who did become heroes, like Field Marshal Sam Maneckshaw and the Marshal of the Air Force Arjan Singh, studiously avoided any political involvement. It was not until the BJP began recruiting retired military leaders into politics that there was any significant presence of military brass within the world of politics and the corridors of power. While the BJP has given greater political prominence to military men and war heroes, this has not always served the cause of raising their profile within the power elite. Consider the case of the former army chief V.K. Singh, who has been a member of Modi's council of ministers. His career ended under a cloud, with controversy about his date of birth and, therefore, date of retirement. Singh further blotted his reputation entering into a pointless argument with a senior editor, calling journalists 'presstitutes'.[21] The image of military leaders has also taken a beating with some retired generals repeatedly appearing on television and participating in shouting matches with all sorts of characters. With the exception of a few senior military men like Admiral Raja Menon and Air Chief Marshal S. Krishnaswamy and a few others, not many military leaders have been able to conduct themselves with dignity in post-retirement public life.

The recent decision of the central government to create the office of chief of defence staff (CDS), and more importantly, to make the CDS the executive head of a newly constituted department of military affairs within the defence ministry has altered, albeit at the margin, the relationship between the civil service and the armed forces within the highest decision-making organization of the government, raising the profile of the latter. This new command structure is still to take concrete shape. As it evolves and systems and procedures get created and established, there will be jockeying for authority and influence between the civil and military officials within the defence ministry. How these equations develop will partly depend on the political leadership and partly on real-life situations. It is only in the midst of a real war that real power equations get settled.

The growing visibility of military leaders in public life, especially in the media, has run parallel to the declining attraction of the defence services to the middle class. Till the 1980s, the children of both civil servants and military brass chose to walk in their parents' professional footsteps. A more recent trend, thanks to the BJP, of celebrating the performance of the armed forces has helped raise the stature of the defence services in public perception. For the moment, this neo-nationalism of the middle class is not yet making the armed services an adequately attractive professional option for the middle class enamoured by financially more rewarding professions. Senior military leaders are worried both about the quality of recruits at the officers' level and the rising dropout rate after a minimum period of service. The military leadership would like lateral movement of middle-level officers into other arms of the government as a way of keeping entry to the services attractive.

Apart from the corridors of the ministry of defence, the other theatre of conflict between the civil and military leadership in Lutyens' Delhi is the Delhi Gymkhana Club. So intense is their power struggle for leadership within the club that a few years back a senior functionary of the PMO had to step in to ensure ceasefire. Officers' clubs are one of the last bastions of privilege of the civil and defence services. After Independence they have also been open to the private sector, a source of revenue for the clubs. The institution of the 'officers' clubs' started during the British Raj to offer a common space outside work for Englishmen and natives in government to socialize. Since these were started as government initiatives, they became entitled to government land. Every district headquarter and cantonment had an officers' club, and Delhi had its Gymkhana and Golf Club. These institutions of privilege survived the end of the Raj but continued in their own ways. One could not enter them in 'Indian attire', as defence minister of India George Fernandes was politely reminded that his kurta-pyjama and chappals attire would debar him from entering any of the clubs of the armed forces. Some of the clubs made membership virtually hereditary and, as a gesture to the erstwhile empire that gave them birth, these clubs allowed access to members from similar clubs around the world. The sun has not yet set on the world of British-era officers' clubs.

An important difference between post-War US and post-Independence India was also the fact that till very recently the domestic private corporate sector was kept outside the defence manufacturing industry. Hence the kind of military-industry nexus that developed in post-War US did not do so, at least till recently, in India. The armed forces sourced all their equipment either from domestic public-sector undertakings or from foreign manufacturers. The heads of defence public-sector undertakings (PSUs) and of the defence research and development organization (DRDO) reported only to civilian leaders, and these organizations were kept apart from the military brass. Thus, the kind of nexus that developed in the US between military and business elites did not develop in India.

The decision of the Modi government to open defence manufacturing to the private sector, including foreign firms with deep pockets, and the trend of hiring retired military brass by private-sector companies may create an Indian version of the military-industrial complex. Media, too, has been playing its role in elevating the social status of military leadership. Retired generals have become a permanent fixture on many television channels, and their views on national security, foreign affairs and even domestic politics are often taken as the last word on the subject and the view of a true nationalist. Another relatively new phenomenon is the possibility of the views of the armed forces getting increasingly publicly articulated by retired brass through a growing number of think tanks, some funded directly by the services and some by the private sector investing in defence manufacturing. Taken together, these trends do assert the growing presence of military brass within the nation's power elite.

While the civil and military brass have succeeded in retaining their power in the face of significant change both within the institutions of the state and in civil society, the social composition of those entering these services has changed in a direction that may have benefited the BJP and its parent organization, the RSS. Extending Indira Gandhi's idea of a 'committed civil service' to a larger ideological commitment to the world view of the ruling dispensation, the RSS and the BJP increasingly seek the allegiance of the civil and military brass to their idea of India. In 1969, when the Congress leadership spoke of a committed civil service, Jagjivan Ram spelt it out as follows: 'Theory of neutral bureaucracy is hardly relevant to Indian conditions. We need a service committed to the ideal of democracy, socialism and secularism.'[22] Today the BJP would, perhaps, drop the word 'secularism' and replace it with 'nationalism'. A series of initiatives with respect to civil service 'reform' taken by the Modi government, including posting non-IAS officers to traditionally IAS postings, increasing the number of 'lateral' entrants into government, and so on, have been interpreted by some senior civil servants as the politicization of a 'neutral' civil service.[23]

The politicization of military leadership came into sharp focus when the former chief of army staff General V.K. Singh joined the BJP and was then inducted into the Union council of ministers. More recently, another chief of army staff, General Bipin Rawat, subsequently appointed the first chief of defence staff, came in for criticism for making adverse comments on those protesting against the Citizenship Amendment Act (CAA).[24] A former Union minister of finance and home, P. Chidambaram, remarked that it is not the business of the army to tell politicians what they should do and that the general should 'mind his business'.[25] If the long-standing politicization of the civil service has dented the meritocratic elitism of the IAS, IPS and the Indian Foreign Service (IFS), the growing instance of military leaders making political statements has also taken the shine off the brass.

9

Policy and Public Intellectuals

*The rearing and guiding of a civilization must depend
upon its intellectual class.*

—B.R. Ambedkar

*Intellectuals remained the main actors in Indian politics
until a few decades ago.*

Ashis Nandy

Four of the first five Indians to be conferred Bharat Ratna, the
nation's highest civilian honour, were middle-class professionals.
The Nobel Prize-winning physicist C.V. Raman, a professor of
philosophy Sarvepalli Radhakrishnan, an engineer Mokshagundam
Visvesvaraya and the educationist and theosophist Bhagwan Das.
While both Radhakrishnan and Das had a political profile, the
former being the republic's first vice president and the latter being
politically active in the national movement, only the first recipient,
C. Rajagopalachari, was a full-time politician. Of the four highly
regarded professionals the least known these days is Visvesvaraya,
one of the founders of the Institution of Engineers. In the four

decades that followed Visvesvaraya's Bharat Ratna, the national honour was bestowed mainly on politicians and political leaders with a couple of honourable exceptions. The second engineer to be so honoured was A.P.J. Abdul Kalam, the missile and rocket engineer who later became president.

It was only decades after engineer Visvesvaraya's contribution to nation-building was recognized with a Bharat Ratna, and another engineer, K.L. Rao, was inducted into the Union cabinet, that twenty-first-century India celebrated the contribution of another engineer, E. Sreedharan, the railways officer who built the Konkan railway and the Delhi metro. He was awarded the Padma Vibhushan in 2008. While Sreedharan was a celebrity because of the Delhi metro, rarely has contemporary India celebrated scientists, engineers, the doers and the makers, as much as it celebrates wealth, power, brand and status. The celebrated engineers of twenty-first-century India are IT professionals who have made their billions, yet there are few scientists and engineers in positions of political power, unlike China where even President Xi Jinping is a qualified chemical engineer. Every time an ISRO rocket goes up into space, the many anonymous space scientists and engineers are cheered and then forgotten. They do not become household names, barring an Abdul Kalam who, too, became nationally famous when he entered the world of politics. In his first six years as PM, Modi has not been able to identify one professional worthy to bestow a Bharat Ratna. The two 'educationists' Modi named—Pandit Madan Mohan Malaviya and Nanaji Deshmukh—were essentially political activists.

The New Brahmins

The standing of academics, scholars and professionals within the nation's power elite has waxed and waned over time. In Nehru's time and even in Indira's, a wide range of professionals across many disciplines entered the ranks of the power elite because of their access to the PM and a national recognition of their contribution.

From Homi Bhabha and Vikram Sarabhai to P.C. Mahalanobis and K.N. Raj, from K.L. Rao to M.S. Swaminathan, scientists, engineers, economists and educationists were treated with great regard. It was partly a legacy of the national movement, for Gandhiji inspired many professionals, educationists and business leaders to lend their weight to the freedom struggle. The spirit of nationalism, of building anew, of self-reliance, gripped the middle classes who came to respect professionals for their contribution to nation-building.

It is not a coincidence that the only British colonial official to have a museum built in his honour and a statue that retains pride of place even to this day happens to be an engineer. Sir Arthur Cotton, the irrigation engineer who built several canals and dams across India, is remembered in Andhra Pradesh for the anicut across the Godavari near Rajahmundhry that has turned this region into a lush rice bowl. Nehru quite understandably called the steel mills and the irrigation dams built in his time the 'temples of modern India'. Middle-class professionals who built and managed them were the priests of these temples and, like the priests of an earlier era, had easy access to the ruler's court and courtiers. This was not merely an upper-caste phenomenon or Brahminism redux. Consider the fact that the most celebrated Dalit leader, Bhimrao Ambedkar, was also a professional, and his statue in almost every village across the length and breadth of India portrays him as a teacher, with a book (the constitution) in hand. Scheduled-caste activists seek inspiration from his life to educate themselves to rise on the social ladder.

This class of professionals was what contemporary analysts would refer to as 'policy intellectuals', as opposed to 'public intellectuals'. Clarifying this distinction in a perceptive analysis of the relationship between knowledge and power, sociologist Shiv Visvanathan defines the 'policy intellectual' as an 'extension of the state'. A 'public intellectual', on the other hand, is someone who provides 'a wide-ranging critique of policy'.[1] The policy intellectual, says Visvanathan, takes his expertise for granted, while the public intellectual questions the nature of expertise. Perhaps one should modify that assertion to suggest that a public intellectual also examines the consequences of such expertise. Visvanathan cites the examples of Sukhamoy Chakravarty, a distinguished economist and adviser to Indira Gandhi, and the scholar Ashis Nandy, as good examples of a policy and a public intellectual.

In a variation on the theme, social historian Mukul Kesavan defines policy intellectuals as the denizens of think tanks, vicariously participating in policymaking by writing to influence policymakers, while he defines public intellectuals as those whose audience is the general public.[2] This classification places both outside the realm of policymaking. One influences policy by writing for a government audience; the other influences policy by writing for the public and hoping they in turn influence the policymakers in government. Either way, Kesavan's definition situates both policy and public intellectuals outside the state, delinking knowledge from power. Visvanathan, on the other hand, views policy intellectuals as being part of the state, as professionals within government—experts in their field bringing knowledge to the exercise of power.

In the post-Independence years, even as the permanent civil service entrenched itself as the principal policy adviser to the political leadership, the latter offered space within the state system to 'intellectuals', professionals, experts and specialists to provide policy inputs, and to even steer policy in critical areas of public policy requiring such inputs. In short, the policy intellectual was not merely an occupant of think tanks and the academic world, trying to 'influence' policymakers, but was a policymaker with a position within government. Nehru conceived the Planning Commission as being one such organization. So was the entire nuclear, space and defence research organization. By bringing specialized knowledge into the government, Nehru not only empowered intellectuals as policymakers but showed appreciation of the fact that knowledge is power. The policy intellectual became the new Brahmin of a republican India.

It is a different matter that the political system rarely allowed professionals to rise up the ladder of political power. It has often been remarked that the pinnacle of political power in China has come to be occupied by scientists and engineers while in India politicians with little professional experience in any other field, barring perhaps the legal profession, occupy the commanding heights of power. Nehru's initial council of ministers had many professionals including B.R. Ambedkar, C.D. Deshmukh and John Mathai. Over the years, few professionals rose to become Union ministers. Historian Nurul Hasan and economist Manmohan Singh were rare exceptions—Manmohan Singh being the only professional who began life as an academic and ended it as the prime minister. Over time, however, professional expertise is increasingly found wanting within the higher councils of government.

The Knowledge Pyramid

Whatever the pros and cons of the Planning Commission and its more recent record as a federal institution, the fact is that for many years it offered space within the government to policy intellectuals, acting as a bridge between knowledge and power. As economist George Rosen has recorded, the Planning Commission became home not just to domestic talent but attracted intellectuals from around the world. India's experiment of seeking development within the framework of a plural democracy attracted the best and brightest of economic policy specialists from across the world.[3] Prime Minister Modi chose to shut down the Planning Commission because he viewed it not merely as an extra-constitutional creation of Nehru but also as an institution that had got used to lecturing to state governments rather than holding their hand and assisting development.

An overwhelming majority of policy intellectuals in government, however, acquired their professional credentials from British and US universities. In British India that was understandable. Even after Independence, the best route to the top of the policymaking establishment for the non-IAS professional was via Oxford and Cambridge universities and subsequently the American Ivy League universities, along with stints at the World Bank and other multilateral organizations. In Nehru's time, a letter of recommendation from someone like Harold Laski, a professor at the London School of Economics (LSE), was adequate not just to get a job in the central government, but to get it after an audience with the PM. With time one did not even require a letter from Laski. The Oxbridge old boy network in India kicked in and began recruiting the next generation of policy intellectuals.

Former Prime Minister Manmohan Singh's first introduction to Nehru was made by Singh's Amritsar neighbour Mulk Raj Anand, a Cambridge scholar who became famous as a novelist and author of short stories focusing on the lives of the poor. Singh came from a humble middle-class background but his entry into India's policymaking elite, as indeed of so many of his generation from K.N. Raj to Amartya Sen, was through the Oxbridge route. Even their left-wing critics of the next generation had Oxbridge lineage.

Nehru's failure, however, was in not appreciating the fact that just like the structure of power, the structure of knowledge too is pyramidical. The broader the base, the higher and more stable the apex. In the early years after Independence, the government did offer opportunities in the policy establishment to Indians trained in India, especially at the three 'presidency' universities—Calcutta, Bombay, Madras—and prominent Indian ones like Allahabad, Delhi, Baroda, Osmania and Benaras Hindu Universities. So, while Nehru's India built its temples of modernity, publicly funded institutions of higher education and research, and attracted talent from overseas into government and the public sector, it failed to invest adequately in the education of the population as a whole, limiting the society's knowledge base. Teaching and research declined in importance as valued professions, and most government-funded institutions of knowledge were overtaken by bureaucracy and mediocrity and privatized over time. Exceptions like the nuclear energy and space research organizations proved the rule. This partly explains the migration of the policy intellectual from government to think tanks which were often foreign funded.

While this was a failure of political leadership, the fact is that even the private sector did not invest enough in research and knowledge-based business activity. As a consequence, there was migration of talent abroad—a secession of the successful that we will explore in a later chapter. Through the 1970s and 1980s, the new policy intellectuals came mostly from US universities and after stints in the UN and related organizations. One thing common to almost all of them was that when they decided to return home to participate in India's development process as policymakers in the government, they moved lock, stock and barrel. Their children accompanied them home and studied in India, and many chose to pursue their professional life working in India. This pattern changed in the past decade when most policy intellectuals returning home on leave from regular employment abroad chose to leave their families behind. They have been viewed as birds of passage seeking to bolster their professional résumés and returning to, often better-paid employment overseas.

If the social value of the 'foreign-returned' policy intellectual of the Nehru and Indira eras was the fact that they had a 'Made in Oxbridge' or 'Made in Ivy League' tag, that of the temporarily returning non-resident Indian (NRI) policy intellectual of the early twenty-first century is that she retains an overseas sinecure with a dollar income assured. This contrast came into sharp relief when the media compared and contrasted the decision of policy intellectuals in government, like a Montek Singh Ahluwalia and a Shankar Acharya, returning home to work for the government with family and possessions, to the recent examples of many overseas Indian economists occupying influential and high-profile policy offices, leaving family and property behind, mostly in the US.

A senior policy position in India is, after all, a good investment while on sabbatical.

The Three Cs of Policy

By the 1970s, as India's politics shifted, and a post-Nehruvian, non-Congress and non-metropolitan political leadership rose to power, a new generation of 'home-grown' intellectuals began to assert their presence in the policy space. It was against the background of Indira Gandhi's radical phase, the emergence of Lohia loyalists in north Indian politics and the assertion of regional identities against New Delhi's globalized metropolitanism of the Nehru era that a truly home-grown educationist, J.P. Naik, provided leadership for the growth of social sciences research institutions. From 1969 to 1978, Naik presided over the Indian Council of Social Sciences Research (ICSSR), funding regional centres of research across the country.

Interestingly, though, while several policy-oriented research institutions sprang up across the country in the 1970s and 1980s, entry into the policymaking corridors of the Government of India remained confined to those trained in the West. Few from these ICSSR institutions were ever hired to senior positions in the government. The few who were hired invariably had a foreign degree. Be it pro-market economists or left economists, including the finance ministers of the Left Front government in West Bengal, almost all policy intellectuals within the government came with foreign degrees. The shift in India's policy outlook from inward orientation to external liberalization naturally attracted more of the Western-trained to take up government employment.

The changing dynamics of provincial politics also influenced the profile of imported policy intellectuals at the state level. In Andhra Pradesh, for example, the influence of overseas Telugus, mainly the Telugus in the United States, was palpable in the Telugu Desam governments of the 1990s. Chief Minister Chandrababu Naidu liked the idea of surrounding himself with US-based Andhra professionals. His decision to seek a structural adjustment loan from the World Bank endeared him to the US administration, and the many members of the Kamma community in the US helped open doors for him across the government and business in the US. The role of foreign-educated professionals increased in states like Andhra Pradesh, Tamil Nadu, Maharashtra, Haryana, Punjab and Karnataka. Interestingly, while West Bengal had for many years an MIT-trained economist, Ashim Dasgupta, as its finance minister, the CPI(M) government in Kerala, too, reached out to Oxbridge economists and expat Malayalis like Gita Gopinath, presently chief economist at the IMF, for policy advice. Left or right, whatever the political hue, the policy intellectual is almost always a 'foreign returned' or overseas-based professional.

While Indian-trained vs foreign-trained was one dimension to the social origins of the policy intellectual, a second dimension has since then been that of the language in which policy is conceptualized and articulated. The issue of the language in which policymakers operated became acutely politicized in the Hindi-speaking states and in Tamil Nadu and West Bengal. An interesting study of the self-perception of the role and status of north Indian intellectuals operating in Hindi, published in 1977, showed that professionals functioning in their mother tongue (Hindi in this case) had higher self-esteem in fields such as education, media and the creative arts. While those in government service and governmental organizations had lower self-esteem since it was generally felt that the language of government and policy was English.[4] This has, of course, changed since. Over the past half century, more of the government, both at the Centre and in the states, functions in the vernacular. English, of course, remains the principal link language for India and there is in fact a growing demand for English-language training, especially in the Hindi states and more so among the less privileged. The interesting point that the 1977 study makes is that English has remained the language of policy and diplomacy and that most writers in Hindi at the time were still viewing themselves as 'translators' rather than writers of original works. Policy, at any rate, was conceived and articulated in the English language.

This conclusion should surprise no one because policymaking in the contemporary world is a source of power and influence, and the globalized elite has taken possession of this process, with multilateral institutions and companies funding, training and deputing such professionals to governments around the world. A perceptive analyst of the phenomenon, Rosabeth Kanter, dubs this global policy elite the 'cosmopolitans'. 'Cosmopolitans are rich in three intangible assets,' says Kanter. 'The three C's that translate into pre-eminence and power in a global economy: *concepts*—the best and latest knowledge and ideas; *competence*—the ability to operate at the highest standards of any place anywhere; and *connections*—the best relationships, which provide access to the resources of other people and organizations around the world. Indeed, it is because cosmopolitans bring the best and latest concepts, the highest levels of competence, and excellent connections that they gain influence over locals.'[5] Whether the 3-C intellectuals brought competence or not, they certainly brought with them concepts and connections that stood them in good stead with politicians in the developing world, in general, and of course in postcolonial India.

The globalized '3-C' policy intellectual acquired a high profile in the policymaking establishments of most Indian prime ministers, but the golden era was the decade of the Manmohan Singh government when Delhi's policymaking world turned into Camelot. Several expert committees were set up which were filled with policy intellectuals on every issue, ranging from agricultural credit to the Kashmir problem, from US–India relations to the building of a knowledge economy; they were also drafted to advise the government. More policy intellectuals were recipients of Padma awards during Singh's decade in the government than in any other decade before him. The policy intellectual was treated with regard within the government if for no other reason than the fact that most of them were friends or students of the prime minister or of people close to him.

This heady world of a knowledge-based power elite was turned upside down when Prime Minister Modi and the BJP began viewing them as members of a power elite that had for generations served in the court of the Nehru-Indira dynasty. The exit of Raghuram Rajan as governor of the Reserve Bank of India (RBI) brought into focus this tension between a new ruling dispensation and the old policy elite. The BJP's decision to bring into government its own intellectuals, committed to its ideology of Hindutva, mirrored the practice of the communist state governments to bring its fellow travellers into policymaking. It mimicked Indira Gandhi's idea of a 'committed bureaucracy', except that as Indira Gandhi matured as a leader she chose to induct into her circle of policy advisers experts with contending perspectives. Her PMO included 'leftists' like Arjun Sengupta and 'rightists' like Montek Ahluwalia. It was a practice that Manmohan Singh followed too, surrounding himself with policy intellectuals of contending ideologies.

Power of Proximity

Policy intellectuals are essentially a creation of the twentieth century with the emergence of privately funded policy institutions, popularly referred to these days as 'think tanks'. The Brookings Institution (USA), founded in 1916, and Chatham House (UK), founded in 1920, are among the earliest think tanks that offered a home to policy intellectuals. Chatham House (Royal Institute of International Affairs) created the practice of non-attribution of comments made in meetings under what has come to be called Chatham House Rules, that enable a non-government venue to facilitate discussion on policy between government officials and diplomats and non-government professionals.

What truly elevated the status of the academic expert as a policy intellectual was the role played by economists in the inter-war and post-war period. The high priest of policy wonks in the West was the economist John Maynard Keynes. The Keynesian revolution in economics contributed to fundamental changes in policy and elevated the status of economists as policy intellectuals within state and society. Keynes' biographer, Robert Skidelsky, subtitled the second of his three-volume biography of Keynes *The Economist as Saviour*, underscoring the pivotal role of professional policy advice in not merely reviving depressed Western economies in the interwar years but rejuvenating crisis-ridden capitalism. If Karl Marx had inspired communist revolutions that had sought the destruction of capitalism, Keynes offered policy advice that helped place Western capitalism on firmer ground.

Skidelsky, in fact, claims that the social sciences developed in the interwar period, mainly because of the 'emergence of an activist intelligentsia, claiming a right of direction, vacated by the aristocracy and the clergy, by virtue of superior intellectual ability and expert knowledge of society. The central claim which emerged from the confluence of these two tendencies was that society was a machine whose working could be improved by deliberate action, with unintended side-effects being equally amenable to correction and control, much as a mechanic fine-tunes an engine.'[6] Keynes, in Skidelsky's view, represented a new generation of intellectuals who saw themselves as 'the front line of the army of progress'.[7]

For the intellectual soldiers of this army of progress to make an impact on the real wielders of power, it is necessary that there is a two-way relationship between the two. The political and bureaucratic leadership has to be interested in and willing to lend an ear to the policy advice of the professional, and the professionals, too, have to be interested in devoting time and resources to that effort. In the war-ravaged Europe of the mid-twentieth century and in post-War US, that two-way relationship between the government and professional opinion outside was created both by social familiarity and physical proximity. The policymakers and the policy intellectuals went to the same schools and colleges and lived in physical proximity, were often related through marriage, and the professionals came to work in institutions close to the seats of power. Skidelsky notes, for example, that as Keynes' influence on policy in London increased, the time he spent in London, and away from Cambridge, also increased.

It is not surprising that both Brookings and Chatham House were located close to the centre of power in Washington DC and London, respectively. In India, too, as the role of policy intellectuals in government increased, the academic institutions in New Delhi began to house more of them. In the intellectual rivalry, for example, between the economists of the DSE (V.K.R.V. Rao, K.N. Raj, Amartya Sen, Jagdish Bhagwati and Sukhamoy Chakravarty) and the Bombay School of Economics (P.R. Brahmananda, C.N. Vakil, M.R. Pai, K.T. Shah and A.D. Shroff), the former established overwhelming influence on national policy not a little because of their social and physical proximity, apart from intellectual affinity, to the Nehruvian power elite.

As New Delhi's role in national policymaking increased, experts in different fields moved to Delhi, inhabiting new institutions, universities and think tanks. In the field of economic policy the denizens of the DSE were joined by fellow travellers at the Institute of Economic Growth, the Delhi campus of the Indian Statistical Institute, National Council of Applied Economic Research, Indian Council for Research on International Economic Relations and so on. The critics of Nehruvian policy, whom we can call 'public intellectuals' as opposed to 'policy intellectuals', inhabited institutions like Centre for Study of Developing Societies, Centre for Policy Research and Council for Social Development, to name a few.

In a bid to de-centre Delhi and take policy intellectuals away from the ivory towers of the Delhi Darbar and closer to the ground where policy makes its impact, both V.K.R.V. Rao and K.N. Raj, the principal architects of the DSE and trusted advisers to Nehru and Indira, utilized the funds provided by J.P. Naik's ICSSR to found new policy-oriented research institutions in state capitals. V.K.R.V. Rao moved to Bangalore and founded the Institute for Social and Economic Change, while K.N. Raj founded the Centre for Development Studies in Thiruvananthapuram. For a brief period, in the 1970s and 1980s, these far-flung institutions did have some influence on policy in Delhi, but after 1991, the Delhi-based institutions once again re-asserted their influence.

This was also aided by the fact that the national media—print and television—became increasingly Delhi-based and gave prominence to the policy intellectuals of Delhi. On any given subject it was the Delhi-based expert whose view was purveyed across the country by the media that was also Delhi-based. There might have been the odd policy wonk from a management institution who had never been to Delhi writing an occasional policy-oriented column, but the vast majority of the policy intellectuals in media would be from Delhi or from London, Washington DC and Singapore—India's overseas intellectual centres. Once again, social and physical proximity and the old boy network—friends from same schools, colleges and clubs—published and read each other.

Platforms of Power

If the policy intellectual is essentially a creature of the twentieth century, the public intellectual, as historian Romila Thapar reminds us, has a much older lineage. The great philosophers of ancient and medieval times across all civilizations were the public intellectuals of their time. If the policy intellectual, as Visvanathan and Kesavan have suggested, lives at the edge of power, seeking to influence its actions, the public intellectual not only lives away from power, but questions and challenges it. Defining an 'intellectual' as someone with a 'recognized professional stature' in any discipline, Thapar suggests that a 'public intellectual' would be someone who seeks 'explanations for public actions from those in authority, even if such explanations required critiquing authority and power'.[8]

The power of the policy intellectual derives, without doubt, from her influence on policy. This, in turn, would be a function of social proximity and professional influence of the individual with respect to the actual wielders of power. The power of the public intellectual would derive both from her public standing and popularity and, paradoxically, ability to get noticed by the wielders of power. Most would imagine that a public intellectual deriving her influence from opposition to power and authority would not be regarded a constituent of the power elite. That would be true for a public intellectual who has no interest in soliciting the attention of the power elite, whose opposition to authority and to the politics and policies of the power elite is based more on an adherence to principle and a desire to influence particular constituencies with no interest in shaping public policy as such. Maoist intellectuals, for example, would be a good example of a group that has no desire to shape state policy. Rather, they question the very legitimacy of the state. In this category one can include the likes of K. Balagopal, who wrote fine prose with a sharp pen, and more recently, the scholar Anand Teltumbde.

Most public intellectuals, in fact, seek to shape public policy and so are often vicarious wielders of power. An early example of such public intellectuals were members of Indira Gandhi's 'kitchen cabinet', like Romesh Thapar, founder-editor of *Seminar*, a journal that lent its pages to both critics of the government as well as those who wished to shape government policy. Raj and Romesh Thapar symbolized Delhi's Nehruvian elite. Hailing from a well-off Lahore family, Romesh went to England for higher education and, like many from the Indian upper class, he returned a communist. He married Raj Malhotra, also an immigrant to Delhi from Lahore and belonging to a business family. They first set up base in Bombay, where Romesh was a journalist, becoming members of the city's social circuit. Moving to Delhi, the couple launched *Seminar* that had an office in Connaught Place in a building owned by Raj's father. Their son Valmik married film actor Shashi Kapoor's daughter Sanjana, and their daughter, Malavika, married writer-editor Khushwant Singh's nephew, Tejbir, also grandson of Sir Shoba Singh, the real estate baron and contractor who built many buildings in Lutyens' Delhi.

It was only natural that such a family would move close to the centre of intellectual and political power in Delhi. It is to the credit of Raj and Romesh that they offered the pages of *Seminar* to both the critics and members of the ruling dispensation. They also sought out talent from across the country, bringing to the attention of Indira Gandhi and her key aides bright and promising individuals doing good work or writing interesting analysis of ground-level change in distant corners of India. The dual role that Romesh Thapar was able to play as a friend and critic of Indira Gandhi ended when Sanjay Gandhi evicted from his mother's inner circle all those who were happy to be its members but were unwilling to accept him as her heir apparent. *Seminar* has continued to offer its pages to the friends and critics of changing ruling dispensations, under the leadership of Thapar's daughter Malavika, a quintessential member of the Lutyens' elite, positioning itself as a platform for the critics of the power elite while being at the same time a long-standing constituent of that very elite.

The more important platform of post-Independence public and policy intellectuals has been the *Economic and Political Weekly* (*EPW*). Launched in 1949 in a modest two-room outfit in Bombay by Sachin Chaudhuri as the *Economic Weekly*, the journal was guided by a 'gang of four'—economists Deena Khatkate, Anand Chandavarkar, V.V. Bhat and former Reserve Bank governor M. Narasimham. It came to be recognized as a respected publication of professional social scientists after its longest-serving editor, Krishna Raj, took charge in the mid-1960s. *EPW* was a nationalist platform that encouraged Indian scholars to publish in India rather than in Western journals. Several generations of social scientists have earned their academic spurs publishing in the *EPW*. The journal took a sharp leftward turn in the 1970s, vehemently opposing the imposition of the Emergency. What made *EPW* a unique publication was that both the policy and the public intellectuals would want to publish in it. Thus, both *Seminar* and *EPW* functioned as important platforms for social scientists to both influence and criticize government policy by offering space for both well-researched academic publications as well as unabashed polemical essays.

Many in the policy circles of Vajpayee's BJP were willing to publish in *Seminar* and *EPW*; however, the new policy elite that has gained influence in Modi's dispensation keep their distance from both. They have launched new publications in print and online like *Swarajya*, *India Foundation Journal* and *Chintan* to put forth their own views on policy and politics.

In the black-and-white world of the powerful, intellectuals are often forced to choose sides. However, in the incestuous world of Lutyens' Delhi, where till recently, both the members and the opponents of the regime in power came from the same social set, one could be a critic of those in government by day, and unwind with the powerful by night. Arguments across political divides were often a continuation of youthful rivalries from the college debating society. It was like the Oxbridge set who drank into the night at a congenial pub arguing about Freud and Sartre and then found themselves in the Lok Sabha years later arguing about Gandhi and Savarkar. Prime-time television discussions had become drawing-room arguments between intellectual adversaries on a first-name basis. Yesterday's establishment intellectual becomes today's anti-establishment radical and vice versa.

This way of viewing the role of a public intellectual places her firmly within the power elite, not outside. Indeed, not all public intellectuals are anti-establishment, in the sense in which one would consider a Naxalite to be. Many of them aspire to be part of the establishment. Most seek public attention and support just like any politician seeking power would. Often, the status of a public intellectual within the ranks of the anti-establishment is defined by her prior status within the establishment. Thus, a retired government official or diplomat, an academic with a foreign degree and an NGO activist with international footprint would be rated higher on a list of anti-establishment public intellectuals. In other words, one's relationship to the matrix of power defined one's status within the ranks of the critics of power. The media, too, plays along, as Kesavan points out wryly:

> The last refuge of unselfconscious, upper-class male privilege is that contemporary parlour game, the listing of public intellectuals. This is peculiarly true of postcolonial countries like India where the gendered elitism that ring-fences these lists is reinforced by the smugness of Anglophone belonging. The typical Indian list will feature upper class, upper caste, middle-aged Hindu men who write and speak in English for that sliver of India's population that reads op-eds in India's English newspapers and websites or watches political wrangling on English news channels.[9]

A more recent entrant into this privileged social set of the 'establishment's anti-establishment' are NRIs living mostly in the US and UK, working mostly at privately funded institutions and living in suburban homes, writing sharp columns in India's English-language media worrying about all that is wrong with a country that they have all but seceded from. The higher one's status within the Western establishment the more privileged one's status within the ranks of the anti-establishment public intellectuals in India. One such radical intellectual once said to me, 'There are only two places in the world I feel truly at home. In my family's ancestral home and in a Paris café!' Demonstrating love for the former was meant to distance him from Lutyens' Delhi, while expressing familiarity with the latter was aimed at elevating his status among the inhabitants of Lutyens' Delhi.

One dimension to the social composition of policy and public intellectuals that has attracted the attention of the BJP is their growing dependence on foreign funding. Increasingly starved of funding by fiscally constrained governments, state and Centre, and unable to impress upon domestic business the need for funding policy research, many research institutions and thinks tanks have become dependent on foreign funding. New Delhi-based Centre for Policy Research (CPR) is a classic example of an influential policy think tank that had 80 per cent of its funding domestically sourced till the early 2000s and is now dependent on foreign sources for almost 90 per cent of funding. In the early 2000s, several US institutions set up shop in India, funding policy research in fields such as public health, population studies, economic and foreign policy. Indian corporates unwilling to fund Indian institutions happily funded these organizations such as the Public Health Foundation of India (linked to McKinsey & Co.), Brookings India and Carnegie India. Perhaps responding to the BJP's growing dislike of such foreign funding of policy research, Brookings India recently Indianized itself, changing its name to Centre for Social and Economic Progress.

It is entirely understandable that the cultural nationalism of Modi's New India is reducing the space available for foreign-funded policy research. However, unless this is matched by liberal domestic support, the space for public intellectuals not willing to depend on government support and seeking non-government support will inevitably shrink unless civil society and corporates step up to the task. The institutions that are attracting funding in the present BJP dispensation are the new think tanks affiliated, directly or indirectly, to the BJP like the Delhi-based Vivekananda International Foundation and the India Foundation. They work closely with the government, promoting rather than critiquing its policy agenda.

The Third Estate

From the early days of the national movement most, of India's political leaders came from the legal profession. After Independence, the profession has contributed both lawmakers and public intellectuals. Over time many have entered the ranks of the power elite at the national and provincial level. Initially, the making and working of a written constitution may have had some role to play in strengthening the link between law and governance. However, with time, it was the intricacies of a highly bureaucratic system of governance, the all-pervasive Licence-Permit-Control Raj and the complex system of taxation, with opportunities for tax avoidance, that made the legal profession increasingly attractive. The paradox of excessive legislation and lawmaking alongside lax implementation gave the legal profession and judiciary the opportunity to accumulate wealth and consolidate power. If lawyers-turned-politicians acquired power and wealth, wealthy lawyers, too, acquired power, turning to politics as a career. There have been any number of jurists and lawyers, from the days of Motilal Nehru to those of Ram Jethmalani, Arun Jaitley, P. Chidambaram, Kapil Sibal and so on, who have acquired wealth and wielded power.

Outside their professional duties, lawyers have sought to influence policy through public articulation of views on policy. The media has amplified their voice, and clever lawyers have used the media both to promote their professional interests and the political or policy cause they advocate. However, what has often added to the wealth and power of the legal profession has been the abdication of institutional responsibility by both the executive and the legislature unwilling to court unpopularity through difficult decisions. Both flailing arms of the state have reached out to the judiciary to bail them out of policy dilemmas. Added to this has been the temptation on the part of the judiciary, at every level, to intervene in policymaking. While many governments have tried to curb the power of the judiciary, Modi has been the first PM since Indira Gandhi to have succeeded in doing so. If the judiciary has often entered a space vacated by the legislature and the executive, the executive has used its powers to influence the judiciary.

———

The BJP's growing suspicion of public intellectuals who reject its ideology is increasingly manifest in its approach to left-wing extremists and radical and fringe Dalit intellectuals who challenge mainstream policy elite. That the ruling dispensation has identified this fringe as a challenge that needs to be snuffed out is not surprising. What is in fact a new development is the emergence of an anti-establishment strain within the establishment represented by the rise of Hindutva politics that bundles up all non-Hindutva intellectuals—pro- and anti-establishment, left, right and Liberal—and classifies them all as the 'power elite' of a westernized India whose status is now being challenged by a resurgent Bharat.

Both the establishment types and the anti-establishment ones in the old regime went to the same schools and colleges and became members of the same clubs—from left-wingers to right-wingers, from the social activists of Sonia Gandhi's National Advisory Council to Manmohan Singh's favourite Oxbridge economists, from Arun Jaitley's friends to Kapil Sibal's, they were all members of the IIC, and everyone had a column in the *Indian Express* or *The Hindu*.

The policy intellectuals with a high profile in media are almost always those who have either wealth, power or international branding. When the coronavirus pandemic hit the country, the more familiar faces on television were not the real subject experts from publicly funded research laboratories but the millionaire business leaders of the healthcare sector—the owners of Medanta and Apollo and other private medical hospitals. If a public institution gets some attention, like the All India Institute of Medical Science (AIIMS), it is because it is in the heart of Lutyens' Delhi.

It took a long time, for example, for the national media to discover Dr Jayaprakash Muliyil, an epidemiologist from Vellore, but no time at all to get through to experts around the world. Even US-based doctors with little professional experience in India were being interviewed in the media. Be it policy intellectuals or public intellectuals, sporting an international tag helps get more attention in the corridors of power and fame. Professional power derives from social and economic status; it is rarely the other way round.

The new 'intellectuals' around an Amit Shah and a Yogi Adityanath belong to a different world. They speak a different language. For them, both a leftist public intellectual like Romila Thapar and a rightist policy intellectual like Montek Ahluwalia are members of the same class—the same social set. Their ideological differences matter little. The new Hindutva elite would view both as 'the establishment' that has since been displaced by a very desi cultural revolution. Pitching this new conservatism as a 'Hindu nationalist intellectual architecture' standing in opposition to the 'pseudo-secular left liberal' Weltanschauung of the old public intellectuals, a Hindutva columnist has claimed that 'Indian conservative thinking process is linked deeply to the Hindu inheritance of the country. The reclaiming of the *dharmic* state is at the heart of the Indian Conservative Thought.'[10] Ironically, though, most of the intellectuals he lists on both sides of the argument have an Oxbridge link—Romila Thapar, Pratap Bhanu Mehta, Ramachandra Guha, all critical of the BJP, on the one hand, and Swapan Dasgupta, Sanjeev Sanyal, Hindol Sengupta, all supporters of the BJP, on the other.

The real cultural revolution and power shift under way, however, is not about displacing one set of intellectuals trained in the English language with another trained in the vernacular, but of the overthrow of globalized, upper-class intellectuals by provincial, middle-class Hindu nationalists. In the world of the conservative Hindu nationalist, policy and public intellectuals would be one and the same, serving the larger cause of the nation and the state.

10

Opinion Makers and Celebrities

The power elite are . . . celebrities because they have prestige,
and they have prestige because they are thought to have power or wealth.

—Wright Mills, *The Power Elite*

There are many apocryphal stories about Samir Jain, vice chairman of Bennett, Coleman and Company Limited, and the legendary brain behind the meteoric rise of the Times of India media group. One of the more enduring tales from the early 1990s is that of a senior editor asking Jain whether the *Times of India* is pro-establishment or anti-establishment. Jain's reply was straightforward: 'We are neither pro-establishment, nor anti-establishment. We are The Establishment.' It was a claim that the country's leading media group could make at a time when the ruling political establishment was in flux. Between 1988 and 1998, when the circulation of the Times group's various publications rose dizzyingly, establishing its dominance across several media markets, the country saw seven prime ministers in office. While prime ministers came and went and editors at the Times group changed seasonally, the group's revenues climbed from peak to peak, making it one of India's most profitable media firms. How could anyone cavil when Jain made that claim?

Samir's entry into the media group his father and father's friends initially built was not smooth. The senior editors whose chairs had become pedestals resented the intrusive ways of someone they regarded an upstart. Their mocking did not discourage Samir. He had devoted time to study modern journalism and was full of ideas. The success of his experiments, like the *Delhi Times* and *Bombay Times* supplement in *Times of India,* the *Brand Equity* supplement in *Economic Times* and other such innovations to newspaper journalism won him the respect of younger journalists. Rising revenues enabled him to pay higher salaries to newer recruits, further cementing his reputation as an innovator and successful media entrepreneur. It was the TOI's financial success that fed its organizational ego.

Ironically though, the *Times of India* began its career in the mid-nineteenth century as a pro-establishment publication, British in ownership and defender of the empire. The nationalist media of British India included *The Hindu* and the *Hindustan Times.* During the Emergency (1975–77), the *Indian Express,* under the leadership of its owner-publisher Ramnath Goenka, became a symbol of protest against curbs on freedom of the press and proudly sported its anti-establishment credentials. At the *Hindustan Times,* on the other hand, the then editor B.G. Verghese, a distinguished journalist and later a scholar at a think tank, was sacked because its publisher K.K. Birla did not approve of his criticism of Indira Gandhi. Birla went on to become a pro-Congress member of Parliament and now has a street named after him at the edges of Lutyens' Delhi, on which the India office of the World Bank is located. The press, both English-language and vernacular, played its part in the national movement, securing for itself a valued social status. The Constitution of free India enshrined freedom of speech and expression as a fundamental right, recognizing the media's role as a 'fourth estate'.

This freedom was met with early scrutiny both by the judiciary and legislature resulting in the very first amendment to the

Constitution, made within the year of its adoption, thereby curbing it. Article 19 (1) of the Constitution had guaranteed the freedom of 'speech and expression' as a fundamental right, but did not specify 'freedom of press' under this clause. Two cases pertaining to the media came up before the judiciary in 1950 requiring clarification of the issue. One pertained to a publication sympathetic to the communists and the other a publication of the Hindu nationalist RSS—both opponents of the ruling Congress dispensation. Both cases raised questions about the extent to which freedom of press was guaranteed as a fundamental right under Article 19(1).

The Congress leadership including Nehru, Patel, Ambedkar and Rajendra Prasad felt it was necessary to impose 'reasonable' restrictions on the freedom of speech and expression so that the media would be restrained from publishing anything seditious or going against the values of the constitution. There was much debate and discussion on the pros and cons, and Ambedkar finally clinched the issue. Intellectually critical of both the communists and the Hindu communalists, Ambedkar strongly favoured some measure of restraint on public expression of extreme views. After considerable debate, Article 19(2) was introduced, imposing what was nebulously termed as 'reasonable restrictions' on the freedom of speech and expression in the interests of national security, sovereignty and integrity of the country, 'friendly relations with foreign states', public order, decency, morality, contempt of court, defamation or incitement to an offence. This was a pretty comprehensive limitation imposed on the freedom of the media very early in India's republican journey, even though at the time the government sought to curb what they viewed as 'anti-national' media and not merely 'anti-government'.

Well into the 1970s no media group could convincingly claim to be a national publication, much less the national establishment. The *Times of India* was among the major publications but its influence was restricted mainly to Bombay. In New Delhi the largest English-language newspaper was the *Hindustan Times*.

In Calcutta this distinction went to *The Statesman* and in Madras it was always *The Hindu*, with the *Indian Express* acquiring marginal presence. In Hyderabad the *Deccan Chronicle* reigned supreme and in Bangalore it was the *Deccan Herald*. My most distinguished predecessor in the office of the media adviser to the prime minister, H.Y. Sharada Prasad, whose term in that office ran parallel to Indira Gandhi's (from the mid-1960s into the mid-1980s) once told me that during his tenure he found it necessary to befriend only five editors so as to ensure favourable press for the PM. The influential five were editors of *Times of India, Indian Express, The Hindu, The Statesman* and *Hindustan Times*.

The cosy relationship between senior media professionals and the government was best exemplified by the latter allotting land and offering subsidized housing to the former. The first generation of post-Independence editors in New Delhi were allotted plots of land to build homes in areas such as Gulmohar Park and Niti Bagh in the heart of Lutyens' Delhi. Some even managed to get office space in and around Connaught Place. The second generation moved farther south to the slightly cramped Press Enclave in Saket. A third generation managed to form a cooperative housing society that was allocated land on the Delhi-Haryana border. Well into the 1990s, many senior journalists were quite happy to accept government accommodation in localities around Khan Market.

Yet, the fact is that many of the newspaper editors of that era came to be regarded with awe and respect. Men like Sham Lal, Girilal Jain, B.G. Verghese, Kuldip Nayar, Gopalan Kasturi, S. Sahay, Nihal Singh and Chalapati Rau were not particularly wealthy but certainly powerful in terms of the respect they commanded. It may be said that many of the well-known editors today may be wealthy but not necessarily powerful. Indeed, over the past quarter century, there has been an inverse relationship between the rising personal wealth of media leaders and their declining credibility, social influence and power. A quarter century ago, Samir Jain could claim that his media empire was in fact 'the' establishment. Today, even the most powerful media group would hesitate to make such a claim, quietly conceding primacy to the ruling dispensation.

Media Power and Credibility

In the summer of 1990, I ran into T.N. Ninan at a neighbour's home in Hyderabad. He had just taken charge as editor of the *Economic Times* after a successful tenure at *India Today*. I was at the time an associate professor of economics at the University of Hyderabad. At the end of an evening of conversation, Ninan asked if I would join his team at ET as an editorial writer, given my training in economics, and the fact that I had some familiarity with journalistic writing based on my occasional writing for newspapers, including *Economic Times*, *Newstime* and *The Hindu*. I gave the invitation some thought and, after a few days, wrote to him conveying my interest. Once I received my offer letter, I applied for a year's leave from my tenured position at the university. Next day, the vice chancellor (VC), Professor Bh. Krishnamurthy, a distinguished and internationally acclaimed professor of linguistics, summoned me. 'You want leave from an academic position to become a journalist? Nonsense! Withdraw your letter.' I was thus admonished and summarily dismissed. I pleaded with the VC. It was an experiment, I told him. I was still young enough to experiment. I had always had an interest in journalism. 'You can experiment, by all means. Go abroad for a post-doctoral. Take up an assignment with government. Why journalism? You will be demeaning yourself and our profession.' The vice chancellor was adamant, and so was I. I withdrew my leave application and resigned. Few favoured my decision. For the middle class, a 'permanent' job with pension was a prized possession. *Economic Times* was offering me only a contractual appointment for three years, with nothing more assured. I took the plunge.

A few years later, Professor Krishnamurthy came to visit me at New Delhi's Times House. I was by then the editorial page editor at the *Times of India*. He was in Delhi to meet his old friend, the polylinguist prime minister, P.V. Narasimha Rao. 'I have been waiting for two days,' he told me. 'I am sure you can get an appointment within a day. You journalists are more influential than we academics.' In saying this Krishnamurthy was pointing to a change in the status of the media. It was not just the new post-Emergency brand of journalism that had made a difference. Journalism was beginning to offer better pay and was attracting more talent. During my time at *Economic Times*, some colleagues used to call the row of cabins seating editorial writers 'Harley Street'—London's street of medical doctors—because a number of us sported the honorific 'Dr' before our names.

Journalism also became more financially rewarding for those who worked with media groups that attracted more advertising revenue. In the pre-Emergency era, newspapers depended mostly on subscription fees and government advertising. Private-sector advertising became an increasingly important source of revenue through the 1980s and certainly after the launch of economic liberalization and the opening up of India to foreign businesses. By 1992, Western media groups began lobbying with the government, seeking the opening up of Indian media space to foreign firms. When the then finance minister, Manmohan Singh, told a gathering of the Foreign Correspondents Club in Delhi that the government was actively considering allowing the *Financial Times* of London to publish from India, the Times of India group went into overdrive, in cahoots with the *Hindustan Times* and other Indian media, to campaign against this. An NGO outfit, called the Nehru Socialist Forum, was launched with their help and it deployed all the required socialist and nationalist jargon to protest the opening up of media business to foreign investment. The mainstream Indian media establishment had established that they indeed were 'The Establishment'.

The Emergency years (1975–77) were the turning point for Indian media. In the years running up to the Emergency, an increasingly restive nation—with a middle class worried about rising and high rates of inflation and students turning violent, influenced by a global trend of campus protests—turned to the media for support, contributing to the emergence of new and powerful voices. Not surprisingly, therefore, Indira Gandhi came down heavily against the media and imposed pre-censorship. The *Indian Express* gained fame and notoriety with its 'journalism of courage' by leaving the space for editorial comment blank rather than having the editorials precleared by government censors.

If the *Indian Express* became the anti-establishment publication that set new standards for the role the media would play in the country's power politics, the newly launched magazine *India Today* tried to create a new journalism of elitist partisanship. Launched originally as an overseas publication, the magazine aimed to whitewash the Emergency and present Indira Gandhi as a symbol of good governance to the world. Its opening editorial, as we have already noted, sang a paean to the prime minister and justified the imposition of Emergency on the grounds that it would end corruption, the unholy alliance between 'babus and baniyas', reduce poverty and inflation, create new employment, and so on. As for freedom of speech and expression, *India Today* said:

> There has been worldwide concern about the curbs put on the press since the Emergency. Mrs Gandhi has repeatedly said that she does not want to muzzle the press. But, the problems for democracies is to decide where freedom begins and responsibility ends . . . As the Emergency continues, press censorship rules, are gradually being relaxed to allow constructive criticism of government policies.[1]

The contrast between the *Indian Express* and *India Today* could not have been starker. The *Express* was run by an earthy dhoti-clad, Tamil-speaking Marwari businessman, Ramnath Goenka, who had participated in the national movement, was elected to

Parliament for a term and supported Jayaprakash Narayan, the Gandhian socialist who became the rallying point for nationwide protests against Indira Gandhi in the early 1970s. *India Today's* founder-editor, Arun Poorie, on the other hand, was a suave Doon School contemporary of Rajiv Gandhi, who then graduated from LSE and trained to be a chartered accountant. Ironically, it was the older, more 'desi' Goenka who became a symbol of media power and freedom, while Poorie became the harbinger of a new trend in journalism—focused on urban lifestyle, entertainment and mindful of the corporate bottom line in publishing. It was Poorie's 'media as business' model that Samir Jain embraced and copied with resounding success.

In the transformation of media from being the 'fourth estate' of democracy to becoming just another business, Poorie and Jain set the trend. Their model got a boost in 1991 with the economic policy taking a new turn, unleashing the 'animal spirits' of Indian enterprise. Till the circulation of Indian-language media picked up, high-value advertising remained largely confined to metropolitan English-language print media. So, when the Indian economy began to record higher rates of growth and corporate-sector profits rose, it was English-language media, especially the financial media, that was able to pay higher salaries and attract better professionals. It was during that period of growth that the Times of India group parted company with most other publications and emerged as the dominant player. Buoyed up by rising revenues, the group spread its wings across the country establishing its presence in almost all major urban centres.

The transformation of media into business did boost revenues and empowered managers over editors. But the process could not go beyond a point once it became clear to owners that professional credibility of journalists remained an important asset in building and retaining brands. An early example of the power of professional credibility even in an increasingly business-oriented media was provided by the experience of the late Dhirubhai Ambani's *Business and Political Observer* (BPO) The decision of one of India's most successful businessmen to launch a newspaper set the cat among the media pigeons in 1990. The decision had itself come after the Ambanis found themselves the target of media attack in the late 1980s. In an implicit recognition of media power, Ambani decided to launch his own publication with the economist–journalist Prem Shankar Jha as its first editor. In the weeks before its October 1990 launch, there was much strategizing at Times House as to how we would deal with a new challenger given the deep pockets of the publisher. BPO had hired some very good journalists, so quality was assured.

On the day when the first edition of BPO landed at our doorstep, a strategy meeting was convened at *Economic Times* to analyse the new competitor in the market and plan our response. Reading through Dhirubhai's letter to the reader on BPO's front page, we took the view that we at *Economic Times* need not be worried. The letter reminded the reader that BPO would be as good a product as the firm's other very good and popular product, Vimal. This newspaper comes from the makers of Vimal, said the letter, and since Vimal is such a popular product in the market, this newspaper would be too. We took the view that newspaper readers still valued credibility and professionalism of journalists. The open identification of a businessman with his paper and the link drawn between a textile brand and a newspaper, we felt would harm the latter. It did. BPO went through a bumpy ride, changed its editor and name, but nothing helped. It was shut down a decade later.

The power of print media, in the final analysis, derives from its credibility. Television is a different ball game. In a country where most families still have only one TV at home, watching it is a family activity and not an individual activity. During prime time, news television competes with entertainment for viewer's attention. Members of a family sitting with a remote in hand surf channels to decide whether to watch the news or a soap opera. It is only natural that news TV often descends to the level of TV soaps to attract and retain, as the jargon goes, eyeballs. The television medium turns journalists into celebrities and thereby devalues their credibility as a source of information. This would account for the survival of print a good two decades after the arrival of news TV in a semi-literate country.

Media and Political Power

To get a better appreciation of the power of media one must look beyond English-language media and consider the size and influence of Indian-language media. After all, unlike the three institutions of the state—the legislature, the executive and the judiciary—the power of the fourth estate is a derivative. It derives from its influence on public opinion. A secondary source of its power, one associated more with a mass medium like television than print, is its potential to create celebrities. The power to influence opinion gets fractured in India by the multiplicity of languages. The audience for English-language media is very different from that for Hindi and other Indian languages. Rising literacy, especially in the Hindi heartland, the spread of television and, most importantly, of digital technology, social media and mobile phone-based news and entertainment, has created new markets for the media and new sources of power. The rapid rise of the India Against Corruption campaign and of the Aam Admi Party (AAP) in 2012–14 was attributed to the new media and the new technology of news dissemination. Narendra Modi was a quick learner who made good use of the new media to quickly evolve from being a regional politician to a national leader.

According to a 2017 KPMG study done for FICCI, though English-language media attracts a bulk of revenue, the growth rate of advertising revenue going to English media in the period 2011–16 was 4.4 per cent, compared to 9.2 per cent for Hindi media and 10.1 per cent for other Indian-language media, pointing to the rising importance of vernacular media. In terms of readership and viewership too, Indian-language media had grown at a faster pace than English-language media through the period 2011–16, with 90 per cent of the population accessing media in their mother tongue. The political influence of local media has been long acknowledged. What has become increasingly commonplace is the nexus between regional business, language and politics.

An early example of a media group influencing the course of local politics was that of the Telugu-language *Eenadu*'s campaign for N.T. Rama Rao's TDP and its subsequent support for NTR's son-in-law Chandrababu Naidu when he staged a political coup against his mentor and father-in-law. *Eenadu* publisher Ramoji Rao, a businessman with interests across finance, film-making, food processing and media, was also the newspaper's editor. That he belonged to Andhra Pradesh's Kamma caste cemented his close partnership with NTR, the state's first Kamma chief minister who challenged and displaced Reddy dominance in the Congress. In many states provincial politicians had business and caste links with local media, but the *Eenadu*-NTR alliance was a new model that demonstrated the power of media in regional politics. In 1993, the Maran family of Tamil Nadu launched Sun TV, a channel loyal to the DMK party in which the Maran family had a leadership position. In 1999, DMK's rival Jayalalitha's All India Anna Dravida Munnetra Kazhagam (AIADMK) launched Jaya TV as the party's media mouthpiece. Not to be left behind, the left parties, too, launched their own TV channel in Kerala in the 1990s.

Most provincial politicians across the country have set up their own media outfits, and most media groups have their political affiliations. Following the *Eenadu* model, former Congress party leader Y.S. Rajashekhar Reddy's son Y.S. Jaganmohan Reddy launched *Sakshi*, print and TV. Hyderabad's *Deccan Chronicle* was for long owned by the Congress party's T. Chandrashekhara Reddy, brother of the high-profile celebrity T. Subbirami Reddy. In Maharashtra, Lokmat group is owned by the Congress party's Darda family, while Sakal has investment from the Sharad Pawar family. In Odisha, politician Jay Panda's wife Jaggi Mangat Pande runs OTV, while Arnab Goswami's Republic TV is funded by a clutch of BJP supporters. Apart from such open political affiliations, there are the less visible ones. *Hindustan Times'* owners K.K. Birla and daughter Shobhana Bharatiya have been Congress party supporters, while *India TV*'s Rajat Sharma has been a BJP supporter. While the *Times of India* has tried hard not to get too close to any political party, its *Times Now TV* channel has been openly pro-BJP. Chennai's *The Hindu* group had a long record of credibility, even after it tilted politically to the left during the editorship of CPI(M)'s N. Ram. The country's largest Hindi newspapers *Dainik Jagran* and *Dainik Bhaskar* tried to play a political balancing act but have increasingly tilted towards the BJP. The very first private English TV channel NDTV was launched with the blessings of the Congress party, enjoying the benefits of a cosy relationship with Rajiv Gandhi in the 1980s and benefited from the family links of many of its senior journalists with various influential persons within and close to the Nehru-Gandhi dynasty. If Prannoy Roy was a favourite of Rajiv Gandhi and had the support of Doordarshan in his early days, Rajat Sharma was a favourite of Atal Bihari Vajpayee and had the support of his family. Links between media celebrities and politicians in power have, more often than not, been all out there in the open and for all to see.

Media's High Society

Do media's close links with politicians give it clout or deprive it of credibility? It would appear that almost every media group makes a trade-off between the two—sacrificing some credibility for either money or power. Indeed, with money comes power, and with proximity to power comes money. The continuing success of the unabashedly partisan, pro-Modi Republic TV is proof. RTV's idiosyncratic anchor, Arnab Goswami, is a thorough professional and a personally amiable fellow. However, when the camera is turned on he becomes an actor, not a professional reporter of news.

His viewers, the mainly urban middle class Hindus who enthusiastically support Modi, lap up all the histrionics on display. Arnab has come to symbolize the headiness of power that the media is capable of conferring on a normal professional.

In the age of private, corporatized television, anchors are not mere journalists; they become brands. Some have even become proprietors. Prannoy Roy set the trend turning from TV anchor to NDTV proprietor. Rajat Sharma and Arnab Goswami have walked in his footsteps. Print media, too, has had its entrants to the world of the power elite. Journalists have entered the corridors of power, joining political parties, becoming members of Parliament and ministers at the Centre and in the states. Then there are the journalists who have graduated into becoming entrepreneurs— successful editors using either their professional position or their political and business contacts to mobilize funds and become owners of media.

The heady mix of media reach, political access and personal wealth has enabled professional journalists to enter the ranks of the power elite. Within less than a decade of launching his Republic TV Arnab Goswami has entered the IIFL Hurun Rich List 2020 with his wealth estimated to be Rs 1300 crore, in the same wealth bracket as K.K. Birla's daughter, Shobhana Bharatiya, the media baroness who owns the venerable daily *Hindustan Times*.[2] The TV anchor's brand and the proprietor's wealth have enabled journalists to own fancy homes in South Delhi, a pricey flat in South Mumbai, farmhouses and getaway homes in the foothills of the Himalayas or in Goa, holidays in Tuscany. The journalists of the pre-Emergency era could never dream of such a lifestyle.

Despite the tremendous growth in media, print and electronic, and the growing wealth and power of its owners and editors, there is a fundamental shift that has taken place with politicians either owning or controlling media more directly. The growing assertion of state power in many states and at the Centre under Modi has forced media to become either more subdued or more partisan, with some honourable exceptions. A quarter century ago when Samir Jain claimed his was 'the' establishment, the sentiment may well have found resonance in the minds of many owner-editors like Arun Poorie, Ramoji Rao, N. Ram, Aveek Sarkar and editor-owners of dominant Indian-language dailies in different provinces. Wealth and power combined to contribute to that feeling of mainstream, traditional media. With the dispersal of media power through the growth of social media and the assertion of state power by authoritarian governments, few in the media would today make Jain's grandiloquent claim.

Modi and 'Lutyens' Media'

Like many political functionaries, especially provincial leaders, Narendra Modi found himself on the margins of this media 'high society' till his elevation to the office of chief minister of Gujarat. In this office, and as a former party spokesperson with contacts in the national media, he could have encashed many media IOUs. However, the events in Gujarat in 2002 and the national media's criticism of his handling of the situation ruptured that relationship. The fact that many BJP leaders in Delhi were also critical of Modi's handling of the Hindu–Muslim tension in Gujarat, and Prime Minister Atal Bihari Vajpayee's reported statement that Modi had not adhered to 'raja dharma'—a ruler's code of conduct—encouraged many in the national media to be even more critical of Modi than they may have normally been. Communal clashes were not new to India. Many Congress chief ministers had presided over equally dastardly events in their states and had not been as severely criticized for it as Modi was.

Modi was particularly incensed with a few Delhi-based journalists including Shekhar Gupta, Rajdeep Sardesai and Karan Thapar. While Thapar had a close social connection to the Nehru-Gandhi family and, with his bow tie and British accent, may have typified an elitism that Modi disliked, the other two were viewed by the BJP as being close to Sonia Gandhi and other non-BJP politicians. It was understandable that during the election campaign of 2014 Modi and the BJP may have wished to undermine the influence of these journalists with their audience. However, by launching a sustained campaign against what he dubbed as 'Lutyens' media', Modi and his media strategists exaggerated the power and influence of Delhi's English-language media even as they sought to marginalize their influence. Their strategy was direct marketing of Modi through social media. Modi became the first politician to bypass mainstream media and deploy social media in his campaign to form a government in Delhi. It worked.

Once in office, becoming the first PM in three decades to secure an absolute majority in the Lok Sabha, Modi could have reached out to the power elite of the national media. He chose not to. As in his campaign mode so too as head of government, Modi opted for social media to communicate with his supporters. Using social media to retain a direct link to the people is good political strategy, but to have shunned New Delhi's mainstream media was misplaced pique. As media adviser to the prime minister, though at a time when social media had not become so pervasive, I found that a dominant segment of the national media could easily be persuaded to be supportive of the PM given that many in the media value access to power and privileged information. I had categorized Delhi's media into four groups: (a) the pure professional (b) pro-government (c) pro-opposition and (d) the corrupt. With the exception of the politically or ideologically committed journalist of category (c), one could ensure adequately favourable media coverage for the PM from the other three.

For his own reasons, Modi and his media strategists not only chose not to seek the support of (a), (c) and (d), but sought to convert as many journalists as they could to join category (b). While their focus was mainly the Hindi media, in the English media they seemed satisfied with purely partisan journalism on the part of the likes of Republic TV, Times Now and India TV.

In the process, though, Modi has sought to obliterate the power of media. His critics, with few exceptions, are corralled within the English-language media. In Indian-language mass media, especially the Hindi-language media, he has ensured overwhelming support. Media's power in a democracy derives from its status as the 'fourth estate'. To play this role, media needs to be independent of political power and willing to speak truth to power. The kind of power this route offers to media is very different from the kind of power that proximity to political and corporate power offers. The battle within media is a constant struggle between these two paths to power. Professional journalists live and die by the power of their byline. Social media dissolves this power by devaluing bylines to the point of ridicule. In the era of fake news, paid news and openly partisan news, the power of professional media is under serious threat.

Media and Celebrity Power

Media also manufactures, makes and breaks celebrities. Film and sports personalities have a hallowed place in the country's power elite, especially when they pair up with business barons and political leaders. Politics, business, cricket and cinema are the arenas on which celebrities test and exercise their power in shaping public opinion and monetizing it. From Nehru's early years till today, prime ministers have made sure they have time for celebrities, each living off the other's popularity and power. All those who succeed, wrote Wright Mills of America a half a century ago, 'No matter what their circle of origin or their sphere of action—are likely to become involved in the world of the celebrity.'[3] 'This world is at once the pinnacle of the prestige system and a big-scale business. As a business, the networks of mass communication, publicity, and entertainment are not only the means whereby celebrities are celebrated; they also select and create celebrities for a profit. One type of celebrity, accordingly, is a professional at it, earning sizeable income not only from working in, but virtually living on, the mass media of communication and distraction.'[4]

Social prestige can have different sources in different societies, at different stages of development in different historical contexts. In a country at war, prestige is attached to bravery and patriotism. In a society on the make, with its pace of change defined by an aspirational middle class, prestige is often associated with being a celebrity. In such a society, suggested Mills:

> Prestige is the shadow of money and power. Where these are, there it is. Like the national market for soap or automobiles and the enlarged arena of federal power, the national cash-in area for prestige has grown, slowly being consolidated into a truly national system. Since the men of the higher political, economic, and military circles are an elite of money and power, they accumulate a prestige that is considerably above the ordinary; all of them have publicity value and some of them are downright eminent; increasingly, by virtue of their position and by means of conscious public relations, they strive to make their names notable, their actions acceptable, their policies popular. And in all this, they tend to become national celebrities.[5]

It is through popular media that the 'power elite' in the world of politics, business, finance and the bureaucracy attach themselves to the celebrities of the worlds of sport and entertainment. In India, Mumbai is the crucible within which the worlds of business, banking, finance, media, entertainment and sports meet. They have to then extend a hand to New Delhi to square the circle of power. All these worlds meet on the cricket field, to be cheered by the multitudes. No institution symbolized the world of this new power elite better than the world of Indian Premier League (IPL) cricket—business billionaires, media barons, celebrity film stars, powerful politicians, ambitious editors, captains of banking and finance. Consider the names of all those who inhabit the world of IPL. Little wonder then that as Union home minister the powerful Amit Shah was happy to see his businessman son joining the Board of Cricket Control of India (BCCI) and Prime Minister Modi does not miss an opportunity to show how popular he is with Bollywood stars. In one of his last gestures to the world of celebrities, Prime Minister Manmohan Singh awarded cricket player Sachin Tendulkar a Bharat Ratna, the Congress party having already made him a member of the Rajya Sabha, whose sessions he rarely attended.

No political leader, business baron, captain of finance or media boss would feel the wedding reception of his offspring is complete without a few film stars, cricketing heroes and fashion designers turning up. From businessman-politician Praful Patel to hotelier-lobbyist Sant Singh Chatwal, anyone and everyone who thinks of himself a celebrity makes sure private jets fly into Udaipur for a wedding at which the power elite dance and drink and make their presence felt. Till the 1980s, celebrity news was confined largely to magazines, and that too, the ones that focused on celebrities, like *Society* and *Filmfare*. In the 1990s, celebrity journalism moved into mainstream media with the *Times of India* launching its city-based colour supplement, *Delhi Times*, *Mumbai Times*, and so on. Not to be left out, other dailies imitated the TOI, and every newspaper now has daily coverage of celebrity lifestyle. Indeed, celebrities have moved up front from supplements to the front page.

Two media institutions have come to symbolize the wedlock between media, entertainment, power and wealth—power lists and annual summits. Every year, the media puts out lists of the 'most this' and the 'most that'. Lobbyists have been enriched in seeking to tweak lists on behalf of their clients. These are referred to as power lists. You do not exist if you are not on one of them at least once in your lifetime. Then there are the annual media 'summits' and 'conclaves'; everyone who matters, from the prime minister to the latest hot film sensation, turn up at these summits. One has to be a guest at the opening dinner to matter at all. From celebrity doctors-turned-CEOs, who are busier partying than conducting surgeries to politicians and business persons seeking glamour, everyone turns up at these events.

Society magazines thrive on the public hunger for a glimpse into celebrity life. Samir Jain was one of the first to tap into this social voyeurism of the aspiring middle class and the celebrity-mania of the power elite by monetizing the public display of power gatherings. TOI's *Delhi Times* and, more recently ET's *ET Panache* have become vehicles that most other dailies have since copied. One can pay and secure space in these pages to display one's lifestyle. Popular media is the stage on which the power elite perform and celebrities widen their audience.

Power and wealth ride on the back of the popularity of the celebrity rather than the other way round. Be it Narendra Modi commissioning Amitabh Bachchan to promote Gujarat in a series of advertisements or Rahul Gandhi naming Sachin Tendulkar to the Rajya Sabha, be it Mukesh Ambani publicly hosting film stars and cricketers at home or K. Chandrashekhar Rao posing for photographs with badminton player P.V. Sindhu, it is almost always the business and political leadership that wants to be seen with celebrities from the world of entertainment and sports. Modi, too, has used film stars and sports personalities to promote government programmes like Swachh Bharat and the use of toilets, abjuring open defecation. From polio eradication to the education of the girl child, many government programmes have been, over the years, promoted by celebrities. In the process, the popularity of the celebrity gets subliminally attached to that of the politician in power. In Tamil Nadu, the power elite are a cocktail of wealthy business, charismatic entertainers, media magnates and politicians. In other parts of the country this mix gets a bit diluted, but everywhere, both wealth and power seek popularity from association with the celebrity, multiplying the latter's wealth and power.

In his political quest to retain the loyalty of the middle class and bolster his popular image, Modi has unabashedly recruited the media and the celebrity to serve his cause. From TV anchors who are openly partisan in support of the PM to celebrities who endorse every one of his slogans, the worlds of entertainment and politics have been brought more close together than ever before. From Hema Malini, Smriti Irani, Anupam Kher, Akshay Kumar and Kangana Ranaut, in Bollywood, to Arnab Goswami and Navika Kumar in news television, Modi's BJP has used the appeal of the celebrity to project its power.

In normal times, a dominant section of opinion makers and celebrities would be expected to be pro-establishment, with an anti-establishment minority that may sometimes acquire a higher public profile but rarely much political clout. In revolutionary and politically unstable times the roles may get reversed. Those wielding state power understand how these equations work and can be manipulated. They expect the pro-establishment majority to fall in line and do the bidding of the powers that be. The Indian ruling elite have not shied away from arm-twisting opinion makers and celebrities. During the Emergency, Indira Gandhi's government even banned the airing of the songs of Kishore Kumar, one of the most popular Bollywood playback singers, on state-run All India Radio (AIR), because he was unwilling to endorse the imposition of the Emergency. This mindless authoritarianism only damaged the credibility of AIR and not the popularity of Kishore Kumar.

The BJP under Vajpayee's leadership was indulgent towards the media elite. However, the BJP under Modi has not hesitated to unabashedly push its ideological and cultural agenda, forcing electronic media to become increasingly partisan and playing political favourites in Bollywood in the name of purging it of dubious sources of funding, inbreeding and alien cultural influences. While Bollywood has generally been kind and supportive of Modi, as PM, it has not yet been converted to the Hindutva political agenda of the BJP and RSS. A campaign of sorts has been unleashed through social media against left-liberal and Muslim actors and directors. Intelligence and security agencies have been deployed in the name of exposing drug use to bring Bollywood into line, at least in part to purge the film industry of those who do not subscribe to the BJP's 'Hindu-Hindi' ideology.

By contrast, the entertainment world's celebrity entertainers were happy to heartily endorse Vajpayee's version of liberal Hindutva. On the occasion of the fiftieth anniversary of Indian Independence, A.R. Rahman composed and sang a new version of the patriotic song '*Vande Mataram*' that many orthodox Muslims have objected to because they view it as an invocation to a Hindu goddess. When he sang the song in Prime Minister Vajpayee's presence in New York in 2000, the PM welcomed Rahman's rendition and said the Mother in the song was not just Mother India but Mother Earth. There are few in Modi's BJP who would today associate themselves with such liberal sentiments. Rather, many would claim victory in having made a Muslim sing '*Vande Mataram*'. The old elites knew how to preserve social and political unity despite India's cultural diversity. The new power elite see no value in that liberal endeavour.

In the past, politicians in power deployed the notion of freedom of press and the power of independent media to ward off allegations of misuse of power. Today, as during the Emergency, politicians in power unabashedly seek the subservience of media and the supplication of celebrities to draw public attention to their own power.

11

Secession of the Successful

If you believe you are a citizen of the world,
you are a citizen of nowhere.

—Theresa May, 2016

On a visit to Washington DC in December 1990, I called on India's ambassador to the United States, Abid Hussain, a fellow Hyderabadi. The ambassador was scheduled to address a dinner meeting of a local NRI community and invited me to join him. His speech was devoted to encouraging US-based NRIs to continue to invest in various foreign currency deposit schemes floated by Indian banks aimed at bolstering India's foreign exchange reserves. These inflows, mainly from the Gulf and the US, had already become an important source of foreign exchange for India. Between 1980–81 and 1988–89, foreign currency deposits from NRIs had increased steeply from a mere Rs 1090 crore to Rs 17,213 crore. However, increasing instability in the Gulf, a decline in remittances from that region and rising oil prices due to tensions in West Asia had triggered a decline in these inflows. Ambassador Hussain was hoping US-based NRIs would make up for the difference by depositing more of their savings in these Indian accounts created specially to attract savings of overseas Indians.

After an inspirational speech by the ambassador, a gentleman in the audience stood up and posed a question to him in a rather aggressive tone. 'Why does India need me now?' he asked. 'India did not need me when I was living there struggling to get a job. None of you government chaps bothered about people like me then. Now you meet us here because America gave us the opportunity to make money. And you come asking us to be patriotic and send our savings to India? Forget it, ambassador!' He shouted, 'I will spend my money here. I owe India nothing.' Many in the audience clapped.

The unwillingness of the NRIs to retain their savings with Indian banks in funds created specially to attract their foreign-currency-denominated deposits was partly responsible for the balance of payments crisis of 1990–91. Over a billion dollars was withdrawn between October 1990 and February 1991 from foreign currency non-resident accounts, depleting India's already atrophied foreign currency reserves and pushing the State Bank of India to the brink of default. The year 1991 marked the low point of trust between the overseas Indians and the motherland.

The gentleman who spoke up at Hussain's dinner meeting had left an India of the 1970s that was not yet offering adequate employment opportunities for highly qualified middle-class professionals like him. People of Indian origin in the US were a mere 12,296 persons in 1960, constituting just about 0.1 per cent of foreign-born population in the US that year. By 1970, the number had increased to 51,000. The 1970s witnessed a significant increase with the total number being 2,06,087 in 1980. That more than doubled to 4,50,406 by 1990. Most of the 1970s and 1980s migrants, before the information technology boom of the late 1990s, were students and middle-class professionals. Tamil Brahmins fleeing a state that was in the grip of Dravidian, anti-Brahmin politics; Andhra doctors not willing to work for the low remuneration that government hospitals were offering, with a non-practising allowance for pocket money; Gujarati and Punjabi entrepreneurs seeking better business opportunities in a freer market. Some of the medical doctors returned home in the 1980s and 1990s to set up private hospitals, while some academics returned to join research and teaching institutions or the government.

The professional middle class that migrated to the US in increasing numbers in the 1960s was different from the working class and the technicians who went to a booming post-oil shock Gulf of the 1970s and 1980s. In the latter's case, families stayed put at home in India and the expat worker remitted most of his income. Most of the working-class migrants who went to the Gulf hailed from Kerala, Maharashtra and Telangana. Lack of employment opportunities at home and the opportunity to save a substantial part of income and invest back home in children's education, a family house and so on made migration to the Gulf very attractive.

Furthermore, these two categories of Indians were very different from the indentured labour of the nineteenth century that was forced to migrate to work on plantations in the Caribbean and the plantation islands of the Indian and Pacific oceans. Many went as soldiers of the British imperial army to Africa and East and South East Asia. Professionals, traders and business persons followed later, especially to Africa. If the post-Independence migrants to the West, especially the US and UK, were mostly urban, upper-caste Indians, the forced migrants of the nineteenth century were mainly from lower castes, often Dalits and tribals.

Hussain's audience in Washington DC comprised largely highly qualified professionals who at the time were also fully alive to the new caste politics that had gripped India in the wake of the 'Mandal agitations' of the 1980s. The V.P. Singh government's decision to implement the recommendations of the B.P. Mandal Commission to extend reservations in educational institutions and government employment to 'other backward classes' had stirred the hornet's nest of caste politics. Why would people send money to an India that not only did not give them jobs, but wanted to deny opportunities to them—the upper-caste Indians? That was the grievance animating Hussain's audience.

Within the year, India took a new turn. The P.V. Narasimha Rao government's decision to open up the economy to greater private investment, domestic and foreign, to liberalize trade and to change India's geopolitical course, moving closer to the US, began to alter US-India relations. The turning point, however, came with Y2K—the year 2000 problem that information technology (IT) and software engineers were called upon to solve. US business, technology and political leadership discovered that the thousands of students that India's engineering colleges were producing could be drafted to help in America's emergence as an IT superpower.

In the summer of 2000, I was invited to spend two months at the East West Center in Honolulu, Hawaii, to write a paper on the impact that the IT and software industry would have on US-India relations.[1] The study drew attention to changes under way in US-India political and economic relations and the growing business traffic, especially in IT and related sectors, and concluded:

> What does all this mean for the Indo-US relationship? Apart from the purely economic aspect of incomes and employment being generated by the e-economy, we must also draw attention to the increased social and cultural interaction this has enabled. The four important areas in which such 'people-to-people' interaction between the two nations has been enhanced by the new economy are—entrepreneurship, internet and IT-enabled services and infotainment.[2]

Till the turn of the century, the out-migration of professional Indians was still a trickle, though even by then almost all students passing out of the prestigious Indian Institutes of Technology (IIT) saw admission to these institutions equivalent to securing a visa to the US. Most of these students came from southern Indian states, especially united Andhra Pradesh, making the Telugu-speaking Indians among the largest group of Indian-Americans in the US. These students were mostly middle class and upper caste, but by no means a part of the power elite. They were the kind who would religiously pray at what came to be called 'visa temples' and saw a passage to the US as the ultimate objective of life.[3] After 2000, the improvement in US-India relations and the easing of visa restrictions on Indians by US authorities seeking to attract more qualified professionals into the US, turned the trickle into a flood. By 2019, it was estimated that there were 4,00,000 Indian students studying in the US.

The Never Returning Indian

From the beginning of humankind till the beginning of the twentieth century, humans have migrated more or less freely, like all other species. This movement was both in response to natural and man-made causes, with pulls and pressures, threats and opportunities shaping it. The spirit of human adventure defined human migration, and so did human tyranny, in the form of slavery and forced labour. After the First World War, governments around the world began restricting the movement of people. Natural migration increasingly gave way to administered movement of people.

Through the twists and turns of history, people of Indian origin ended up inhabiting far corners of the world. Addressing the University of Oxford in July 2005, Prime Minister Manmohan Singh made the point that while it used to be said that the sun never set on the British Empire and Indians had managed to put the adage out of use, the one phenomenon on which the sun would never set 'is the world of the English-speaking people, in which the people of Indian origin are the single-largest component'.

Earlier, in January 2003, Prime Minister Atal Bihari Vajpayee decided to celebrate the love of the overseas Indian community—the Indian 'diaspora' as it came to be increasingly called—for their motherland, by declaring the day Mahatma Gandhi returned home after years of living in Britain and South Africa— 9 January 1915—as the Pravasi Bharatiya Divas (The home-returning Indian Day). This was partly a recognition of the growing economic and diplomatic value of the overseas Indian, especially the growing influence of Indian-Americans in the US. Overseas Indians had not helped India in 1990–91, but by 1999, they had stepped up to the plate and subscribed handsomely to the Resurgent India Bonds (RIBs) floated by the Vajpayee government to raise dollars after the US imposed economic sanctions, responding to India's Pokhran-II nuclear tests.

The Pravasi Bharatiya Divas also fit into the BJP's world view of regarding Hindus—no matter where they lived—as the children of Mother India. Ironically, though, it is a view that mimics the Muslim concept of 'ummah'—a global community united by ideology and sentiment even if divided by political boundaries. Ghazal singer Pankaj Udhas captured the heartfelt sentiment of the overseas Indian with his song '*Chitthi Aayi Hai*' that sent tears flooding down the cheeks of overseas Indians and their families back home. Even though they had left Indian shores, people of Indian origin discovered their emotional connection with the motherland. It was a mix of these sentiments that Atal Bihari Vajpayee tapped into declaring 9 January as Pravasi Bharatiya Divas. However, the 'pravasi Bharatiya' was, like Gandhiji, the home-'returning' Indian, whom Udhas's song touched deeply, while the world of People of Indian Origin (PIOs) and overseas Indians comprised three very different groups.

The group most Indians are familiar with is the NRI—non-resident Indian. These are PIOs with an Indian passport. Then there are PIOs whose ancestors left the subcontinent but who are now citizens of other countries. They should in fact be viewed as a very different kind of NRIs—Not Really Indian. They live in island nations across the Indian, Pacific and Atlantic Oceans, in

Africa and across Asia—some even in Europe. The third category of PIOs lived mainly in the developed, English-speaking countries—the Not-Returning Indians. This group includes those who have secured citizenship of the host country or are waiting to, the green card holders in the US, the permanent residents of Singapore and such like. At the annual Pravasi Bharatiya Divas all three categories of Indians turn up. The ones most often celebrated are in fact the non-pravasi, 'never-returning', Indians.

A recent estimate of the Indian ministry of external affairs puts the total number of PIOs (including NRIs) at over 32 million, with close to 19 million PIOs and over 13 million NRIs living in over 200 countries.[4] The largest numbers, mostly blue- and white-collar workers, are based in the Gulf. The more qualified Indians flock mainly to developed English-speaking countries.[5] Most of the dollar remittances India earns come mainly from white- and blue-collared salariat from the Gulf as well as the less-qualified H1-B workers—the foot soldiers of the knowledge economy. The upper ranks of the better-qualified migrants keep their savings where they live.

It is not surprising that it was in fact an Indian-American, Sabeer Bhatia, an NRI, who developed the first no-cost email service—Hotmail.Com. Telephone calls to family back home in India, and calls from India to the US were found to be the item of highest monthly expenditure for many NRIs and their families back home. Bhatia's pioneering Hotmail, and subsequent internet-based communications, reduced that cost to nothing.

No Indian politician has milked this overseas sentiment of the diaspora for domestic political ends better than Modi. However, he is not the first. The Congress and many regional parties have made use of overseas Indians to enhance their domestic standing. The only difference is that Modi has done so with greater focus and success. In fact, he commandeered the support of scores of overseas Indians in the election campaign of 2014. Professionals like Suresh Gupta and Manoj Ladwa in the UK, Adapa Prasad, Vasudev Patel and Ramesh Shah in the US, and Smita Barooah in Singapore, dedicated themselves to helping Modi's campaign and overseas engagement. The hope of the Indian politician has always been that greater global acceptance and popularity, even if within the Hindu diaspora, is helpful in boosting domestic image. Analysts across disciplines ranging from foreign affairs to economics and politics have offered explanations for Modi's more high-profile engagement of the diaspora. The fact is that many overseas Indians played an important role in mobilizing public opinion and funding and extending logistical support in the run-up to the 2014 Lok Sabha elections. Modi was not yet in control of the party organization and could not rely only on the Delhi-based leadership to help him realize his political goal of becoming PM. Literally hundreds of overseas Indians reportedly took time off their work and academic schedules to help Modi win. Apart from this, there is the RRS/BJP desire to create a global Hindu community.[6]

There is also the other possibility that Modi understood very well the obsession of the Indian middle class—especially its elite sections—with all that is foreign, especially Western. The measure of good quality has for long been that a product should be imported. Foreign branding had also become a measure of success for the middle class. Securing the approval of the overseas Indian may well have been Modi's subliminal desire in his bid to win over India's westernized power elite who were still viewing him as just another provincial politician. Whatever the motivations, the fact is that the diaspora has acquired a high profile in Modi's politics.

If India's economic rise made overseas Indians take pride in their Indian origins, would India's economic slowdown and internal political dissensions create new tensions? The divisions within the overseas Indian community, especially in the US and UK, between pro-Modi and anti-Modi sections has created a new political division within the diaspora that could weaken the case for deploying the diaspora as an instrument of Indian foreign policy. This issue has come to the fore with sections of overseas Indians lobbying US and UK political parties to be critical of the Modi government.

Promoting Brain Drain

As early as in 1972, economist Jagdish Bhagwati co-authored an influential paper on the price developing countries were paying for out-migration of talent to the developed world, especially the US, famously advocating the imposition of a 'brain drain tax'.[7] The idea was that when a professionally qualified person from a developing country migrated to the developed, he would pay a 'brain drain tax', apart from local income tax in the host country, which would be collected by a UN agency and remitted back to the home country of the migrant. The proposal caught the imagination of economists and policymakers, and international conferences were organized through the early 1970s to flesh out the proposal. Pakistan even went ahead and imposed a 'brain drain tax', only to withdraw it within a couple of years.

While nothing came of the proposal, the idea that talent migration from the developing world to the developed was detrimental to the former and something had to be done to compensate the developing country for the investment it had made in creating that talent in the first place, retained some popularity among development economists. The sharp increase in remittances being sent home by migrant populations pushed the tax idea aside since developing countries were now benefiting from foreign currency savings of migrants. Both Prime Minister Manmohan Singh and Prime Minister Modi have referred to overseas Indians—the Indian diaspora—as a 'brain bank' on which the home country can draw. In fact, chairing a lecture by Bhagwati in New Delhi in 2010, Singh spoke of the trade economists' early work on brain drain and added, 'The problem of "brain drain" has been converted into an opportunity of "brain gain". We are drawing on the global "brain bank" of people of Indian origin worldwide.'[8] Modi endorsed this premature celebration of 'brain gain' more cautiously by hopefully claiming to an audience of techies at San Jose, California, in 2015, 'Brain drain is actually a "brain deposit" that will serve India at an appropriate time.'

Over the years, India has elevated the idea of the export of human capital to high principal, actively promoting brain drain. The physical cross-border movement of productive labour can be defined as the export of human capital stock. Skilled workers in the Gulf and H1-B visa holders in the US e-economy are examples of such export. There is then the export of services based on labour performed within Indian borders—like work in back offices based on business process outsourcing by multinational corporations (MNCs) and research work, research work conducted in India by Indians for foreign companies and overseas laboratories. This constitutes a flow of brain power based on human capital stock. Indian trade negotiators have fought hard to secure multilateral, plurilateral and bilateral trade agreements that facilitate such export. There is income flowing into India from all this activity, but brain power is going out, contributing to the building of knowledge economies elsewhere.

Many saw the rising inward foreign currency remittances that had risen from a trickle in the 1980s to US$12 billion by 2000 and close to US$90 billion in 2018 as the reward for export of talent. But the remittances that came home to India came largely from the less-qualified workers and technicians in the Gulf and software professionals on H1-B visas in the US. The IIT graduates and other more talented Indians rarely remitted money home, since they were all absorbed into the host country workforce and settled down in the US. In any case, the issue is not one of converting Indian brain power into dollar remittances. The real 'brain drain' that has been happening now for close to a half century is the out-migration of highly qualified Indians who are today contributing to the knowledge economy of the developed world, leaving the home country bereft of high-quality talent. Names like Satya Nadella and Sundar Pichai are familiar to many Indians but there are hundreds of others like them, contributing their brain power to the creation of wealth and knowledge in the US and other host nations. It is a moot question, though, whether and how the home country can make good use of that talent. Given the bureaucratization and politicization of higher education and the low investment in research and development, both by government and private sector, much of this exported Indian brain power may not have blossomed and been productively utilized at home the way in which it is in the more knowledge-based economies.

A new generation that is coached from early in life on how to qualify to leave India has come into being. This class will rave and rant against any 'Bhagwati tax' on brain drain, for, after all, many among them come from families that routinely evade and avoid taxes even at home. These are not the hard-working professional middle class that put their children through the grind of early-morning tuition before regular schooling hours, followed by evening tutorials. This class represents the upwardly mobile, social ladder-climbing Indians who can afford to pay their way to educational institutions overseas. The former may have been the real 'brain drain' but the latter represent the 'secession of the successful'—India's power elite, who have increasingly hitched their wagon to distant economic engines.

Since 1976, as many as 176 'world schools' have come up across India that offer International Baccalaureate (IB) certificates that help qualify Indian children for graduate education abroad. The fee charged by IB world schools can range from around Rs 75,000 per month to Rs 1,50,000 a month. Many of them employ experienced, elderly British and European teachers retired from institutions in their countries. The rising number of such schools and enrolment is partly due to the increasing number of professional Indians working around the world leaving their children back home in India to study at boarding schools. Many IB schools are indeed such boarding schools. Once schooling is over, their non-resident parents take the child away to some college overseas for higher education. Many others at these schools come from financially well-off families—both the 'old wealthy' and the 'nouveau riche'—who prepare their young for higher education overseas.

It is not just the IB schools that prepare students to go abroad for higher education. Data collected from a couple of high-profile private schools in New Delhi show that while around the turn of the century around 20 per cent of school-leaving children went abroad for graduate studies, this number shot up to close to 50 per cent by 2010 and to 70 per cent in 2019. In December 2020 the *Indian Express* reported the results of a study it had conducted that showed that over half of the first rankers in Class X and Class XII examinations (conducted by the Central Board of Secondary Education and the Council for Indian School Certification Examination) during the two decades of 1996–2015 had migrated and were employed overseas, mostly in the US.[9] While the largest numbers still go to the US, other popular destinations include Britain, Canada, Australia and Singapore. This flight of students does not necessarily constitute brain drain since many of them pay their way to admission at private colleges abroad because of their inability to get admission based on merit into public institutions in India. It is in response to this demand that the number of private educational institutions, with affiliations to foreign institutions, has been rising in India.

Rather than the government earning any income through a Bhagwati-like 'brain drain tax' on emigrating Indians, the latter end up paying annually billions of dollars in tuition fees to overseas institutions. An RBI estimate placed the figure at close to $3 billion in 2018, but an earlier study of Assocham placed the amount at three to four times that number, anywhere between $10 to $13 billion.[10] The Assocham study estimates that around 1,50,000 students go abroad for post-school education every year. Assuming the length of stay is three years, the number of students at any one time studying abroad is around 4,50,000. Some students go abroad to study, paying a lot of money, because they can afford to. Some go because they have not been able to secure admission into any good institution in India, given the paucity of good-quality higher education institutions. Some go because their families see no future for them in India.

Flight of the Elite

Reacting to the change wrought in American society by Reaganomics and what came to be called 'neo-liberal' economics, with its mythology of the benefits of economic growth and wealth creation 'trickling down' from the rich to the poor, economist Robert Reich wrote a sharp and influential polemic in January 1991 on the growing social divide in America, drawing attention to what he dubbed the 'secession of the successful'.[11] After George Bush Sr lost his re-election bid despite his 'Read my lips—no new taxes' promise, Reich became secretary of labour in the Bill Clinton administration. Following up his *New York Times* (*NYT*) essay with an influential book, *The Work of Nations*, Reich observed that this secession:

> 'Is more dramatic because the highest earners now inhabit a different economy from other Americans. The new elite is linked by jet, modem, fax, satellite and fiber-optic cable to the great commercial and recreational centers of the world, but it is not particularly connected to the rest of the nation. That is because the work this group does is becoming less tied to the activities of other Americans. Most of their jobs consist of analyzing and manipulating symbols—words, numbers or visual images. Among the most prominent of these "symbolic analysts" are management consultants, lawyers, software and design engineers, research scientists, corporate executives, financial advisers, strategic planners, advertising executives, television and movie producers, and other workers whose job titles include terms like "strategy," "planning," "consultant," "policy," "resources" or "engineer".'[12]

Reich concluded that the retreat of this class into their suburban enclaves and their overseas tax havens signified the 'secession of the successful'.

This has been a familiar binary in India—the divide between India and Bharat—and much has been written over the years. Diplomat-writer-politician Pavan Varma wrote evocatively and passionately about the 'aggressive, selfish, insular' lifestyle of the urban rich, raising high walls around their homes to cut themselves off from the milieu around, securing water from borewells within the walls and electricity from diesel-powered generators.[13] The Indian power elite had seceded from their surroundings. Varma noted in passing a phenomenon that has since not just multiplied but has also transformed. 'Some of the best and brightest students study here but their dominant interest is to go West, to somehow enhance their marketability by acquiring a Western degree.' Since the time Varma wrote this, hundreds of thousands of bright young Indians as well as the wealthy ones who could afford it have left India to study overseas, and to try and settle down there.

There have been many waves of migration out of India. The post-Independence migration gathered momentum only in the 1980s. Till the turn of the century, the assumption was that most would return home some day. That assumption still holds for migrants to the Gulf, especially non-Muslims, because of the nature of Gulf societies and the desire of these migrants to retain their family links to India. It no longer holds for Indians migrating to the developed English-speaking world. Well into the 1990s, it was expected that Indians living in the West would return home. They rarely do so now.

More interestingly, it is no longer the middle-class migrant that prefers to stay put in the developed world. Even children from the business class have begun to live abroad and visit India when they need to. New residence and tax laws allow promoters of Indian companies to reside abroad, as NRIs, while remaining fully in control of their businesses in India. A typical NRI businessman living in a fancy home with a lovely garden outside London would have his children studying at a boarding school in Oxfordshire, his wife shopping at Harrods, and would only visit India for board meetings and other corporate formalities. Many business families have come to operate multiple homes with different members of the family residing in different places overseas. The most popular alternative homes of Indian business families outside India are to be found in England, Singapore, Dubai and Switzerland. In February 2021, the *Times of India* reported a study on 'global wealth migration' conducted by Henley & Partners that showed that India topped the world in the emigration of the wealthy in 2019 with nearly 7000 high net worth individuals (HNWI) relocating out of India. In 2020 there was a 62 per cent rise over 2019 in the number of enquiries made by Indian HNWIs planning to leave the country. An increasing number are seeking investment-linked migration.[14]

It should surprise no one that in the midst of the preoccupation with the Covid pandemic, the virtual paralysis of the economy, the plight of internal migrants caught between home and hearth, the Union finance ministry found the time to address the concern of the NRIs 'stuck in India due to the lockdown' so that their tax status would not be hurt by their extended stay in India and their inability to fly out in time to their tax shelter![15]

Since 2009–10, the RBI has been publishing more detailed information on outward foreign exchange remittances from India made by resident Indians through its window Liberalised Remittance Scheme (LRS). Data is available on forex outflow on account of education abroad, foreign travel, maintenance of close relatives overseas and medical treatment abroad. The total annual outflow through the LRS route in the five-year period, 2009–14, was US$1.07 billion. After rising fourfold in 2014–15 to $4.62, the sum doubled to $8.17 bn in 2015–16, $11.33 bn in 2017–18, $13.78 bn in 2018–19 and to as much as $18.75 billion in 2019–20. Resident Indians are taking increasing amounts of dollars out of India, with the annual average outflow rising from a mere $1.07 bn in 2009–14 to $11.33 in 2014–20. Two items on the list have come to dominate the total—payments for studies abroad and for maintenance of close relatives. Taken together, these two items accounted for an average of around 30 per cent of outward remittances under LRS in the period 2009–14. In the period 2014–20, the share of these two items accounted for 47 per cent of outflows. The rising numbers of school-leaving children paying for graduate education overseas in order to eventually migrate and their rising share in India's outward foreign exchange remittances are as good a proxy as any for the secession of the successful.

Till the 1990s, professionals working overseas and opting to take up assignments in India would move back home with family in tow. Their children would move from a school in Chevy Chase, Washington DC, to one in Vasant Kunj, New Delhi. Few saw an appointment to a senior position in government as a sabbatical from a tenured job in the US. But in more recent years it has become commonplace for Indians resident abroad to take a break from employment overseas to spend a little time in India advising the country how it should run itself and in the process burnishing their biodata to return to the US for better jobs in multilateral organizations on Wall Street or at Ivy League institutions. Most senior government officials, diplomats, politicians and business persons are increasingly making sure that their children study, live and work overseas. The parents may be part of India's power elite, but the future of their children is in the hands of a foreign government. The next generation has all but seceded from India.

Former British Prime Minister Theresa May described the class aptly when she said, 'Today, too many people in positions of power behave as though they have more in common with international elites than with the people down the road, the people they employ, the people they pass on the street. But if you believe you are a citizen of the world, you are a citizen of nowhere.'[16] While nationalism tinged with pride in their Hindu civilizational heritage has gripped the Indian middle class at home and overseas, Modi's political constituency, and the middle class is happy to mouth slogans like 'Vocal for Local' aimed at establishing an 'Atmanirbhar Bharat', the prayers at the temple of the visa gods continue.

12

A Changing Balance of Power

The smoothness of the transfer of power in British India and from most Indian kingdoms to the new Indian state enabled the elites of pre-Independence India to continue to enjoy much of the power they had even in the new republic. While the constitution bestowed new rights on the hitherto repressed and downtrodden, the balance of social, political and economic power remained with the traditional elites—the upper castes, the landed gentry and the emerging business class. The INC became the umbrella party of the business, the peasantry and the middle classes, with the communists and socialists rallying whatever opposition there was to the left of the Congress. A feeble attempt was made to build a right-wing opposition, in the form of the Swatantra Party, but intra-elite differences led to its quiet decline, with G.D. Birla telling his business colleagues, 'Swatantra politics are not good businessmen's politics.'

The real alternative to the Congress came from regions and castes that jostled for greater space within the 'Congress System'— Dravidian mobilization in Tamil Nadu challenged not just the dominance of the Tamil upper castes but of the Hindi-speaking north-Indian-dominated Congress. In Uttar Pradesh—Nehru's own home turf and the epicentre of Congress power—the party's secular decline began with the departure of the Jats, under

Charan Singh's leadership, then the Yadavs, under Mulayam Singh's, and, finally, the Dalits and Muslims, under Mayawati. Once Brahmins and Kayasthas had also crossed over to the BJP, the Congress was left with Raebareli and Amethi, the Nehru family's pocket boroughs. The rise of the Communist Party in Bengal, Kerala and Andhra Pradesh had a touch of regionalism, with language and culture playing a big part in mass mobilization. By the 1980s, the decline of the Congress was largely on account of the rise of regional and caste-based political parties. Walking out of the large Congress umbrella, its voters splintered, gathering under many foldable ones.

The decline of the Congress in a large number of states also meant that the regional elite shifted their loyalties to regional parties. In Bengal, Marwari businessmen began to get used to Jyoti Basu's leadership, just as the Brahmins and Chettiars of Tamil Nadu learnt to live with Dravidian leadership. In UP, Dalit leader Mayawati managed to win over Brahmins. Losing its support among a rising regional elite, a shrinking Congress depended increasingly on the support of big business and the Lutyens' elite.

The end of the Congress era was followed by an 'era of coalitions' whose caste, class and regional composition varied over the years. After the 'centralizing' leaderships of Nehru, Indira and Rajiv, three 'consensus-based' leaderships followed with Narasimha Rao, Vajpayee and Manmohan Singh. All these political transitions and the shifts in power relations were reasonably smooth. Barring the aberration of the Emergency, the democratic process proceeded smoothly even as democratic institutions became weaker. The political power elite corrupted and captured all the institutions of the state—the bureaucracy, the police, the judiciary and the media. Aborted land reforms preserved landlord power, tariff protection and the Licence-Permit-Control Raj sustained monopolies and public expenditure, and subsidies kept the middle class happy.

Despite all these shortcomings, the economy performed reasonably well. The average annual rate of growth of national income rose from 3.5 per cent during 1950–80 to 5.5 per cent in

1980–2000 and 7.5 per cent thereafter. A rising economy created
wealth that was shared unequally across regions, castes and classes,
further empowering the elite. Those still dissatisfied with the pace
of change and extent of opportunity emigrated. Through this era
of rising economic growth, the Congress failed to remobilize itself
and re-emerge as the dominant national party, nor was the left able
to enter the space vacated by the Congress. Rather, regional and
caste-based parties, on the one hand, and the 'Hindu–Hindi' BJP,
on the other, occupied the Congress space.

The BJP had the option of becoming a Congress-like umbrella
party, seeking allies among regional parties. That was the path
Vajpayee chose to take. His defeat in 2004 was taken as proof of
failure of such an enterprise. The RSS and the BJP hardliners opted
for Hindu majoritarianism. Once the BJP secured a majority of its
own in Parliament and across several states, it chose to implement
its Hindutva manifesto. What made this shift possible was the
fact that a growing aspirational middle class from an increasingly
urbanizing India was ready to accept the BJP's Hindutva agenda in
the name of nationalism. The BJP then secured agrarian support,
adopting a strategy first tried by Indira Gandhi in the 1970s, of
turning the terms of trade between industry and agriculture in
the latter's favour. It then made a distinction between small and
medium business and big business, winning both of them over with
different policy instruments. With time, Modi has succeeded in
ensuring that the power elite that constituted the foundation of
Congress power would now bolster BJP's.

The BJP targets every institution that the Congress had
managed to bend to do its bidding, now including non-government
organizations (NGOs) and the 'new media', creating an intrusive
state that many view as the thin end of an authoritarian one. If
Indira Gandhi sought a 'committed civil service', so does Narendra
Modi. The police and other paramilitary forces, the investigative
agencies and the intelligence apparatus have long learnt to kneel
when asked to bend by the political masters of the day. In seeking

an accommodative judiciary, the BJP is once again learning from Indira's Emergency precedent. Be it crony capitalists, media barons or the leadership of the armed forces, every member of the power elite accommodates itself to the new power dispensation.

Ideology, Power and National Interest

If there is a difference between the old 'Congress System' and the new BJP system, it lies in the latter's ideology-driven power politics. The Congress thrived as an all-inclusive party adopting and adapting political platforms with the sole purpose of securing power. It remained committed to pluralism, but its commitment to values such as secularism and socialism was contingent upon their political benefits. The BJP, under Modi, also seeks power and all the perks of power, but it has an overriding commitment to the ideology of Hindu majoritarianism. Unveiling the statue of Swami Vivekananda on JNU campus, in November 2020, Modi did say 'One thing that has done great harm to the democratic system of our country is to give priority to ideology over national interest.'[1] However, it was not clear if he was only referring to the ideologies of the left and liberal, that the BJP has campaigned against, or if his message was also aimed at his own party's bigoted ideologues.

Even as the BJP tries to build a wider national base with Hindutva, it has to contend with the interests of a regional power elite. While a weak left has not been able to mobilize on the basis of class, powerful regional leaders have been able to use caste and language as buffers to ward off the challenge of Hindu consolidation. It is in dealing with all these complexities that Modi has used his anti-elitism, attacking 'Lutyens' Delhi', to consolidate the BJP's hold. For how long, remains to be seen. It will depend critically on how the economy performs over the remainder of his term, for that is what matters to every segment of the people and the power elite.

The elite in a multilayered, multidimensional society like India's would of course not be a homogenous group either in social composition or cultural outlook. Unlike many societies of the West and the East, India is defined by its plurality and diversity. Even Hinduism is defined by its plurality. Diversity and plurality of experience is inherent to a civilizational nation of continental proportions. However, all societies are hierarchical and power relations are defined by these social, cultural and economic hierarchies. What makes India different, if at all, is the multiplicity of its hierarchies. Caste, class, language, region, ethnicity and even the colour of skin define the hierarchies of power. Even Dalits— scheduled castes in the Constitution—now argue on who among them has benefited more from affirmative action. Many, not all, of these hierarchical structures have endured despite significant social, political and economic change within the framework of a democracy. Caste certainly has, even if attitudes and even equations are changing. While class endures despite half a century of democratic socialism, language remains an important marker of power and elitism.

The sources and use of power differ between rural and urban India and across different regions of India. Given the diversity of Indian social structure, one can identify a 'regional' elite, a 'national' elite and a 'globalized' elite, each with different caste composition and different cultural practices, social values and even economic capabilities. Thus, it is possible to suggest that the morphology of the power elite outlined here may not fully capture the complexity of the Indian reality. Unlike countries that have experienced social revolutions or military occupation that have in turn had a lasting impact on social relations, upsetting existing hierarchies and creating new ones, India's 'gradual revolution' has ensured that long-standing social hierarchies have endured. New layers of social and cultural practice rest uneasily on old ones. The transition from a colonial and feudal past to a democratic and republican present has not obliterated these old hierarchies. The big business and the big landlords of the pre-Independence period continue to be the wealthy of today, even if new groups have entered their ranks. Within this overall structure of continuity in power relations there has also been some change, as we have noted in this book.

Radical social revolutions disrupt, destroy and rebuild. Gradual and consensual change, as we see in India, reshapes and reconfigures. In each epoch a nation's social, political and economic elite tries to control change, preserving its privilege and power, by promoting a grand idea that it is capable of defining and deploying to ensure its dominance. The British Empire was run on that principle. A small minority of aliens operated a vast empire by asserting the hegemony of an idea that the majority came to accept. After securing Independence, the builders of the republic wrote a constitution that enabled the nation's power elite to remain in positions of economic privilege, while granting equality of constitutional status to all. The ideas were new and in consonance with the times—democracy, equality, socialism, secularism—but their implementation was such as to preserve existing relations of power and privilege.

Over the years, new ideas have been deployed to perpetuate old hierarchies while managing change at the margin. The constitutional derecognition of untouchability and reservations for the scheduled castes and tribes has wrought major social changes, yet it has not altered the basic structure of power and the nature of elitism defined by caste as an institution. Similarly, all manner of welfare schemes and social protection have empowered workers, but the class relations between owners of capital and the owners of labour power endure. The spread of education has empowered new social groups, and yet access to education remains a privilege.

Democratic socialism and state-funded development ensured political stability during what has come to be known as the Nehruvian era. When that process ran out of steam, technological change and economic liberalization unleashed pent-up energies in the rural and urban economies, fuelling a new phase of

development. The Green Revolution in agriculture, in the
1970s, and trade and industrial policy liberalization, in the 1980s
and 1990s, increased incomes and empowered new social classes,
providing the social context for the new turn in Indian economic
and foreign policy after 1991.[2]

The post-Nehruvian paradigm, 1991 to 2014, has also run its
course. If the Nehruvian era created and sustained its own power
elite, so did the post-Nehruvian era. Across fields of business,
culture, media and politics, new caste and social groups rose to
social dominance and acquired political power. As we noted earlier,
the names among the top twenty business groups in the year 2000
were significantly different from the top twenty of 1980. Political
parties and leaders unheard of in 1980 had become national players
by 2000. The big guns of the 1970s media had fallen silent by
the end of the century while new brands and banners had come
to dominate. It was a period of significant change, yet the basic
principles of the republic enshrined in the Constitution had not yet
been questioned.

That paradigm, too, is beginning to shift. A significant majority
no longer swears either by 'socialism' or 'secularism'. Prime
Minister Modi's rise to political dominance is now increasingly
viewed as the beginning of a second republic, if not a third. The
assertion of Hindutva in politics, society and culture and the pursuit
of an 'Atmanirbhar Bharat' is said to define a 'New India'. How
deep and enduring this change will be remains to be seen, but it is
already reshaping the hierarchy of power and the notion of elites
and elitism.

Is BJP really turning India into a Hindu nation, or is the
focus on religion a tactic used by the politically and economically
powerful elite to hide their failure in ensuring sustained and
equitable economic growth and development for all? Is the
Hindutva assertion a moment of awakening of a dormant people,
or an attempt to prevent that awakening by an elite intent on
retaining political power, even as the poor bear the brunt of

poverty, ignorance and disease? Our analysis of power and elitism raises such questions.

All populist ideologies blunt the rough edges of reality. Be it Maoism during the Chinese Cultural Revolution and Xi Jinping Thought today, Islamic radicalism in the highly unequal West Asian feudal kingdoms and in a military-dominated Pakistan, or Trump's call for a White-dominated America, ideological movements of various kinds—some secular, some religious—appear to be ways in which an old elite seek to retain power, unable to deliver on their promise of development and justice.

Even if the ideologues of the RSS sincerely believe in Hindutva, is the power play of Modi and Shah really defined by the ideology of Hindu nationalism, or is it merely aimed at securing and retaining power? How then is the BJP's Hindutva any different from Indira Gandhi's socialism and secularism, whose aim was merely to capture and retain power, reshaping a social reality with the hope of perpetuating not just individual power but the power of the social classes that support the leader? Has an old and enduring elite found a new idea to retain hegemony?

If wealth and power is all that the power elite seek, ideology becomes nothing more than a veil. Beneath the surface of rising communal consciousness, long-enduring inequalities and inequities remain, and the power elite seek to retain their privileges in the face of the challenge these pose. Even as a new cultural nationalism seeks to unite a diverse society, it also has the effect of papering over enduring social and economic divisions. The success of the democratic experiment has been that it has managed to ensure political and social stability despite economic inequality. The elite are often frustrated by the gradual pace of change and those who feel alienated have successfully seceded, either leaving the country or retreating into enclaves that have been created to prevent the dualism of a 'Bharat and India' from destabilizing the republic. One must recognize that it is this very gradualism of change that has not just ensured political and social stability, but also the perpetuation of the social and economic foundations on which the elite have constructed their powers and privileges.

Many years ago a development administrator familiar with the ground reality of change in a traditional society suggested that those who seek rapid and speedy change do not quite appreciate the fact that Indians are quite amenable to gradual change as long as that change is in a positive direction for their own families and for themselves.[3] Contemporary India may envy China's high rates of growth and rapid transformation; however, that order of change can destabilize an inherently unequal society seeking to function within a democratic system. Gradualness of change and empowerment has the advantage of not drawing attention to the extremes of inequality and the concentration of wealth and power that rapid growth entails, as it has in so many fast-growing economies. The power of the Indian elite has endured because, notwithstanding the vulgarity of wealth, the corruption of politics, the prejudices of casteism and communalism and the secession of the successful, a vast majority has come to accept the gradualness of change in their own lives. Their acquiescence in this gradualness contributes to the resilience of the power elite.

Acknowledgements

I should first thank Ranjana Sengupta of Penguin Random House for persuading me to write this book. I am equally grateful to Meru Gokhale for her encouragement and support as I made my way through multiple drafts. I owe a special debt of gratitude to Francine Frankel and Harsh Sethi for patiently reading through an earlier draft and suggesting improvements. Aparna Kumar has been a very efficient editor and so my thanks are due to her too.

Most of this book was written during the months of the Covid-19 lockdown. I am deeply grateful to Rama and Tanvika for all their love and support in managing our household and working together through the long lockdown months. This was also a difficult period for the family because I lost both my father and father-in-law, two important intellectual influences on me, in June 2020. To them, and my mother, Seshu, and mother-in-law, Shanta, I owe more than just this book.

Notes

Preface

1. Saeed Naqvi, *The Last Brahmin Prime Minister of India*, Har-Anand Publications, New Delhi, 1996.
2. Sanjaya Baru, 'Economic Policy and the Development of Capitalism in India: The Role of Regional Capitalists and Regional Political Parties', Francine Frankel, Zoya Hasan, Rajeev Bhargava and Balveer Arora (ed.), *Transforming India: Social and Political Dynamics of Democracy*, Oxford University Press, New Delhi, 2000. The central thesis of this essay was taken forward in an interesting book by Harish Damodaran, *India's New Capitalists: Caste, Business, and Industry in a Modern Nation*, Permanent Black, New Delhi, 2008.

A Cultural Revolution?

Chapter 1: Bombard the Headquarters

1. 'Anil Ambani Lifts Modi to the League of "King of Kings"', *Indian Express*, 12 January 2013.
2. 'PM Modi's Only Regret, "I Could Not Win Over Lutyens' Delhi"' *Economic Times*, 2 January 2019.
3. From Rashtriya Swayamsevak Sangh website, www.rss.org.
4. Kancha Ilaiah, 'Dalits and English', anveshi.org.in.
5. Edgar Snow, *The Long Revolution*, Hutchinson, London, 1973, p. 66.
6. Kenneth Lieberthal, 'The Great Leap Forward and the Split in the Yan'an Leadership, 1958–65', in Roderick MacFarquhar (ed.), *The Politics of China, 1949–89*, Cambridge University Press, USA, 1993, p. 124.

7. MacFarquhar, 1993, p. 298.
8. Snow, 1973, pp. 69–70.
9. Ibid.
10. Ram Manohar Lohia, 'Towards the Destruction of Castes and Classes', *Lokayan Bulletin*, September-October 1996, cited in D.L. Sheth, 'Ram Manohar Lohia on Caste in Indian Politics', in Ghanshyam Shah (Editor), *Caste and Democratic Politics in India*, Permanent Black, New Delhi, 2002, p. 122.
11. C. Wright Mills, *The Power Elite*, 1956, p. 3.
12. Bertrand Russell, *Power: A New Social Analysis*, Unwin Paperbacks, London, 1985, p. 11.
13. Raj Kamal Jha and Ravish Tiwari, 'Khan Market Gang Hasn't Created My Image, 45 Years of Tapasya Has . . . You Cannot Dismantle It', *Indian Express*, 13 May 2019.

Chapter 2: Modi's Metaphors

1. Rajmohan Gandhi, *The Good Boatman: A Portrait of Gandhi*, Viking, Penguin Books India, 1995, p. 370.
2. Rajni Kothari, 'The Congress "System" in India', *Asian Survey*, Vol. 4, No. 12, University of California Press, December 1964, pp. 116–117.
3. Francine Frankel, *India's Political Economy 1947–1977: The Gradual Revolution*, Oxford University Press, Delhi, 1980.
4. Ranjana Sengupta, *Delhi Metropolitan: The Making of an Unlikely City*, Penguin Books India, Delhi, 2007.
5. Pavan Varma, 'Lutyens' Elite and English Apartheid', *Deccan Chronicle*, 29 July 2018.
6. Ranjana Sengupta, 'Literature's Delhi', *Seminar*, 2002.
7. 'Rahul Gandhi Slams Sam Pitroda for His "Hua Toh Hua" Remark over 1984 Riots', *Hindustan Times*, 10 May 2019.
8. Personal correspondence with Jairam Ramesh, 30 July 2018.
9. 'Saving the Nehru Memorial Museum and Library', *Economic and Political Weekly*, Vol. 44, No. 26/27, 27 June–10 July 2009, p. 2.
10. Kal Friese, 'Modifying Lutyens', *India Today*, 23 May 2020.
11. Gautam Bhatia, 'Daring to Recast a Vision in Stone', *The Hindu*, 31 December 2019.
12. Sarah Cascone, 'Anish Kapoor Slams India's Prime Minister and His "Fascist Government" for Planning to "Destroy" Delhi's Historic Parliament Building', news.artnet.com.

Digression into Concepts

Chapter 3: Power and Elitism

1. Kalecki, Michal, 'Observations on Social and Economic Aspects of "Intermediate Regimes"', in Kalecki, Michal, *Collected Works of M. Kalecki,* Vol. V, Clarendon Press, Oxford, 1993.
2. Max Weber, *Max Weber: Essays in Sociology* (translated and edited by H.H. Gerth and C. Wright Mills), Oxford University Press, New York, 1946, pp. 179–80.
3. Bertrand Russell, *Power: A New Social Analysis,* Unwin Paperbacks, London, 1985, Chapter 2.
4. Russell, 1985, Chapter 3.
5. Russell, 1985, p. 11.
6. Vilfredo Pareto, *Mind and Society: A Treatise on General Sociology,* Jonathan Cape, London, 1935.
7. Gaetano Mosca, *The Ruling Class,* McGraw-Hill, New York, 1939, p. 50.
8. K. Marx and F. Engels, 'The Ruling Class and the Ruling Ideas', in K. Marx and F. Engels, *Collected Works,* Vol. 5, Progress Publishers, Moscow, 1976, p. 44.
9. Antonio Gramsci, *Selections from the Prison Notebooks,* (Translated and edited by Quintin Hoare and Geoffrey Nowell Smith), International Publishers, New York, 1971, p. 57.
10. A useful summary of academic literature is offered by Surinder Jodhka and Jules Naudet in their editors' 'Introduction' to the book *Mapping the Elite: Power, Privilege and Inequality,* Oxford University Press, 2019, pp. 1–33. Some of the essays in this volume present interesting case studies of elitism in India.
11. C. Wright Mills, *The Power Elite,* New York, 1956, Chapter 1.
12. Mills, 1956, p. 11.
13. Mills, 1956, p. 9.
14. Mills, 1956, p. 18.
15. Pierre Bourdieu, *Distinction: A Social Critique of the Judgement of Taste,* Harvard University Press, Cambridge, USA, 1984, pp. 482–83.
16. Swapan Dasgupta, 'What the Spin Doctor Could Recommend for Vajpayee', *India Today,* 11 January 1999.
17. P.V. Narasimha Rao, *The Insider,* Viking, Penguin Books India, New Delhi, 1998.
18. Andre Beteille, *Caste, Class and Power: Changing Patterns of Stratification in a Tanjore Village,* University of California Press, Los Angeles, 1965.

19. M.S.A. Rao, 'Some Conceptual Issues in the Study of Caste, Class and Ethnicity and Dominance', in Francine Frankel and M.S.A. Rao (ed.), *Dominance and State Power in Modern India: Decline of a Social Order*, Volume 1, Oxford University Press, New Delhi, 1989, pp. 40–41.
20. Srinivas, M.N., *Religion and Society amongst the Coorgs of South India*, Clarendon Press, Oxford, 1952.
21. Francine Frankel, 'Conclusion', in Frankel and Rao, 1989, p. 516.

Chapter 4: Social Dominance and Political Power

1. The four tiers of the varna caste pyramid in descending order are Brahmins, Kshatriyas, Vaishyas and Shudras. The Dalit or Scheduled Castes, the so-called 'outcastes' remain subordinated outside the varna classification. Brahmins are the priestly caste, Kshatriyas the warrior caste, Vaishyas are merchants and moneylenders, and Shudras are various types of working people ranging from land-tilling peasants, including rich peasants, to weavers and carpenters.
2. See, for example, Imtiaz Ahmed (ed.), *Caste and Social Stratification among Muslims*, Manohar Book Service, Delhi, 1973; *Encyclopedia Britannica*, 'Christian Caste: India', www.britannica.com.
3. D.L. Sheth, 'Caste and Class: Social Reality and Political Representations', Ghanshyam Shah (Editor), *Caste and Democratic Politics in India*, Permanent Black, New Delhi, 2002, p. 212.
4. See Ghanshyam Shah, 'The BJP and Backward Castes in Gujarat', in Ghanshyam Shah, 2002, p. 295.
5. Rajmohan Gandhi, *Modern South India: A History from the 17th Century to Our Times*, Aleph Book Co., New Delhi, 2018, Chapter 3.
6. Frankel, 1989, p. 2.
7. Ram Manohar Lohia, 'Towards the Destruction of Castes and Classes', *Lokayan Bulletin*, September-October 1996, cited in D.L. Sheth, 'Ram Manohar Lohia on Caste in Indian Politics', Ghanshyam Shah, 2002, p. 131.
8. Lohia, 1996, p. 122.
9. Kancha Ilaiah, 'Dalits and English', *Deccan Herald*, 14 February 2011.
10. Fukuyama, Francis, *Political Order and Political Decay: From the Industrial Revolution to the Globalisation of Democracy*, Profile Books, London, 2014, p. 464.
11. Yogendra Yadav, 'Electoral Politics in the Times of Change: India's Third Electoral System, 1989–99', *Economic and Political Weekly*, 34:34/35, 21 August–3 September 1999.

12. See, for example, Chiranjib Sen, *Curbing Crony Capitalism in India*, Working Paper No. 5, Azim Premji University, April 2017; Raghuram Rajan, 'Right Guy at Wrong Time', *HT Mint*, 13 August 2012; Aseema Sinha, 'India's Porous State: Blurred Boundaries and the Evolving Business-State Relationship', in Christophe Jaffrelot, et al., (ed.), *Business and Politics in India*, Oxford University Press, New Delhi, 2019.

13. K. Srinivasulu, *Caste, Class and Social Articulation in Andhra Pradesh: Mapping Differential Regional Trajectories*, Working Paper No. 179, Overseas Development Institute, London, September 2002.

14. Lohia, 1996, p. 113.

15. M.N. Srinivas, *Religion and Society among the Coorgs of South India*, Oxford University Press, New Delhi, 1952.

16. D.L. Sheth, 'Caste and Class: Social Reality and Political Representations', Shah, 2002, p. 221.

The Wielders of Power

Chapter 5: Business and the State

1. Mills, 1956, p. 165.
2. Mills, 1956, p. 167.
3. See, for example, Chiranjib Sen, *Curbing Crony Capitalism in India*, Working Paper No. 5, Azim Premji University, April 2017.
4. See, for example, Claude Markovits, *Indian Business and Nationalist Politics, 1931–39: Indigenous Capitalist Class and the Rise of the Congress Party*, Cambridge University Press, UK, 1985, Chapters 4 and 5; Sanjaya Baru, *The Political Economy of Sugar: State Intervention and Structural Change*, Oxford University Press, New Delhi, 1990, Chapter 3.
5. Baru, 1990, p. 65.
6. See, for example, A.K. Bagchi, *Private Investment in India 1900–1939*, Cambridge University Press, 1972; Francine Frankel, *India's Political Economy 1947–2004: The Gradual Revolution*, Princeton University Press, 2005; Lloyd and Susanne Rudolph, *In Pursuit of Lakshmi: The Political Economy of the Indian State*, University of Chicago Press, 1987.
7. Markovits, 1985, p. 177.
8. The document was titled *A Brief Memorandum Outlining a Plan of Economic Development for India (Vols I and II.)*, Penguin, London, 1945. The original document is reprinted in Sanjaya Baru and Meghnad Desai (Editors), *The Bombay Plan: Blueprint for Economic Resurgence*, Rupa Publications, New Delhi, 2018.

9. Sanjaya Baru, 'Business, Government and Politics: From Plan to Plea', Baru and Desai, 2018, pp. 124–47.

10. Amal Sanyal, 'The Making of a Mythical Forerunner', Baru and Desai, 2018, pp. 19–63.

11. Amal Sanyal, 'The Making of a Mythical Forerunner', Baru and Desai, 2018, p. 42.

12. See Baru and Desai, 2018, p. 91.

13. Baru and Desai, 2018, p. 92.

14. Baru and Desai, 2018, pp. 95–97.

15. Baru and Desai, 2018, p. 95.

16. Baru and Desai, 2018, p. 324

17. Markovits, 1985, p. 180.

18. On L'affaire Teja, see Sumit Mitra, 'Jayanti Dharma Teja: An Unheralded Comeback', *India Today*, 31 March 1983.

19. Santhanam Committee report cited in Stanley A. Kochanek, *Business and Politics in India*, University of California Press, 1974, p. 292.

20. Kochanek, 1974, pp. 36–37.

21. Both quotes cited in H.L. Erdman, *Swatantra Party and Indian Conservatism*, Cambridge University Press, UK, 1967, pp. 172–73.

22. *Mitrokhin Archive II and the Indian Congress Party*; Also see: Dilip Bobb, 'Book on KGB Unveils Russian Agency's Ops in India during Cold War', *India Today*, 3 October 2005; *The Soviets in India: Moscow's Penetration Programme*, CIA Archives, archives.

23. Mitu Sengupta, 'Making the State Change Its Mind—The IMF, the World Bank, and the Politics of India's Market Reforms', *New Political Economy*, Vol. 14, No. 4, 2009.

24. Constance Roger, 'Indo-French Cooperation: Friends in Need or Friends Indeed', *IPCS Research Papers,* Institute of Peace and Conflict Studies, New Delhi, India. March 2007, pp. 6–7.

25. Sanjaya Baru, 'Economic Policy and the Development of Capitalism in India: The Role of Regional Capitalists and Political Parties', Francine Frankel, Zoya Hasan, Rajeev Bhargava and Balveer Arora (Editors), *Transforming India: Social and Political Dynamics of Democracy*, Oxford University Press, New Delhi, 2000.

26. P.V. Narasimha Rao, *The Insider*, Viking Penguin India, 1998, p. 675.

27. For an analysis of the role of caste in the rise of Andhra communists, see Selig S. Harrison, 'Caste and the Communists', *American Political Science Review*, Vol. 50, No. 2, June 1956, pp. 378–404.

28. Sanjaya Baru, 'Capitalism in Agriculture and Growth of Manufacturing: Some Issues with Reference to Andhra Pradesh', in Y.V. Krishna Rao

(Editor), *Peasant Farming and Growth of Manufacturing in Indian Agriculture*, Visalandhra Publishers, Vijayawada, 1984, pp. 207–30.

29. Baru, 2000; Harish Damodaran, *India's New Capitalists: Caste, Business and Industry in a Modern Nation*, Permanent Black, India, 2008.

30. Dennis J. Rajakumar and John S. Henley, *Growth and Persistence of Large Business Groups in India*.

31. IIFL Wealth Management Ltd and Hurun India Rich List 2020, *The Richest People in India*, 29 September 2020.

32. A good recent collection is Christophe Jaffrelot, Atul Kohli and Kanta Murali (Editors), *Business and Politics in India*, Oxford University Press, New Delhi, 2019.

33. Josy Joseph, *The Feast of Vultures: The Hidden Business of Democracy in India*, HarperCollins Publishers, New Delhi, 2018. Other books include Edward Luce, *In Spite of the Gods: The Rise of Modern India*, Abacus, London, 2006; James Crabtree, *The Billionaire Raj*, HarperCollins, India, 2018.

34. Rahul Devulapalli, 'Ties with Ambani, Lobbying, Dissolution of Council: What Jagan's Choice of RS Candidates Reveals', *Week*, 10 March 2020.

35. Quoted in Aseema Sinha, 'India's Porous State: Blurred Boundaries and the Evolving Business-State Relationship', in Jaffrelot, et al, (Ed.), 2019. pp. 88–92.

36. Sinha, 2019, pp. 58–68.

37. Joseph, 2018, Chapters 5 and 7.

38. N. Sahoo and N. Tiwari, 'Financing Elections in India: A Scrutiny of Corporate Donation', *India Matters*, April 2019, Observer Research Foundation, New Delhi.

Chapter 6: The Landed and the Feudals

1. P.V. Narasimha Rao, *The Insider*, Viking, Penguin Books India, 1998, p. 304.

2. Rao, 1998, p. 766.

3. Baru and Desai, 2018, p. 307.

4. Rudolph and Rudolph, 1987, pp. 49–51.

5. Rudolph and Rudolph, 1987, p. 50.

6. Pradhan H. Prasad, 'Rise of Kulak Power and Class Struggle in North India', *Economic and Political Weekly*, Vol. 26, No. 33, 17 August 1991, pp. 1923–26.

7. See website of Ministry of Agriculture and Farmers' Welfare, Government of India, agriculture.gov.in

8. Ashok Mitra, *Terms of Trade and Class Relations*, Frank Cass and Co. Ltd, London, 1977, p. 101.
9. Mitra, 1977, p. 103.
10. 'Ruling BJP Got 95% of Funds', *Business Standard*, 5 April 2019, Accessed on 2 April 2020.
11. Sukhdeep Kaur, 'Land Deal Cemented Badal-Chauthala Family Ties', *Hindustan Times*, 12 October 2014.
12. 'FIR against Robert Vadra and Bhupinder Hooda over Gurgaon Land Deals', *Outlook India*, 2 September 2018.
13. 'What Is Panama Papers? Here Is Everything You Need to Know', *Indian Express*, 8 April 2016.
14. William L. Richter, 'Princes in Indian Politics', *Economic and Political Weekly*, Vol. 6, No. 9, 27 February 1971, p. 535.
15. The Air India Brands, www.airindia.in
16. Nikita Doval, 'A Raja's 43-year Battle to Reclaim Ancestral Property', *HT Mint*, 19 July 2017.

Chapter 7: Shifts in Political Power

1. Vilfred Pareto, *The Mind and Society: A Treatise on General Sociology*, (1935), Dower, New York, 1963, p. 1430.
2. I owe the term 'gradual revolution' to Francine R. Frankel, *India's Political Economy 1947–1977: The Gradual Revolution*, Oxford University Press, Delhi, 1980.
3. Rajni Kothari, 'The Congress System in India', *Asian Survey*, Vol. 4, No. 12, December 1964, p. 1163.
4. Kothari, 1964, p. 1170.
5. Gyan Prakash, Lawful Suspension of Law, in *Democracy Interrupted: The Emergency, 1975–77*, Penguin Viking, New Delhi, 2019, p. 132.
6. As quoted by his son Ravi Visvesvaraya Sharada Prasad, 'Multiple Narratives Exist for Why Indira Gandhi Lifted the Emergency', *Indian Express*, 23 February 2019.
7. These remarks on the Emergency are from Sanjaya Baru, 'Introduction', *Democracy Interrupted: The Emergency, 1975–77*, Penguin Viking, New Delhi, 2019. pp. x–xi.
8. Jay Dubashi, '100 Days of Morarji Desai's Government', *India Today*, 15 July 1977.
9. Editorial, *India Today*, 15 December 1977.
10. See, for example, Christophe Jaffrelot, 'The Rise of the Other Backward Classes in the Hindi Belt', *Journal of Asian Studies*, Vol. 59, No. 1, February 2000, pp. 86–108.

11. Jay Dubashi, 'Centre-State Relations: Tussle for Fiscal Power', *India Today*, 15 April 1978.

12. For a discussion along these lines, see T.V. Satyamurthy, 'Impact of Centre-State Relations on Indian Politics, An Interpretative Reckoning, 1947–87', *Economic and Political Weekly*, Vol. 24, No. 38, 23 September 1989, pp. 2133–347.

13. Report of the Sarkaria Commission, Inter-State Council Secretariat, Ministry of Home Affairs, Govt of India, 1988.

14. See, for example, Milan Vaishnav, *When Crime Pays: Money and Muscle in Indian Politics*, HarperCollins Publishers, Delhi, 2017; Devesh Kapur and Milan Vaishnav, *Costs of Democracy: Political Finance in India*, Oxford University Press, Delhi, 2018.

15. Association of Democratic Rights, *Analysis of Criminal Background, Financial, Education, Gender and other Details of Winner*.

16. For a study of data from Hindi states alone, see Christophe Jaffrelot and Giles Verniers, 'In Hindi States: Upper Castes Dominate New Lok Sabha', *Indian Express*, 27 May 2019.

17. Niranjan Sahoo and Niraj Tiwari, 'Financing Elections in India: A Scrutiny of Corporate Funding', *India Matters*, 9 April 2019, Observer Research Foundation.

Chapter 8: Bureaucracy and the Military

1. Hansard, Proceedings of the House of Lords, UK, 26 February 1924.

2. St. Catherine's Society Magazine, September 1939.

3. Zareer Masani, *Macaulay: Pioneer of India's Modernisation*, Random House India, 2012, pp. 205–06.

4. Kautilya, *Artha Shastra*, [Two, VII, 20].

5. Quoted in Sandro Serpal and Carlos Miguel Ferreira, 'The Concept of Bureaucracy by Max Weber', *International Journal of Social Science Studies*, Vol. 7, No. 2, March 2019.

6. Satya Deva, 'State and Bureaucracy in Kautilya's "Arthasastra"', *Economic and Political Weekly*, Vol. 19, No. 19, 12 May 1984, p. 814.

7. Sardar Patel, Address to IAS Probationers, 21 April 1947.

8. Record of Proceedings of the Constituent Assembly of India, Thursday, 4 November 1948.

9. S.R. Maheshwari, 'The Indian Bureaucracy: Its Profile, Malady and Cure', *Indian Journal of Political Science*, Vol. 31, No. 3, July–September 1970, p. 226.

10. For a representative set of essays on the IAS as a constituent of the power elite, see: P.S. Appu, 'The All-India Services. Decline, Debasement and

Destruction', *Economic and Political Weekly*, Volume 40. Number 9, 2005, pp. 826–32; Balveer Arora and Beryl Radin, *The Changing Role of the All-India Services. An Assessment and Agenda for Future Research on Federalism and the All-India Services*, Centre for the Advanced Study of India, New Delhi, 2000.

Dan Banik, 'The Transfer Raj: Indian Civil Servants on the Move', *The European Journal of Development Research*, Volume 13, Number 1, 2001, pp. 106–34; Dalal Benbabaali, 'Questioning the Role of the IAS in National Integration'.

11. Quoted in Maheshwari, 1970, p. 222.

12. Maheshwari, 1970, p. 227.

13. Ibid.

14. See, for example, S.K. Das, *Public Office, Private Interest: Bureaucracy and Corruption in India*, Oxford University Press, New Delhi, 2001, Chapter 5.

15. Ajit Jha, 'Lord of the Files', *India Today*, 22 September 2018.

16. N.N. Vohra, *Safeguarding India: Essays on Security and Governance*, HarperCollins, New Delhi, 2016.

17. Ajit Jha, 2018.

18. Vohra, 2016, The N.N. Vohra Committee (Ministry of Home Affairs, Government of India, 1993) was the first official inquiry into links between criminals, politicians and security agencies. The report has never been published but a brief official note on it is available at adrindia.org

19. Wright Mills, *The Power Elite*, 1956, p. 224.

20. The most recent, and excellent, addition to the literature on civil–military relations in India is Anit Mukherjee's *The Absent Dialogue: Politicians, Bureaucrats, and the Military in India*, Oxford University Press, 2020. Mukherjee also offers a comprehensive review of existing literature on the subject.

21. 'V.K. Singh in New Row: Calls Media "Presstitutes"', *Times of India*, 8 April 2015.

22. Jagjivan Ram quoted in Maheshwari, 1970, p. 222.

23. See, for example, Sanjay Dhingra, 'Modi Government Is Shaking the Foundations of India's IAS-led Civil Service', Print, 16 September 2019; D. Shyam Babu, 'Neither New nor Desirable', *The Hindu*, 21 June 2018.

24. The Citizenship (Amendment) Act, 2019, passed by Parliament in December 2019, permits the granting of Indian citizenship to illegal migrants of Hindu, Sikh, Buddhist, Jain, Parsi and Christian faiths who have arrived in India before December 2014, allegedly fleeing persecution

in Muslim majority Pakistan, Bangladesh and Afghanistan. The act was criticized for linking citizenship to religious affiliation, contrary to the spirit of the Indian Constitution.

25. 'Congress MP Asks President to Sack Army Chief', *Indian Express*, 30 December 2019, Accessed on 26 August 2020.

Chapter 9: Policy and Public Intellectuals

1. Shiv Visvanathan, 'A New Public Policy for a New India', *The Hindu*, 6 April 2015, Accessed on 27 April 2020 at: https://www.thehindu.com/opinion/lead/a-new-public-policy-for-a-new-india/article7070831.ece

2. Mukul Kesavan, 'Who Is an Indian Public Intellectual?', *Telegraph*, 31 August 2019.

3. George Rosen, *Western Economists and Eastern Societies: Agents of Change in South Asia, 1950–70*, Oxford University Press, Delhi, 1985.

4. *Yogendra K. Malik,* 'North Indian Intellectuals' Perceptions of Their Role and Status', *Asian Survey*, Vol. 17, No. 6, June 1977, pp. 565–80.

5. Rosabeth M. Kanter, 'World Class: Thriving Locally in the Global Economy', *Long Range Planning*, Vol. 30, No. 1, 1997, pp. 142–43. Quoted in Jivanta Schoettli and Markus Pohimann, 'A "New" Economic Elite in India: Transnational and Neoliberal?', *Samaj*, 2017.

6. Robert Skidelsky, *John Maynard Keynes: The Economist as Saviour, 1920–1947*, Macmillan, London, 1992, p. 406.

7. Skidelsky, 1992, p. 408.

8. Romila Thapar, 'Searching for the Public Intellectual', *Seminar*, January 2015.

9. Kesavan, 2019, op. cit.

10. Manishankar Prasad, 'On Your Right: Configuring the Hindu Nationalist Intellectual Architecture', *Tilak Chronicle*, 25 December 2019.

Chapter 10: Opinion Makers and Celebrities

1. 'In-depth Study: The Emergency Situation in India and Its Effects on People', *India Today*, 15 December 1975.

2. IIFL Wealth Hurun India Rich List 2020, The Richest People in India, October 2020.

3. Mills, 1956, p. 71.

4. Mills, 1956, p. 74.

5. Mills, 1956, p. 83.

Chapter 11: Secession of the Successful

1. Sanjaya Baru, 'IT and the E-economy: A Ballast for India–US Relations', Chapter 37 in Sanjaya Baru, *Strategic Consequences of India's Economic Performance*, Academic Foundation, New Delhi, 2006.
2. Baru, 2006, p. 316.
3. On the phenomenon of 'Visa Temples', see 'Visa Temples of India'.
4. Data accessed on 7 May 2020 at: https://mea.gov.in/images/attach/NRIs-and-PIOs_1.pdf
5. Tish Sanghera, 'As India Becomes Wealthier, 17 Mn Leave the Country to Settle Abroad', *Business Standard*, 25 November 2018.
6. See, for example, 'Elections 2014: Overseas Indians Travel Home to Support Narendra Modi', *Deccan Chronicle*, 5 May 2014; Preetha Nair, 'Friends from Afar: Meet the Army of BJP's NRI Supporters', *Outlook*, 8 April 2019.
7. Jagdish N. Bhagwati, 'Taxing the Brain Drain', *Challenge*, Vol. 19, No. 3, July/August 1976, pp. 34–38.
8. 'Manmohan Singh, India Converted 'Brain Drain" into "Brain Gain"', *Hindustan Times,* 2 December 2010.
9. Indian Express Investigation, '20 Years On, Where Are the Board Toppers? Over Half Are Abroad, Most in Science and Technology', *Sunday Indian Express*, 27 December 2020.
10. Prakash Nanda and Asit Ranjan Mitra, 'More Indians Going Abroad for Studies', *LiveMint*, 17 August 2018.
11. Robert B. Reich, 'Secession of the Successful', *New York Times*, 20 January 1991.
12. Robert B. Reich, *The Work of Nations: Preparing Ourselves for 21st-Century Capitalism*, Alfred Knopf, New York, 1992.
13. Pavan K. Varma, *The Great Indian Middle Class*, Viking India, 1998.
14. Lubna Kably, 'Indian rich top world in looking to leave country', *Times of India*, 13 February 2021, p. 1.
15. Shishir Gupta, 'Stranded Indians Won't Lose NRIs Status, Don't Need to File Returns: Govt', *Hindustan Times,* 9 May 2020.
16. 'Theresa May's Conference Speech', *Telegraph*, London, 5 October 2016.

Chapter 12: A Changing Balance of Power

1. 'Narendra Modi, "Ideology Not Above National Interest"', *Indian Express*, 13 November 2020.

2. For a detailed discussion, see Sanjaya Baru, *1991: How P.V. Narasimha Rao Made History*, Rupa Publications, New Delhi, 2016.

3. Najinyanupi, 'Some Philosophic Aspects of the Approach', *Economic and Political Weekly*, Vol. 8, No. 4/6, Annual Number, February 1973, pp. 141–43. 'Najinyanupi' means 'surrounded' in the native language of the Lakota, an American Indian tribe. My late father, B.P.R. Vithal, used that name as his pseudonym for a series of articles he published in the 1970s in the *Economic and Political Weekly*. Economist Raj Krishna coined the term 'Hindu Rate of Growth', referring to the gradualness of Indian growth, based on this essay. (For a cross reference see Arvind Panagariya, *India: The Emerging Giant*, Oxford University Press, New Delhi, 2008, p. 463). However, Raj Krishna's term 'the Hindu rate of growth' has been interpreted by many as a pejorative, suggesting that a Hindu India is not capable of delivering higher growth. That is not the interpretation to be derived from Vithal's original essay. Vithal was suggesting that the Hindu view of life allows a nation to sustain itself even at low rates of change because Hinduism views change as a gradual process and one in which each individual compares her present with her past and not with the 'Joneses next door'. Every individual and family subsumes its identity within that of a larger social community. The gradualness of change and the resilience of the mind and spirit have ensured political stability in a changing and unequal society.